Lecture Notes in Computer Science   11610

Commenced Publication in 1973
Founding and Former Series Editors:
Gerhard Goos, Juris Hartmanis, and Jan van Leeuwen

Editorial Board Members

David Hutchison
  Lancaster University, Lancaster, UK
Takeo Kanade
  Carnegie Mellon University, Pittsburgh, PA, USA
Josef Kittler
  University of Surrey, Guildford, UK
Jon M. Kleinberg
  Cornell University, Ithaca, NY, USA
Friedemann Mattern
  ETH Zurich, Zurich, Switzerland
John C. Mitchell
  Stanford University, Stanford, CA, USA
Moni Naor
  Weizmann Institute of Science, Rehovot, Israel
C. Pandu Rangan
  Indian Institute of Technology Madras, Chennai, India
Bernhard Steffen
  TU Dortmund University, Dortmund, Germany
Demetri Terzopoulos
  University of California, Los Angeles, CA, USA
Doug Tygar
  University of California, Berkeley, CA, USA

More information about this series at http://www.springer.com/series/8851

Ngoc Thanh Nguyen · Ryszard Kowalczyk ·
Fatos Xhafa (Eds.)

Transactions
on Computational
Collective Intelligence XXXIII

Springer

Editor-in-Chief
Ngoc Thanh Nguyen
Wroclaw University of Technology
Wroclaw, Poland

Co-Editor-in-Chief
Ryszard Kowalczyk
Swinburne University of Technology
Hawthorn, VIC, Australia

Guest Editor
Fatos Xhafa
Technical University of Catalonia
Barcelona, Spain

ISSN 0302-9743   ISSN 1611-3349 (electronic)
Lecture Notes in Computer Science
ISSN 2190-9288   ISSN 2511-6053 (electronic)
Transactions on Computational Collective Intelligence
ISBN 978-3-662-59539-8   ISBN 978-3-662-59540-4   (eBook)
https://doi.org/10.1007/978-3-662-59540-4

This Springer imprint is published by the registered company Springer-Verlag GmbH, DE
part of Springer Nature
The registered company address is: Heidelberger Platz 3, 14197 Berlin, Germany

Transactions on Computational Collective Intelligence TCCI XXXIII

Editorial Preface

Volume XXXIII of LNCS *Transactions on Computational Collective Intelligence* (TCCI) covers research topics such as Performance Optimization in IoT, Big Data, Reliability, Privacy, Security, Service Selection, QoS and Machine Learning, among others. The volume includes nine interesting and original papers, which have been selected via the peer-review process. In the papers, the authors present new findings and innovative methodologies as well as discuss issues and challenges in the field of collective intelligence from big data and networking paradigms while addressing security, privacy, reliability, and optimality to achieve QoS to the benefit of final users.

The nine papers of this volume are arranged as follows.

The first paper, "Performance Optimization in IoT-based Next-Generation Wireless Sensor Networks," by Behzad et al. proposes a novel framework for performance optimization in Internet of Things (IoT)-based next-generation wireless sensor networks. The aim is to overcome certain bottlenecks appearing in such systems, namely, drainage of battery and data degradation. The proposed framework comprises mechanisms to ensure the efficient and optimized use of resources. The framework is analyzed both mathematically and by extensive simulation results to sustain the claims of optimization and efficiency.

Kyriazis, in the second paper "Enabling Custom Security Controls as Plugins in Service-Oriented Environments," analyzes the concerns of non-adopters of service-oriented environments related to privacy and security. The use of security controls as plugins that can be ingested in service-oriented environments are proposed. The aim is to allow users to tailor the corresponding security and privacy levels by utilizing security measures that have been selected and implemented by themselves. The challenges and an architecture with the corresponding key building blocks that address these challenges are presented. Trustworthy requirements within the proposed approach are also discussed.

The third paper, "A Flexible Synchronization Protocol to Learn Hidden Topics in P2PPS Systems," by Nakamura et al. considers hidden topics in P2PPS (peer-to-peer type of topic-based publish/subscribe) models where each peer process can publish and subscribe event messages with no centralized coordinator. In such settings illegal information flow to the target peer may occur. The authors propose a flexible synchronization for hidden topics protocols. By experimental evaluation, it is evidenced that the fewest number of event messages are prohibited from being received in the proposed protocol when compared with the other protocols.

Bhattacharya and Choudhury, in the fourth paper "QoS Preservation in Web Service Selection," discuss the challenge of delivering a QoS solution satisfying the requirement of a consumer with minimum possible execution time, whereby many conflicting

QoS objectives increase the complexity of the problem. Therefore the problem may be formulated as a multi-objective, NP-hard optimization problem. The authors propose a goodness measure that replaces all QoS metrics by a single one, aiming at dimension reduction while satisfying all the QoS requirements of a consumer in most of the cases. The experimental results substantiate the claims of the proposed model.

In the fifth paper, "File Assignment Control for a Web System of Contents Categorization," Kohana et al. deal with the effect of the controlling file assignment on the file transfer time for a Web-based content categorization system. The authors propose an algorithm that estimates categories of contents based on the terms and the content categories already added. The longer file transfer time issue is solved by a distributed Web system that uses multiple calculation machines by controlling the file assignment. Thereby the large files are assigned to the Web browser process while the smaller files are assigned to the calculation machines over the network.

The sixth paper, "Byzantine Collision-Fast Consensus Protocols," by Saramago et al., analyzes Byzantine failures in atomic broadcast protocols, which are fundamental building blocks used in the construction of many reliable distributed systems. By observing that the collision-fast atomic broadcast algorithm, which uses m-consensus to decide and deliver multiple values in the same instance, is not Byzantine fault-tolerant, a requirement for many a modified version of the algorithm is presented to handle Byzantine failures. The authors prove that there are no Byzantine collision-fast algorithms in an asynchronous model as traditionally extended to solve consensus. Finally, the authors present a Byzantine collision-fast algorithm that bypasses the stated impossibility by means of a unique sequential identifier generator trusted component.

Calzarossa et al. in the seventh paper, entitled "A Methodological Approach for Time Series Analysis and Forecasting of Web Dynamics," address the problem of modelling and predicting Web dynamics in the framework of time series analysis and forecasting. The authors present a general methodological approach that allows the identification of the patterns describing the behavior of the time series, the formulation of suitable models, and the use of these models for predicting the future behavior. Also, aiming to improve the forecasts, a method for detecting and modelling the spiky patterns that might be present in a time series is proposed and analyzed through the temporal patterns of page uploads of the Reuters news agency website over one year. It is shown that the overall model of the upload process accurately fits the data, including most of the spikes.

In the eighth paper, "Static and Dynamic Group Migration Algorithms of Virtual Machines to Reduce Energy Consumption of a Server Cluster," Duolikun et al. envision the green society and the need to reduce the consumption of electric energy for information systems, especially servers in clusters like cloud computing systems. The authors identify some energy-related issues in a process migration approach to reducing the total electric energy consumption of clusters by migrating virtual machines. Both static and dynamic migration algorithms where a group of virtual machines migrate from a host server to a guest server are discussed. In the evaluation, the authors show the total electric energy consumption of servers can be reduced more in the dynamic setting algorithm compared with other algorithms.

Dawoud et al., in the last paper "Unsupervised Deep Learning for Software Defined Networks Anomalies Detection," analyze security and vulnerability threats in software-defined networks (SDN), where a centralized network controller is a target for the attackers. Providing security measures is a crucial procedure to leverage the SDN's model capabilities. The authors analyze the detection of network anomalies in view of recent advances in machine learning and of deep learning, in particular. Then, an intrusion detection framework based on unsupervised deep learning algorithms is proposed. The experimental results showed a significant improvement in detection accuracy.

I would like to sincerely thank all the authors for their valuable contributions to this TCCI volume and the reviewers for their timely and constructive feedback. I would like to thank the Editor-in-Chief of TCCI, Prof. Ngoc Thanh Nguyen, for the opportunity to edit this volume. The support by the managerial team of TCCI is highly appreciated.

April 2019   Fatos Xhafa

Transactions on Computational Collective Intelligence

This Springer journal focuses on research in applications of the computer-based methods of computational collective intelligence (CCI) and their applications in a wide range of fields such as the Semantic Web, social networks, and multi-agent systems. It aims to provide a forum for the presentation of scientific research and technological achievements accomplished by the international community.

The topics addressed by this journal include all solutions of real-life problems for which it is necessary to use CCI technologies to achieve effective results. The emphasis of the papers published is on novel and original research and technological advancements. Special features on specific topics are welcome.

Editor-in-Chief

Ngoc Thanh Nguyen   Wroclaw University of Technology, Poland

Co-editor-in-Chief

Ryszard Kowalczyk   Swinburne University of Technology, Australia

Editorial Board

John Breslin   National University of Ireland, Galway, Ireland
Longbing Cao   University of Technology Sydney, Australia
Shi-Kuo Chang   University of Pittsburgh, USA
Oscar Cordon   European Centre for Soft Computing, Spain
Tzung-Pei Hong   National University of Kaohsiung, Taiwan
Gordan Jezic   University of Zagreb, Croatia
Piotr Jędrzejowicz   Gdynia Maritime University, Poland
Kang-Huyn Jo   University of Ulsan, South Korea
Yiannis Kompatsiaris   Centre for Research and Technology Hellas, Greece
Jozef Korbicz   University of Zielona Gora, Poland
Hoai An Le Thi   Lorraine University, France
Pierre Lévy   University of Ottawa, Canada
Tokuro Matsuo   Yamagata University, Japan
Kazumi Nakamatsu   University of Hyogo, Japan
Toyoaki Nishida   Kyoto University, Japan
Manuel Núñez   Universidad Complutense de Madrid, Spain
Julian Padget   University of Bath, UK
Witold Pedrycz   University of Alberta, Canada
Debbie Richards   Macquarie University, Australia
Roman Słowiński   Poznan University of Technology, Poland

Contents

Performance Optimization in IoT-Based Next-Generation Wireless Sensor Networks

Muzammil Behzad[1,2]([⊠]) [ID], Manal Abdullah[3], Muhammad Talal Hassan[2],
Yao Ge[4][ID], and Mahmood Ashraf Khan[2]

[1] University of Oulu, 90014 Oulu, Finland
`muzammil.behzad@oulu.fi`
[2] COMSATS University Islamabad, Islamabad 44000, Pakistan
`{talal,mahmoodashraf}@comsats.edu.pk`
[3] King Abdulaziz University, Jeddah 21589, Kingdom of Saudi Arabia
`maaabdullah@kau.edu.sa`
[4] The Chinese University of Hong Kong, Shatin 999077, Hong Kong
`yge@ee.cuhk.edu.hk`

Abstract. In this paper, we propose a novel framework for performance optimization in Internet of Things (IoT)-based next-generation wireless sensor networks. In particular, a computationally-convenient system is presented to combat two major research problems in sensor networks. First is the conventionally-tackled resource optimization problem which triggers the drainage of battery at a faster rate within a network. Such drainage promotes inefficient resource usage thereby causing sudden death of the network. The second main bottleneck for such networks is the data degradation. This is because the nodes in such networks communicate via a wireless channel, where the inevitable presence of noise corrupts the data making it unsuitable for practical applications. Therefore, we present a layer-adaptive method via 3-tier communication mechanism to ensure the efficient use of resources. This is supported with a mathematical coverage model that deals with the formation of coverage holes. We also present a transform-domain based robust algorithm to effectively remove the unwanted components from the data. Our proposed framework offers a handy algorithm that enjoys desirable complexity for real-time applications as shown by the extensive simulation results.

Keywords: Coverage holes · Denoising · Energy efficiency ·
Energy holes · Sparse representations · Wireless sensor networks

1 Introduction

Recent technological-accelerations for surging advancements regarding industrial applications in Internet-of-Things (IoT) based wireless communication have

This research work was funded in part by the Higher Education Commission of Pakistan under the research grant number 288.67/TG/R&D/HEC/2018/25181.

N. T. Nguyen et al. (Eds.): TCCI XXXIII, LNCS 11610, pp. 1–31, 2019.
https://doi.org/10.1007/978-3-662-59540-4_1

significantly aided major scientific and research platforms, where the main focus is to propose exceptionally elegant and convenient systems in terms of computational cost, design and practical execution. With these tremendous efforts available at hand, the consumer electronics industry have been made confident to manufacture wireless devices with economical value, tiny structure, and the capability of effectively utilizing the in-hand battery resources. Toward this end, sensors-based wireless networks have earned significant attention in the unlimited development of information and communication technologies [1]. However, since many of these devices are restricted by the resources available to them at hand, the communication overhead and power consumption are, hence, critical areas of research for analysis, manufacturing and development of such wireless networks in order to achieve efficient management in IoT.

Wireless sensor networks (WSNs) are made up of small, portable and energy-restricted sensor nodes deployed in an observation venue. These nodes carry the baggage of transmitting vital information using wireless radio links. Such information can have the form of multi-dimensional signals, and are of critical importance in many world-wide applications. The development of such networks demands extensive planning strategy along with superior tactical approaches for its working capabilities. This effective development motivates the existence of many real-time application scenarios such as environmental control [2], underwater networks [3], battlefield surveillance [4], medical and health-care systems [5,6], and many more [7–11].

1.1   Underlying Structure of WSNs

As a function of the underlying transmission mode, WSNs can be categorized by two types of communication mechanisms: (1) direct or single-hop, and (2) multi-hop, as shown in Fig. 1. In the former method, the nodes in a network transmit their data directly to the base station (BS), also known as the sink. This in turn drains-up the battery life of the nodes, hence, resulting in an early death of the network. Therefore, this type of communication is not recommended for efficient and practical approaches. On the other hand, the later approach suggests a much more promising deal. In this method, the nodes are not needed to communicate with the BS directly, and can instead send their data to BS in multiple steps. This ultimately lessens the burden on each node, and allows the network to remain stable for a longer period of time.

Similarly, another distribution of WSNs is based on the type of the response that the nodes usually exhibit. Specifically, WSNs can be designed as either proactive or reactive. In a proactive mode, the nodes keep their transmitters continuously active, and periodically transmit the data independent of any parameters. Consequently, such power-hunger transmissions result in an inefficient energy utilization. On the contrary, in the reactive mode, the nodes respond only to the events that, for example, exceeds a certain threshold or when a specific event has been triggered. Since the nodes only respond to drastic changes and keep their transmitters turned-off otherwise, this yield a practically convenient system with an elongated network lifespan.

1.2   Research Developments in WSNs

The first step in establishing a WSN is the initialization and distribution of sensor nodes around the observation field. Many researchers have advocated normal distribution of the statically deployed nodes as the optimal distribution (e.g., see [12]). The deployment of nodes in the network field area is then followed by transmission of the required data. Since these nodes are left unattended, with limited resources at hand, efficient utilization of the available resources becomes a key operation factor to form a vigorous and standalone network.

To tackle this, many protocols recommended clustering of the network area, a pioneer contribution by W.B. Heinzelman [13]. Fundamentally, clustering divides the field into multiple smaller observation versions thereby making resource management a comparatively convenient task [14–17]. However, this requires free and fair election of cluster heads (CHs) in each cluster. These CHs are responsible for data fusion, i.e., they receive data from their respective clusters' normal nodes, and transmit them to the BS.

Traditionally proposed protocols for WSNs focus mainly on performance improvements via effective selection criterion for CHs, the choice of single-hop or multi-hop communication between nodes, and whether the clustering scheme should be static or dynamic. Even though an optimal combination of the above factors yield interesting results, however, impressive results can be achieved by looking into more exciting parts of the problem. Furthermore, another much concerned and barely discussed side of the problem is the degradation due to environment. A common form of such inevitable degradation affecting the data sent over radio links is that of additive white Gaussian noise (AWGN). Several designed protocols discard this important issue and just focus on minimizing

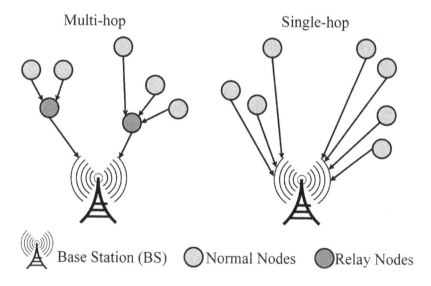

Fig. 1. Multi-hop vs. Single-hop communication mechanism

the energy consumption by assuming that the data received by nodes have not experienced any noise addition due to the environment.

1.3   Notations

In the rest of the paper, we use the following notations. We represent all the vectors used in our work with small case and bold face letters (e.g., $\mathbf{y}$), while all the scalars with small case normal font letters (e.g., y). We reserve upper case and bold face letters (e.g., $\mathbf{Y}$) for matrices, whereas calligraphic notations (e.g., $\mathcal{N}$) are used for sets. Additionally, we use $\mathbf{y}_i$, $y(j)$ and $\mathcal{N}_k$ to denote ith column of matrix $\mathbf{Y}$, jth element of vector $\mathbf{y}$ and a subset of $\mathcal{N}$, respectively.

1.4   Recoveries via Sparse Representations

Contrary to the traditional Nyquist-Shannon sampling theorem, where one must sample at least double the signal bandwidth, compressive sensing (CS) has emerged out as a new framework for data acquisition and sensor design in an extremely competent way. The basic idea is that if the data signal is sparse in a known basis, a perfect recovery of the signal can be achieved leading to a significant reduction in the number of measurements that need to be stored.

According to CS, the following model can be used to recover an unknown vector $\mathbf{v}$ from an under-determined system:

$$\mathbf{x} = \boldsymbol{\Phi}\mathbf{v} = \boldsymbol{\Phi}\boldsymbol{\Psi}\boldsymbol{\theta} = \boldsymbol{\Theta}\boldsymbol{\theta}, \tag{1}$$

where $\mathbf{x} \in \mathbb{C}^M$, $\mathbf{v} = \boldsymbol{\Psi}\boldsymbol{\theta} \in \mathbb{C}^N$ are observed signal and unknown vector, $\boldsymbol{\theta} \in \mathbb{C}^N$ is unknown sparse signal which, for example, a node will collect, representing projection coefficients of $\mathbf{v}$ on $\boldsymbol{\Psi}$, $\boldsymbol{\Theta} = \boldsymbol{\Phi}\boldsymbol{\Psi}$ is an $M \times N$ reconstruction matrix $(M < N)$. The measurement matrix $\boldsymbol{\Theta}$ is designed such that the dominant information of $\boldsymbol{\theta}$ can be captured into $\mathbf{x}$.

Reconstruction algorithms in CS exploit the fact that many signals are genetically sparse, therefore they proceed to minimize ℓ_0, ℓ_1 or ℓ_2-norm over the solution space. Among them, ℓ_1-norm is the most accepted approach due to its tendency to successfully recover the sparse estimate $\hat{\boldsymbol{\theta}}$ of $\boldsymbol{\theta}$ as follows:

$$\hat{\boldsymbol{\theta}} = \arg\min_{\boldsymbol{\theta}} \|\boldsymbol{\theta}\|_{\ell_1}, \quad \text{subject to} \quad \mathbf{x} \approx \boldsymbol{\Phi}\boldsymbol{\Psi}\boldsymbol{\theta}. \tag{2}$$

In this regard, however, the inevitable presence of noise in wireless channels is always a challenging task to combat. Consequently, the system is modeled as

$$\mathbf{y} = \mathbf{x} + \mathbf{n} = \boldsymbol{\Theta}\boldsymbol{\theta} + \mathbf{n}, \tag{3}$$

where $\mathbf{y} \in \mathbb{C}^M$ is the noisy version of the clean signal $\mathbf{x} \in \mathbb{C}^M$ which is corrupted by the noise vector $\mathbf{n} \in \mathbb{C}^M$ with i.i.d. zero mean Gaussian entries having variance $\sigma_{\mathbf{n}}^2$, i.e., $\mathbf{n}(.) \sim \mathcal{N}(\mathbf{0}, \sigma_{\mathbf{n}}^2\mathbf{I})$. A depiction of this model is shown in Fig. 2.

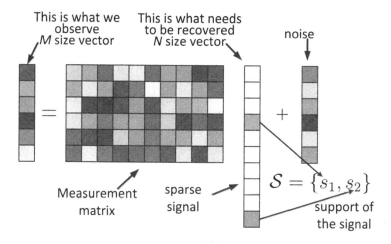

Fig. 2. Sparse model

1.5   Contribution

A part of this work has already been published in [18], and this is the extended version of our previous work. In [18], we introduced a novel framework to tackle two major concerns in WSNs: (1) performance optimization via efficient energy utilization, and (2) combating the unavoidable presence of Gaussian noise, added as a result of multiple communications among the nodes via wireless channel. We proposed a fast and low-cost sparse representations based collaborative system enriched with layer-adaptive 3-tier communication mechanism. This is supported by an effective CHs election method and mathematically convenient coverage model guaranteeing minimization of energy and coverage holes. A computationally desired implementation of our framework is an added benefit that makes it a preferable choice for real-world applications.

To tackle AWGN, the data is transmitted in spatial-domain form and its sparse estimates are later computed at the receiver side. For a much better denoising, we let the nodes situated at a single-hop to mutually negotiate with each other for better collaboration. The data denoising is further refined by a specially designed averaging filter.

In this paper, we extend the concept of image denoising in wireless sensor networks. Specifically, we propose to use region growing based efficient denoising mechanism where we divide the entire image into various sub-regions based on their intensities, and apply smoothening filter. Motivated by this, we also extend our current framework for color images where we are especially interested in exploiting inter-channel correlation of each color image. This effective piece of information plays a crucial role in identifying the noisy components, and thereby helps discarding those components. Our proposed protocol lends itself the following salient features:

- The implementation of a mathematically efficient coverage model along with an adaptive CHs election method help avoiding coverage holes to a greater extent.
- Our proposed layer-adaptive 3-tier communication system greatly reduces energy holes.
- To compute denoised data signals, we compute support-independent sparse estimates which relieves us from finding distribution of the sparse representations first, hence, giving it a support-agnostic nature.
- Prior collaboration enjoyed by the nodes for communication yields an effectively significant energy minimization.
- The use of a fast sparse recovery technique allows a desired computational complexity of our algorithm.
- The use of inter-channel correlation among red, green and blue channels of color images not only makes it a suitable choice for denoising of color images, but also provides a convenient solution for fast and practical image denoising applications.

Rest of the paper is structured as follows: Sect. 2 presents an overview of the related work done in this area. We describe our proposed framework and its complexity in Sects. 3 and 4, receptively, while the results from various simulations are discussed in Sect. 5. Finally, Sect. 6 concludes the paper.

2   Related Work

Presently, researchers are fundamentally concentrating on the technologically-enriched tools for performance optimization of network structure, as a result of which the lifetime of WSNs is possible to increase. This possibility provides a roadway for scientists working in this research domain to propose low-cost, energy-efficient and optimized algorithms [19].

This includes a trend-setter work by W.B. Heinzelman, et al., proposing a multi-hop energy efficient communication protocol for WSNs, namely LEACH [20]. The objective was to reduce energy dissipation by introducing randomly elected CHs resulting in, however, unbalanced CHs distribution. Nevertheless, the partition of network area into different regions via clustering yielded a significant increase in system lifetime. As a principal competitor, a new reactive protocol, named as TEEN, was proposed by authors of [21] for event-driven applications. This protocol, even though constrained to temperature based scenarios only, proposed threshold aware transmissions thereby outperforming LEACH in terms of network lifespan.

In comparison with the aforementioned homogeneous WSNs, the authors of [22] and [23] proposed SEP and DEEC, respectively, introducing heterogeneous versions of the WSNs by allowing a specific set of nodes, defined as advanced nodes, to carry higher initial energy than other normal nodes. SEP used energy based weighted election to appoint CHs in a two-level heterogeneous network ultimately improving network stability. As a stronger contestant to SEP, DEEC deployed multi-level heterogeneity and improvised CHs election measure to attain extended lifespan of the network than SEP.

A. Khadivi et al., proposed a fault tolerant power aware protocol with static clustering (FTPASC) for WSNs in [24]. The network was partitioned into static clusters, and energy load was distributed evenly over high-power nodes, resulting in minimization of power consumption, and increased network lifetime. Another static clustering based sparsity-aware energy efficient clustering (SEEC) protocol is proposed in [25]. This protocol used sparsity and density search algorithms to classify sparse and dense regions. A mobile sink is then exploited, specifically in sparse areas, to enhance network lifetime.

As opposed to static clustering, authors of [26] presented centralized dynamic clustering (CDC) environment for WSNs. In this protocol, the clusters and number of nodes associated with each cluster remains fixed, and a new CH is chosen in each round of communication between clusters and BS. CDC showed better results than LEACH in terms of communication overhead and latency. In a similar fashion, G.S. Tomar, et al., proposed an adaptive dynamic clustering protocol for WSNs in [27], which creates a dynamic system that can change topology architecture as per traffic patterns. Mutual negotiation scheme is used between nodes of different energy levels to form energy efficient clusters. Periodic selection of CHs is done based on different characteristics of nodes. Another work proposed to use the cooperative and dynamic clustering to achieve energy efficiency [28]. This framework ensured even distribution of energy, and optimization of number of nodes used for event reporting thereby showing promising results.

D. Jia et al., tackled the problem of unreasonable CHs selection in clustering algorithms [29]. The authors considered dynamic CH selection methods as the best remedy to avoid overlapping coverage regions. Their experimental results showed increased network lifetime than LEACH and DEEC. Another energy efficient cluster based routing protocol, termed as density controlled divide-and-rule (DDR), is proposed in [30]. The authors tried to take care of the coverage and energy holes problem in clustering scenarios. They presented density controlled uniform distribution of nodes and optimum selection of CHs in each round to solve this issue. Similarly, a cluster based energy efficient routing protocol (CBER) is proposed in [31]. This protocol elects the CHs on the basis of optimal CH distance and nodes' residual energy. CBER reported to outperform LEACH in terms of energy consumption of the network, and its lifetime.

3 Proposed Framework Design

In this section, we provide the readers with detailed understanding of our proposed routing protocol. Here, we broadly discuss the widely accepted radio model for communication among nodes. This is then followed by a comprehensive explanation of our adopted network configuration and its operation details for energy efficiency and denoising of the data.

3.1 Wireless Communication Model

For transmission and reception of required data among sensor nodes via wireless medium, we assume the simple and most commonly used first order radio communication model as given in Fig. 3. In this figure, we present the energy consumed by a node while transmitting and receiving data. We show that a packet of data traveling over radio waves has to combat against degrading factors such as noise, multi-path fading, etc. Thus, we also take into account the d^2 losses that almost all chunks of data has to face. This is mathematically explained in terms of the following expressions:

$$E_{Tx}(k,d) = \begin{cases} k \times (E_{elec} + \epsilon_{fs} \times d^2), & d < d_o \\ k \times (E_{elec} + \epsilon_{mp} \times d^4), & d \geq d_o \end{cases} \tag{4}$$

$$E_{Rx}(k) = E_{elec} \times k, \tag{5}$$

where d_o is a reference distance, k is the number of bits in packet, d is the transmission distance which varies every time for each node, E_{elec} is the energy used for data processing, ϵ_{fs} and ϵ_{mp} are channel dependent loss factors[1], E_{Tx} is the energy used by a node for transmission, and E_{Rx} is the energy used by a node for data reception. As shown, the d^r losses may change from $d^r|_{r=2}$ to $d^r|_{r=4}$ forcing a higher value of E_{Tx}. A similar increase is then observed in the E_{Rx} values to process a highly corrupted data when assuming a noisy environment, as in our case. The generally used energy dissipation values for a radio channel are presented in Table 1.

Table 1. Energy dissipation measurements

Dissipation source	Amount absorbed
E_{elec} of Rx and Tx	50 nJ/bit
Aggregation energy	5 nJ/bit/signal
Tx amplifier ϵ_{fs} for $d^r|_{r=2}$	10 pJ/bit/4 m^2
Tx amplifier ϵ_{mp} for $d^r|_{r=4}$	0.0013 pJ/bit/m^4

3.2 Network Configuration

For the configuration model, we use a network consisting of L number of nodes deployed randomly. Unlike the traditional models, we adopt a spherically-oriented field, and propose to use an optimized version of area division via adaptive clustering. For a much better understanding, see the network model shown

---

[1] It is worth noting that over larger distances, such loss factors demand a higher amount of energy yielding sudden death of the network. This is often missed by traditional protocols assuming lossless channel. Therefore, avoiding these power-hungry transmissions significantly optimize resources.

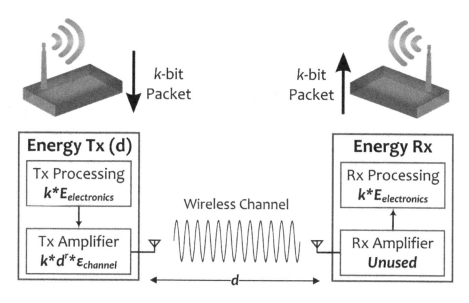

Fig. 3. Radio model

in Fig. 4. Here, for the sake of simplicity and understanding, we use the field area $A = \pi 150^2$ m^2, i.e., the diameter $D = 300$, with a total of $L = 100$ deployed nodes. To avoid formation of energy holes, and thus the death of network, we place the BS in the center of the network at coordinates $< i, j >= (0,0)$. This is followed by the clustering of network field into various coronas which are then further classified into different sensing-based reporting regions. The prior computation of number of coronas, represented by η, is a function of field area A, which itself is depending on D, and the number of nodes L. As a sound approximate, we propose $\eta = D/L$. Hence, in our case we use $\eta = 3$ coronas, denoted accordingly by η_1, η_2 and η_3.

Once the η number of coronas are formed, the next step is to divide each corona into various sensing regions as shown in the figure. However, for a much better network performance, the distribution is such that each sensing region in the upper level corona η_α surrounds two sensing regions in lower level corona $\eta_{\alpha-1}$. This is shown in Fig. 4(a), where for example region R_7 in η_3 covers both R_2 and R_3 in η_2, hence, avoiding coverage holes by satisfying the following expression for a general network configuration[2]:

$$A = \pi(D/2)^2 = \sum_{\alpha=1}^{\eta} A_{\eta_\alpha} = \sum_{\alpha} A_{R_\alpha}, \qquad \alpha \in \mathbb{Z}^+, \tag{6}$$

---

[2] Here, we presented calculations for $A = \pi 150^2$ m^2 and $L = 100$ merely for the ease of understanding. However, for any other small or large scale network configuration, the computations can be done in a similar fashion using the proposed expressions.

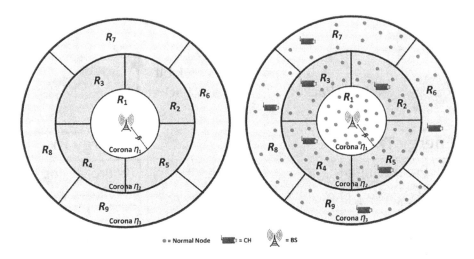

Fig. 4. Network model: (a) Network Configuration, (b) Nodes Deployment

where A_{η_α} and A_{R_α} represented area of each corona and sensing region, respectively. It is worth noting that we do not divide the corona surrounding BS further, η_1 in our case, to avoid unneeded and poor use of available resources. Thus, we can safely write:

$$A_{\eta_1} = A_{R_1} = \pi\beta^2, \text{ where } \beta \in \mathbb{R}^+. \tag{7}$$

3.3 Nodes Deployment and Layer-Controlled CHs Nomination

As soon as the network is clustered out into various coronas and sensing regions, the next step is to distribute the nodes randomly over these regions. To optimize resources, a sensible decision is to deploy an equal percentage of nodes over different regions to ensure minimization of coverage holes, and elongation of network lifetime. Therefore, in this scenario, we propose to deploy 20% of the nodes in region R_1 and the rest 80% of the nodes to be distributed evenly over $R_{2,3,...,8,9}$ regions as shown in Fig. 4(b). This nodes' deployment always depend upon the network field area and number of nodes. Hence, for any other network configuration, an adjusted percentage can be calculated to optimize communication among nodes, and to avoid energy and coverage holes.

Following the deployment of nodes and prior network initialization, the election of CHs is carried out in all $R_{2,3,...,8,9}$ regions. Since the use of CHs in clustering techniques plays an important role to improve network lifespan, effective criterion for CHs election is equally necessary for further improving performance of the network. The most commonly used measures for electing CHs are residual energy and distance from BS. We propose a blend of both to increase the life of each node. Furthermore, we introduce a layering-based election of CHs. This means that the election will take place in lower level coronas η_α first, and will then move to high level coronas $\eta_{\alpha+1}$ for higher level CHs. The reason to adopt this is the effectiveness noted in CHs election. Thus, in each round, all the nodes are assessed based on their residual energies and top 5% of the nodes having highest residual energies in their respective regions are shortlisted. These shortlisted nodes then contest against each other where the node with smallest distance to the CHs of both associated regions in lower level corona is elected as CH. The nodes in η_2 are evaluated in a similar fashion based on the residual energy but having minimum distance with the center of their respective region.

3.4   Layer-Adaptive 3-Tier Communication Mechanism

For transfer of data among various nodes, we propose a layer-adaptive 3-tier architecture. Our communication mechanism is enriched with distance-optimized transmissions to avoid wastage of energy. The nodes use a multi-hop scheme instead of directly transmitting the data of interest to BS. In tier-1 phase, all the normal nodes gather data, and send it to the nearest CH. This CH may not necessarily be the same region CH. Here, we allow nodes in η_α to transmit the data to CHs of even $\eta_{\alpha-1}$. This is the reason why we distributed the sensing regions in such a way that each region in upper level corona is bordered with two regions in lower level corona. However, the nodes of a region in η_α cannot transmit to another region on the same corona, i.e., it must either send data to its own CH in η_α, or any other nearest CH in the two bordered regions on lower level corona $\eta_{\alpha-1}$ as explained in Fig. 5.

In the next tier-2 phase of communication, the CHs of η_α aggregate their data and then send it to the CHs of $\eta_{\alpha-1}$. Note that even though the CH of R_3 is receiving data from CHs of both R_7 and R_8, this is blessing in disguise. This is because, as shown in the figure, the CHs of both R_7 and R_8 have not received data from all the nodes in its region, since some nodes find another nearest CH, so these CHs are aggregating and then forwarding a comparatively smaller amount of load thereby not overburdening themselves. Also, the CHs change in each round based on the election criterion, so it ultimately saves energy. Finally in tier-3 phase, all the CHs in lower level coronas send their data to the BS, hence, completing the data transmission process.

3.5   Coverage Model

For reduction in coverage holes, we express the coverage scenario of nodes by a mathematical model. All the deployed sensor nodes are represented in set notation as $\kappa = \{\mu_1, \mu_2, \mu_3, ..., \mu_L\}$. The coverage model of one alive node μ_α belonging to the set κ can be expressed as a sphere centered at $< i_\alpha, j_\alpha >$ with radius h_α. We let a random variable $\aleph_\alpha$ define an event when a data pixel $< a, b >$ is within the coverage range of any node μ_α. As a result, the equivalent of likelihood of the event $\aleph_\alpha$ to happen, as denoted by $P\{\aleph_\alpha\}$, is represented as $P_{cov}\{a, b, \mu_\alpha\}$. A decomposed version of the above is given as follows:

$$P\{\aleph_\alpha\} = P_{cov}\{a, b, \mu_\alpha\} = \begin{cases} 1, & (a - i_\alpha)^2 + (b - j_\alpha)^2 \le h_\alpha^2 \\ 0, & \text{otherwise} \end{cases} \tag{8}$$

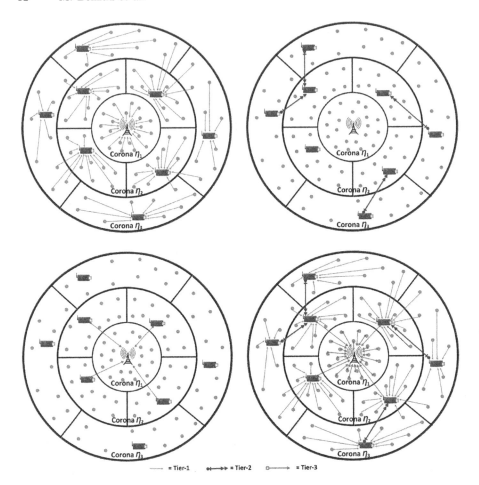

Fig. 5. 3-tier communication architecture

where the equation translates that a data pixel $< a, b >$ is surrounded by the coverage range of any random node μ_α if the distance between them is smaller than the threshold radius h_α. However, since the event $\aleph_\alpha$ is stochastically independent from others, this means h_α and h_γ are not related $\implies \alpha, \gamma \in [1, L]$ and $\alpha \neq \gamma$. This gives us the following conclusive equations:

$$P\{\overline{\aleph_\alpha}\} = 1 - P\{\aleph_\alpha\} = 1 - P_{cov}\{a, b, \mu_\alpha\}, \tag{9}$$

$$P\{\aleph_\alpha \cup \aleph_\gamma\} = 1 - P\{\overline{\aleph_\alpha} \cap \overline{\aleph_\gamma}\} = 1 - P\{\overline{\aleph_\alpha}\}.P\{\overline{\aleph_\gamma}\}, \tag{10}$$

where $P\{\overline{\aleph_\alpha}\}$ denotes the statistical complement of $P\{\aleph_\alpha\}$ which means that μ_α failed to assist data pixel $< a, b >$. Importantly, this data pixel is given coverage if any of the nodes in the set is covering it otherwise a coverage hole would form. Hence, the following expressions denote the probability such that data pixels would be within the coverage range of at least one of the nodes in the set to minimize coverage holes:

$$P_{cov}\{a, b, \kappa\} = P\{\bigcup_{\alpha=1}^{L} \aleph_{\alpha}\} = 1 - P\{\bigcap_{\alpha=1}^{L} \overline{\aleph_{\alpha}}\},$$

$$= 1 - \prod_{\alpha=1}^{L} (1 - P_{cov}\{a, b, \mu_{\alpha}\}). \quad (11)$$

For further facilitation, we present the coverage rate as fraction of area under coverage, denoted by Q, and the overall area of the observation field as follows:

$$P_{cov}\{\kappa\} = \sum_{\alpha=1}^{L} \sum_{\gamma=1}^{L} \frac{P_{cov}\{a, b, Q\}}{A} \quad (12)$$

3.6   Data Denoising

After taking care of the energy efficiency, second major problem is retrieving the original data back. This is because the received data is generally degraded by AWGN so it is of no use unless denoised. For this purpose, we propose denoising of the data samples via Bayesian analysis based sparse recovery techniques. To do so, we take into account the data correlation of various adjacent nodes, and use this as an important piece of information for collaboration among nodes.

We use three stages for CS based sparse recovery technique to denoise the data. In doing so, received data is converted to sparse domain first (e.g., wavelet transform for images data). This is followed by computing similar and correlated data by adjacent nodes, giving them weights based on the similarity extent. Using equivalent sparse representations of data samples, probability of active taps is computed giving us the location of undesired corrupted support locations [32]. With the help of correlation information, an averaging based collaborative step is performed to remove the unwanted noisy components as shown via flowchart in Fig. 6. Here, we denote the initially denoised image by $\bar{\mathbf{X}}_d$.

Finally, we apply a specially developed averaging filter to further smooth out the data as discussed in the later sections. This filter fundamentally works on finding similar data samples, and then averaging those samples to provide a clean estimate of the data. Using a CS based pre-determined dictionary, a reverse transform is applied to give back the denoised data in spatial-domain representation as $\hat{\mathbf{x}} = \boldsymbol{\Theta}\hat{\boldsymbol{\theta}}$.

Similarity via Distance Vs. Correlation: For the similar and correlated data, we first compute samples from the data, for example, overlapping patches or blocks in images. Once the overlapping patches are formed, the next step is to find a certain number of similar patches, for each patch, that would be used during collaboration. The grouping of patches in such a way using a similarity measure has led to a number significant improvements in a wide range of application like signal/image/bio-medical processing, computer vision, machine intelligence, etc. (e.g., see [32–39]).

A number of techniques for similarity based grouping of patches have been proposed in the literature. Some of those include self-organizing maps [40], vector quantization [41], fuzzy clustering [42] and a review on these [43]. The recently developed denoising algorithms use a distance based measure where similarity between different signals are realized in terms of the inverse of the point-wise distance between them. Therefore, a smaller distance between the signals would imply a higher similarity and vice versa. The generally used distance based similarity measure is the Euclidean distance as used by the state-of-the-art denoising image algorithms like NL-means [44], BM3D [45], etc.

However, despite being an effective way of finding similarity, Euclidean distance based similar-intensity grouping has a limitation; it limits the search for number of similar patches. For instance, even though natural images have some similarity in their structure, the number of similar patches vary. Consequently, in an image having a smaller number of similar patches, the collaboration is not that effective thereby disturbing the performance of denoising, especially in case of high noise. This creates a bottleneck specifically for lower resolution images where finding similar-intensity patches becomes a difficult task.

To tackle this case and have a similarity measure that can be used globally even in lower resolution images or images having a smaller number of similar-intensity patches, novel methods are being proposed to find better ways of collaboration by using efficient grouping of similar patches. For example, the authors in [46] search the similar patches by using not only a patch itself but the noise too where they propose the concept of noise similarity, while the authors in [47] propose sequence-to-sequence similarity (SSS) which is an essential way of preserving the edge information.

In our case, we take care of the aforementioned problem by introducing intensity-invariant grouping. The idea is to stack all the patches that have a similar inherent structure without relying on the intensity values as shown in the Stage 01 of Fig. 6. The correlation coefficient serves as the best tool to be utilized for the said purpose. For two random signals $\mathbf{y}_\alpha$ and $\mathbf{y}_\gamma$, the correlation coefficient is given as,

$$r(\mathbf{y}_\alpha, \mathbf{y}_\gamma) = \frac{cov(\mathbf{y}_\alpha, \mathbf{y}_\gamma)}{\sigma_{\mathbf{y}_\alpha} \sigma_{\mathbf{y}_\gamma}}, \tag{13}$$

where $-1 \leq r(\mathbf{y}_\alpha, \mathbf{y}_\gamma) \leq 1$. A value close to 1 or -1 means larger positive and negative correlation, respectively, while a value close to 0 means smaller correlation.

Selection of the Measurement Matrix: Since we will be denoising the image patches by using the sparse estimates from collaborative filtering in the transform domain, the use of an appropriate measurement matrix or dictionary also serves as a key step. Generally, the dictionary mainly consist of basis vectors through which any random patch can be represented as a linear combination of the basis elements. In our case, we are representing any patch using the obtained sparse vector and the dictionary as already shown in Fig. 2.

Decorrelation of the Measurement Matrix: Each patch can be written as linear combination of basis elements from the dictionary. The columns of this dictionary are derived from wavelet basis and are normalized to have unit norms. Prior finding support sets of $\widehat{\theta}_\alpha$ via sparse estimation of patches, we will reduce the correlation between dictionary columns for a robust computational and performance ability. Consequently, we remove weak supports by rejecting highly correlated columns as the information they encode could easily be encoded by other columns which correlate with them. We denote it by the decorrelator operator as follows

$$\Theta = \Gamma_\tau(\Theta') \tag{14}$$

where $\Gamma_\tau(.)$ is the de-correlation operator that removes all the columns of Θ' with correlation greater than τ.

Gaussianity Property: This should be noted that the Gaussianity property of the noisy data received and then aggregated at the receiver (e.g., CHs or BS) should remain intact. This is because, even though our proposed Bayesian analysis based denoising algorithm is agnostic to support distribution of the sparse coefficients, it does need the data samples to be corrupted by Gaussian noise collectively. A concise version of this is provided in the following Lemma 1 to support the accuracy of our denoising algorithm.

Lemma 1. *The aggregated data samples received at either CHs or BS keep the Gaussianity property intact, hence, we can denoise the cumulative version of the AWGN corrupted data.*

Proof. To show this, we consider two independent Gaussian random data samples P and Q sent by nodes μ_α and μ_γ, both $\in \kappa$. For data aggregated by CH, we let $Z = \rho P + \delta Q$. Without loss of generality, let ρ and δ be positive real numbers because for $\rho < 0$, P would be replaced by $-P$, and then we would write $|\rho|$ instead of ρ. The commutative probability function can be written as:

$$F_Z(z) = P\{Z \le z\} = P\{\rho P + \delta Q \le z\}$$
$$= \int\int_{\rho P + \delta Q \le z} \varphi(p)\varphi(q)dpdq \tag{15}$$

where $\varphi(.)$ represents the unit Gaussian density function. However, as the integrand $(2\pi)^{-1}\exp(-(p^2 + q^2)/2)$ possesses circular symmetry, the numerical

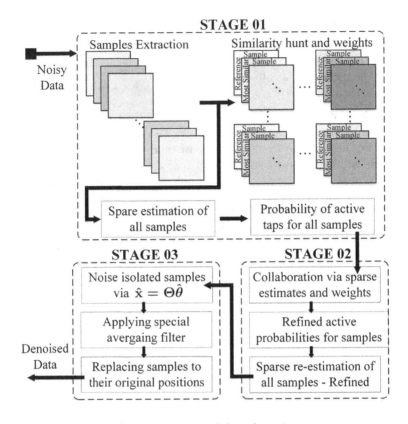

Fig. 6. Flowchart of data denoising

property of this integral is a function of length of the origin from $\rho p + \delta q = z$. Consequently using coordinates rotation, we can conclude

$$F_Z(z) \quad = \quad \int_{p=-\infty}^{\zeta} \int_{q=-\infty}^{q=\infty} \varphi(p)\varphi(q)dpdq \quad = \quad \Delta(\zeta) \quad (16)$$

where $\zeta = \frac{z}{\sqrt{\rho^2 + \delta^2}}$, and $\Delta(.)$ shows standard Gaussian CDF. Hence, the CDF of $Z|_{L=2}$ is a zero-mean Gaussian random variable having total variance equal to $\rho^2 + \delta^2$.

3.7   Region Growing Based Smoothening Filter

As a final step for removing out the noisy components from the image, we perform region growing method on the output image resulted from the previous process. For this image, we store the pixels in different number of bins based on their intensity levels. For instance, we assign group 1 to the pixels that have, for example, intensity range from 0–3, group 2 to pixel intensities from 4–7, and

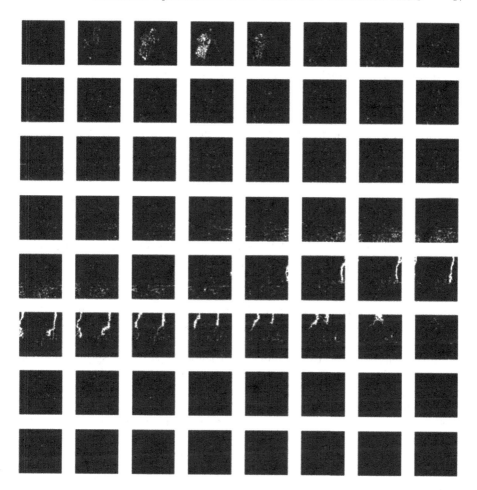

Fig. 7. An example of dividing the Cameraman image into 64 different groups/bins (left to right): first row; group 1–8, second row; group 2–16, third row; group 17–24, fourth row; group 25–32, fifth row; group 33–40, sixth row; group 41–48, seventh row; group 49–56, 8th row; group 57–64

so on. We do this for all the pixels and as a result we create different bins with pixels and their locations stored within those bin groups. We show an example of applying such intensity-leveling on the *Cameraman* image in Fig. 7. In this figure, we display all the intensity groups/bins as binary images where the white pixels correspond to the pixels of the *Cameraman* image belonging to the relevant group.

For each bin, we apply the region growing algorithm to find the connected pixels within that bin. This means that the local similar intensity pixels are identified first. Afterwards, if the number of connected pixels in each bin exceed a certain threshold, then we replace those connected pixels by their mean.

Similarly, we repeat this process for all the bins which ultimately provides us with the region growing based processed image that we denote by $\bar{\mathbf{X}}_r$. Finally, we get our final denoised image $\bar{\mathbf{X}}$ using the weighted average of the image $\bar{\mathbf{X}}_d$ from denoiser and the region growing processed image $\bar{\mathbf{X}}_r$ as follows

$$\bar{\mathbf{X}} = \varrho_1 \bar{\mathbf{X}}_d + \varrho_2 \bar{\mathbf{X}}_r, \tag{17}$$

where ϱ_1 and ϱ_2 are the weights which are a function of the noise variance.

3.8   Effective Collaboration via RGB Channels of Color Images

As opposed to the case of grayscale single channel images, color images having three R, G and B channels that provide a more advanced way through which the patches can collaborate. Since finding similar patches using more effective approaches is the key for such collaboration, the three channels of a color images supply an important piece of information in the form of the channel correlation that can be used to identify similar patches.

To understand this, consider the three R, G and B channels of the standard Mandrill image as shown in Fig. 8 as separate images. Since the additive white Gaussian noise is independent in all three channels of the image, we denoise the color image by denoising each channel separately. This results in formation of rectangular patches for all three channels. To denoise a patch in a specific channel of the observed color image, once the patches are extracted, similar patches are grouped together by taking into account information from both reference channel and the other two channels.

For example in Fig. 8, to denoise the reference patch, denoted by 'R', from the red channel, similar patches are grouped together from the red channel firstly. This ensures the identification of patches as similar and gives a set containing the information of similar patch numbers. Using this set from the red channel, the similar patches from other channels, for this specific patch, are also identified. Then, the reference patch in the red channel may collaborate with the patches from all channels. Since the idea is to refine the probabilities of active taps by using the sparse vectors that may share the same support, finding similar patches using all three channels can be very effective. These grouped patches for all channels can then ultimately be used to effectively estimate the sparse vectors that are in turn used to obtain denoised patches. These steps are performed for all the patches in all the three channels which ultimately provide us with a denoised color image.

4   Computational Complexity

The computational complexity of our proposed framework is dominated by that of the sparse recovery algorithm that we use, which fortunately has a low computational complexity when compared to other similar existing algorithms for sparse recovery. With the dimensions of our problem at hand, the complexity

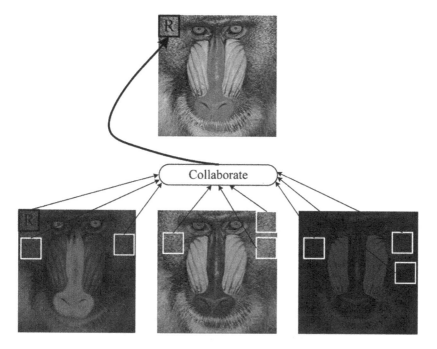

Fig. 8. A depiction of collaboration among patches across all three channels

for estimating one θ_α via the sparse recovery algorithm is of order $\mathcal{O}(MN^2\Upsilon)$ where Υ is the expected number of non-zeros that is generally a very small number.

5   Results and Discussions

In this section, we compare our proposed scheme with the state-of-the-art and traditional routing protocols such as LEACH [20], TEEN [21], SEP [22], DEEC [23] and DDR [30]. We use the values given in Table 1, and our experimentation is divided into two main scenarios: (1) efficient resource utilization, and (2) data denoising. The comparison is carried out over $L = 100, 1000$ and 10000 nodes with following metrics: stability and instability period, network lifetime, energy consumption, computational complexity, peak signal-to-noise ratio (PSNR) and structural similarity (SSIM) index.

A comparison of stability period for $L = 100$ is shown in Fig. 9. This figure demonstrates the number of alive nodes over 8000 sensing rounds. It is evident from the figure that our proposed scheme significantly outperforms all the protocols, and shows promising results. The first node die time of our approach is around 2900, while that of LEACH, TEEN, SEP, DEEC and DDR is around 800, 1900, 1600, 2000, and 1400, respectively. Similarly, Fig. 10 illustrates the all node die time (ADT) of these protocols for $L = 100$. It can be clearly seen that

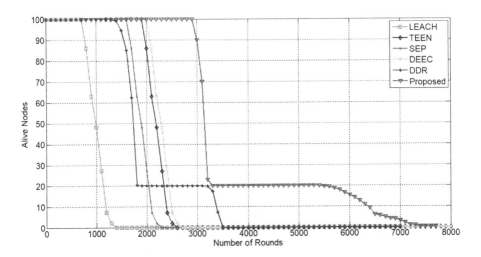

Fig. 9. Stability period

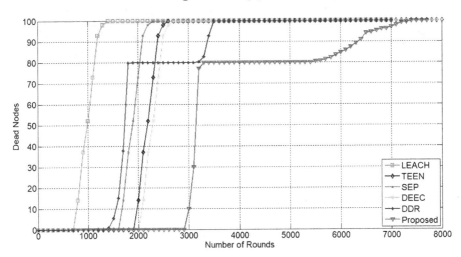

Fig. 10. Instability period

the ADT of our method is ~6390, ~5290, ~5490, ~5190 and ~4290 better than LEACH, TEEN, SEP, DEEC and DDR, respectively. We show that our scheme provides the best ADT, and hence, is the most suitable candidate for practical applications.

We provide a comparison of energy efficient resource utilization in Fig. 11. Here, we show that all protocols start with same energy levels. However, based on the optimized communication method, our scheme demonstrates outstanding results beating all the contestants. In Fig. 12, we compare the network lifetime of our proposed method with LEACH and DDR for $L = 100, 1000$ and 10000.

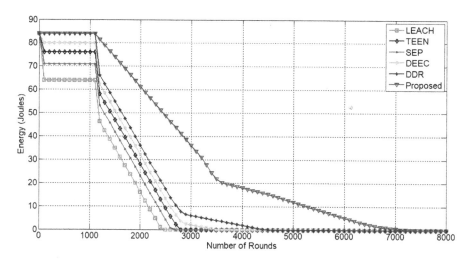

Fig. 11. Energy utilization comparison

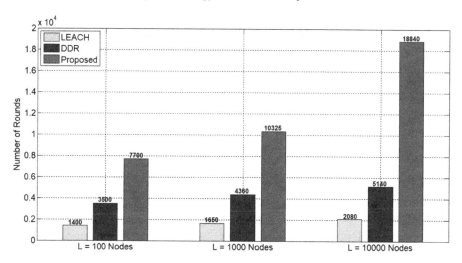

Fig. 12. Network lifetime

It is validated that our protocol is equally competitive on large scale network scenarios outperforming each of the traditional methods.

The complexity of our approach is dominated by the communication yielding a convenient implementation of our method as compared with other protocols as shown in Fig. 13. We compare the computational time consumed by the contestant methods using a 2.20 GHz Intel Core i7-3632QM machine for different number of nodes. This figure proves the robustness of our protocol by showing superior performance, hence, lending itself the most preferable choice for real-time applications.

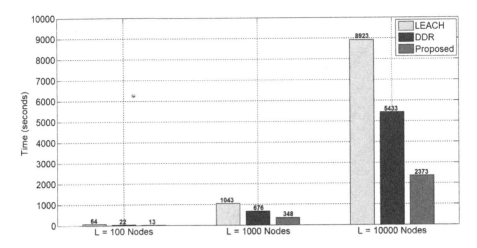

Fig. 13. Computational overload comparison

Table 2. Comparison of denoising image data samples in terms of PSNR/SSIM

Noise level σ_n		10	15	20	50	100
Lena	Noisy	28.03/0.76	24.63/0.66	22.16/0.58	20.13/0.50	08.13/0.11
	Denoised [18]	32.64/0.90	30.44/0.86	28.77/0.82	23.97/0.62	20.50/0.48
	Proposed	**35.54/0.96**	**33.65/0.94**	**32.65/0.91**	**26.21/0.76**	**23.01/0.61**
Barbara	Noisy	28.18/0.87	24.59/0.77	22.09/0.69	14.10/0.33	08.21/0.13
	Denoised [18]	31.88/0.94	29.56/0.91	27.93/0.88	22.75/0.68	20.11/0.50
	Proposed	**35.36/0.97**	**32.34/0.93**	**29.09/0.91**	**25.67/0.79**	**23.21/0.61**
House	Noisy	28.07/0.51	24.57/0.44	22.02/0.38	14.03/0.19	08.09/0.07
	Denoised [18]	35.28/0.67	32.63/0.61	31.33/0.58	25.80/0.45	22.14/0.27
	Proposed	**38.34/0.79**	**35.74/0.69**	**33.90/0.64**	**29.04/0.53**	**24.03/0.29**
Peppers	Noisy	28.08/0.81	24.72/0.72	22.13/0.63	14.17/0.33	08.16/0.13
	Denoised [18]	32.00/0.92	29.74/0.89	28.11/0.85	23.09/0.68	19.62/0.49
	Proposed	**35.03/0.94**	**32.44/0.90**	**20.95/0.88**	**27.34/0.73**	**21.34/0.54**
Boat	Noisy	28.08/0.75	24.59/0.63	22.05/0.53	14.17/0.24	08.10/0.09
	Denoised [18]	31.59/0.86	29.11/0.76	27.48/0.69	23.42/0.45	20.64/0.26
	Proposed	**33.97/0.89**	**31.34/0.84**	**28.98/0.75**	**26.34/0.59**	**22.34/0.42**
C-man	Noisy	28.07/0.53	24.56/0.45	22.09/0.40	14.13/0.21	08.18/0.10
	Denoised [18]	33.28/0.75	31.21/0.69	29.23/0.63	24.19/0.45	20.67/0.25
	Proposed	**35.53/0.86**	**34.34/0.74**	**32.34/0.71**	**26.53/0.55**	**22.24/0.30**
Room	Noisy	28.21/0.80	24.62/0.68	22.07/0.58	14.19/0.25	08.10/0.09
	Denoised [18]	31.59/0.86	29.11/0.76	27.48/0.69	23.42/0.45	20.64/0.26
	Proposed	**33.53/0.92**	**31.64/0.89**	**29.53/0.85**	**25.30/0.63**	**22.11/0.41**
Mandrill	Noisy	27.99/0.80	24.56/0.66	21.98/0.54	14.16/0.20	08.18/0.06
	Denoised [18]	30.88/0.85	28.51/0.75	27.09/0.67	24.17/0.47	21.30/0.28
	Proposed	**34.87/0.91**	**31.51/0.76**	**29.93/0.73**	**26.54/0.53**	**23.87/0.30**

Finally, the detailed denoising results of various standard images are shown in Figs. 14, 15, 16, 17, 18, 19 and 20, and summarized in Table 2. We opt globally adopted PSNR and SSIM as evaluation metrics to prove that the denoising section of our proposed framework produces equally promising outcomes. The provided table summarizes denoising results[3] of a number of images, as PSNR/SSIM, over a range of noise levels, i.e., $\sigma_n = [10, 15, 20, 50, 100]$. Similarly, we also present the extensive denoising results of color images in Fig. 21. As can be seen by in these figures and table, the recovered images are a very good approximation of original images thereby verifying the effectivenesses of our proposed framework.

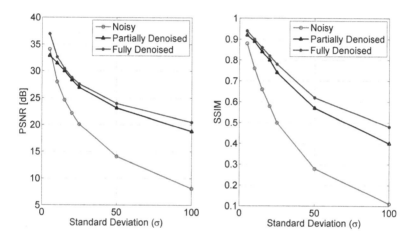

Fig. 14. Denoising 256×256 grayscale *Lena* standard test data images over noise $\sigma = [5, 10, 15, 20, 25, 50, 100]$ when received at a node μ_α. The graphical results show PSNR [dB] and SSIM results in the form of graphs.

For experimentation, we transmitted various images among deployed nodes and showed that the resultant images received at the receiver suffers from Gaussian noise. The PSNR and SSIM values of the corresponding received noisy images are shown in the table. In comparison with our denoised images, we show that a significant amount of improvement is achieved in terms of the noise being removed, and the actual data is recovered to a greater extent. Consequently, these results confirm that our proposed framework is indeed an effective and robust model for real-time scenarios in WSNs which outperforms many traditionally proposed routing protocols.

---

[3] Due to space limitations, a detailed version of these results along with their pictorial representations [48, 49] are available at: https://arxiv.org/abs/1806.09980.

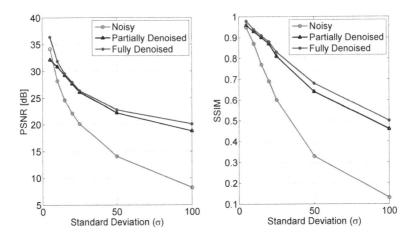

Fig. 15. Denoising 256×256 grayscale *Barbara* standard test data images over noise $\sigma = [5, 10, 15, 20, 25, 50, 100]$ when received at a node μ_α. The graphical results show PSNR [dB] and SSIM results in the form of graphs.

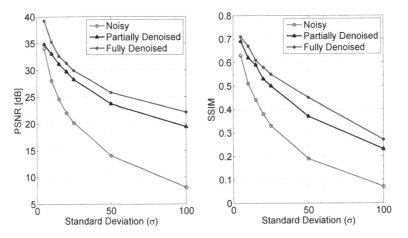

Fig. 16. Denoising 256×256 grayscale *House* standard test data images over noise $\sigma = [5, 10, 15, 20, 25, 50, 100]$ when received at a node μ_α. The graphical results show PSNR [dB] and SSIM results in the form of graphs.

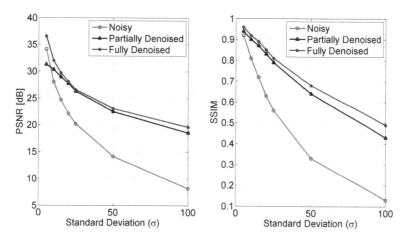

Fig. 17. Denoising **256 × 256** grayscale *Peppers* standard test data images over noise $\sigma = [5, 10, 15, 20, 25, 50, 100]$ when received at a node μ_α. The graphical results show PSNR [dB] and SSIM results in the form of graphs.

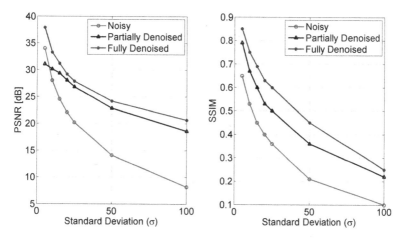

Fig. 18. Denoising **256 × 256** grayscale *Cameraman* standard test data images over noise $\sigma = [5, 10, 15, 20, 25, 50, 100]$ when received at a node μ_α. The graphical results show PSNR [dB] and SSIM results in the form of graphs.

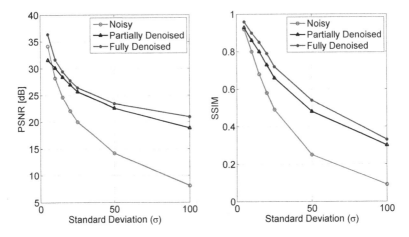

Fig. 19. Denoising **256 × 256** grayscale *Living Room* standard test data images over noise $\sigma = [5, 10, 15, 20, 25, 50, 100]$ when received at a node μ_α. The graphical results show PSNR [dB] and SSIM results in the form of graphs.

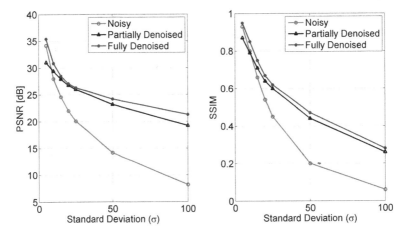

Fig. 20. Denoising **256 × 256** grayscale *Mandrill* standard test data images over noise $\sigma = [5, 10, 15, 20, 25, 50, 100]$ when received at a node μ_α. The graphical results show PSNR [dB] and SSIM results in the form of graphs.

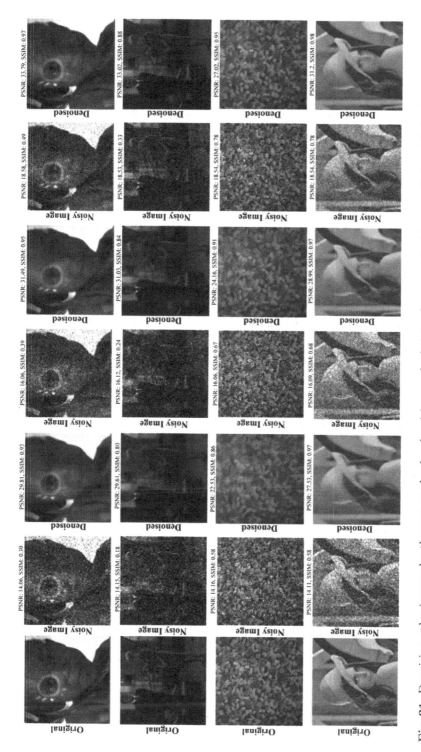

Fig. 21. Denoising color images by the proposed color denoising method. 1st column: original images, 2nd and 3rd columns: noisy and denoised images at $\mathcal{N}(0, 40)$, 4th and 5th columns: noisy and denoised images at $\mathcal{N}(0, 50)$, 6th and 7th columns: noisy and denoised images at $\mathcal{N}(0, 30)$,

6 Conclusions

In this work, we discussed our proposed framework that ensures energy-efficiency and data-denoising in a wireless sensor network. Our system is enriched with a layer-adaptive method that uses a 3-tier communication mechanism for effective and energy-efficient communication among the nodes ultimately minimizing the energy holes. Our presented mathematical coverage model effectively dealt with the formation of coverage holes thereby yielding a robust network. For combating noise in the data, we proposed a collaborative transform-domain based denoising algorithm to take care of the unwanted components. As shown with the help of many simulation results, our framework outperformed traditional algorithms by a significant margin, and provided a computationally-desirable algorithm for real-time applications.

As a future direction, the current work can be enhanced using recently-proposed deep learning models for carrying out the denoising task. Specifically, since there are still some traces of noise in the data, low level deep features from Convolutional neural networks (CNNs) can come in handy to effectively represent patches of the corrupted images. Another interesting direction, as inspired by the CNNs, is to extract the features from transform domain and feed them as input to the CNNs instead of the images itself. This would help the model train well by learning the underlying structures within the images.

References

1. Sheng, Z., Mahapatra, C., Zhu, C., Leung, V.C.M.: Recent advances in industrial wireless sensor networks toward efficient management in IoT. IEEE Access **3**, 622–637 (2015)
2. Mois, G., Folea, S., Sanislav, T.: Analysis of three IoT-based wireless sensors for environmental monitoring. IEEE Trans. Instrum. Meas. **66**(8), 2056–2064 (2017)
3. Umar, A., et al.: On enhancing network reliability and throughput for critical-range based applications in UWSNs. Procedia Comput. Sci. **34**, 196–203 (2014)
4. Grumazescu, C., Vluaduțua, V.A., Subașu, G.: WSN solutions for communication challenges in military live simulation environments. In: International Conference on Communications, pp. 319–322 (2016)
5. Salem, O., Liu, Y., Mehaoua, A.: Anomaly detection in medical WSNs using enclosing ellipse and chi-square distance. In: IEEE International Conference on Communications (ICC), pp. 3658–3663, June 2014
6. Jha, S.S., Nair, S.B.: On a multi-agent distributed asynchronous intelligence-sharing and learning framework. In: Nguyen, N.T. (ed.) Transactions on Computational Collective Intelligence XVIII. LNCS, vol. 9240, pp. 166–200. Springer, Heidelberg (2015). https://doi.org/10.1007/978-3-662-48145-5_9
7. Behzad, M., et al.: Design and development of a low cost ubiquitous tracking system. Procedia Comput. Sci. **34**, 220–227 (2014)
8. Sandhu, M.M., Akbar, M., Behzad, M., Javaid, N., Khan, Z.A., Qasim, U.: Mobility model for WBANs. In: 2014 Ninth International Conference on Broadband and Wireless Computing, Communication and Applications (BWCCA), pp. 155–160. IEEE (2014)

9. Sandhu, M.M., Akbar, M., Behzad, M., Javaid, N., Khan, Z.A., Qasim, U.: REEC: reliable energy efficient critical data routing in wireless body area networks. In: 2014 Ninth International Conference on Broadband and Wireless Computing, Communication and Applications (BWCCA), pp. 446–451. IEEE (2014)

10. Behzad, M.: M-BEHZAD: minimum distance based energy efficiency using hemisphere zoning with advanced divide-and-rule scheme for wireless sensor networks. arXiv preprint arXiv:1804.00898 (2018)

11. Behzad, M., Adnan, N., Merchant, S.A.: Technology-embedded hybrid learning (2018)

12. Sibeko, N., Mudali, P., Oki, O., Alaba, A.: Performance evaluation of routing protocols in uniform and normal node distributions using inter-mesh wireless networks. In: World Symposium on Computer Networks and Information Security (WSCNIS), pp. 1–6, September 2015

13. Heinzelman, W.B.: Application-specific protocol architectures for wireless networks. Ph.D. thesis, Massachusetts Institute of Technology (2000)

14. Behzad, M., et al.: TSDDR: threshold sensitive density controlled divide and rule routing protocol for wireless sensor networks. In: Ninth International Conference on Broadband and Wireless Computing, Communication and Applications, pp. 78–83, November 2014

15. Saleem, F., et al.: IDDR: improved density controlled divide-and-rule scheme for energy efficient routing in wireless sensor networks. Procedia Comput. Sci. **34**, 212–219 (2014)

16. Behzad, M., Ge, Y.: Performance optimization in wireless sensor networks: a novel collaborative compressed sensing approach. In: IEEE 31st International Conference on Advanced Information Networking and Applications (AINA), pp. 749–756, March 2017

17. Behzad, M., Javaid, M.S., Parahca, M.A., Khan, S.: Distributed PCA and consensus based energy efficient routing protocol for WSNs. J. Inf. Sci. Eng. **33**(5), 1267–1283 (2017)

18. Behzad, M., Abdullah, M., Hassan, M.T., Ge, Y., Khan, M.A.: Layer-adaptive communication and collaborative transformed-domain representations to optimize performance in next-generation WSNs. In: IEEE 32nd International Conference on Advanced Information Networking and Applications, pp. 101–108 (2018)

19. Jurenoks, A., Novickis, L.: Analysis of wireless sensor network structure and life time affecting factors. In: Communication and Information Technologies (KIT), pp. 1–6, October 2017

20. Heinzelman, W.B., Chandrakasan, A., Balakrishnan, H.: Energy-efficient communication protocol for wireless microsensor networks. In: Proceedings of the 33rd Annual Hawaii International Conference on System Sciences, January 2000

21. Manjeshwar, A., Agrawal, D.P.: TEEN: a routing protocol for enhanced efficiency in wireless sensor networks. In: Proceedings 15th International Parallel and Distributed Processing Symposium (IPDPS), pp. 2009–2015, April 2001

22. Smaragdakis, G., Matta, I., Bestavros, A.: SEP: a stable election protocol for clustered heterogeneous wireless sensor networks. Technical report, Boston University Computer Science Department (2004)

23. Qing, L., Zhu, Q., Wang, M.: Design of a distributed energy-efficient clustering algorithm for heterogeneous wireless sensor networks. Comput. Commun. **29**(12), 2230–2237 (2006)

24. Khadivi, A., Shiva, M.: FTPASC: a fault tolerant power aware protocol with static clustering for wireless sensor networks. In: IEEE International Conference on Wireless and Mobile Computing, Networking and Communications, pp. 397–401, June 2006)

25. Azam, I., et al.: SEEC: sparsity-aware energy efficient clustering protocol for underwater wireless sensor networks. In: IEEE 30th International Conference on Advanced Information Networking and Applications (AINA), pp. 352–361, March 2016

26. Bajaber, F., Awan, I.: Centralized dynamic clustering for wireless sensor network. In: International Conference on Advanced Information Networking and Applications (AINA) Workshops, pp. 193–198, 2009

27. Tomar, G.S., Verma, S.: Dynamic multi-level hierarchal clustering approach for wireless sensor networks. In: 11th International Conference on Computer Modelling and Simulation, pp. 563–567, March 2009

28. Naeem, M.K., Patwary, M., Abdel-Maguid, M.: Universal and dynamic clustering scheme for energy constrained cooperative wireless sensor networks. IEEE Access **5**, 12318–12337 (2017)

29. Jia, D., Zhu, H., Zou, S., Hu, P.: Dynamic cluster head selection method for wireless sensor network. IEEE Sens. J. **16**(8), 2746–2754 (2016)

30. Ahmad, A., Latif, K., Javaidl, N., Khan, Z.A., Qasim, U.: Density controlled divide-and-rule scheme for energy efficient routing in wireless sensor networks. In: 26th IEEE Canadian Conference on Electrical and Computer Engineering (CCECE), pp. 1–4, May 2013

31. Mammu, A.S.K., Sharma, A., Hernandez-Jayo, U., Sainz, N.: A novel cluster-based energy efficient routing in wireless sensor networks. In: IEEE 27th International Conference on Advanced Information Networking and Applications (AINA), pp. 41–47, March 2013

32. Behzad, M., Masood, M., Ballal, T., Shadaydeh, M., Al-Naffouri, T.Y.: Image denoising via collaborative support-agnostic recovery. In: 2017 IEEE International Conference on Acoustics, Speech and Signal Processing (ICASSP), pp. 1343–1347, March 2017

33. Krause, A.F., Harischandra, N., Dürr, V.: Shape recognition through tactile contour tracing. In: Nguyen, N.T., Kowalczyk, R., Duval, B., van den Herik, J., Loiseau, S., Filipe, J. (eds.) Transactions on Computational Collective Intelligence XX. LNCS, vol. 9420, pp. 54–77. Springer, Cham (2015). https://doi.org/10.1007/978-3-319-27543-7_3

34. He, K., Sun, J.: Image completion approaches using the statistics of similar patches. IEEE Trans. Pattern Anal. Mach. Intell. **36**(12), 2423–2435 (2014)

35. Liu, H., Xiong, R., Ma, S., Fan, X., Gao, W.: Gradient based image/video softcast with grouped-patch collaborative reconstruction. In: IEEE Visual Communications and Image Processing Conference, pp. 141–144, December 2014

36. Wang, M., Yu, J., Sun, W.: Group-based hyperspectral image denoising using low rank representation. In: IEEE International Conference on Image Processing (ICIP), pp. 1623–1627, September 2015

37. Yang, W., Liu, J., Yang, S., Quo, Z.: Image super-resolution via nonlocal similarity and group structured sparse representation. In: IEEE Visual Communications and Image Processing, pp. 1–4, December 2015

38. Bahrami, K., Shi, F., Zong, X., Shin, H.W., An, H., Shen, D.: Reconstruction of 7T-like images from 3T MRI. IEEE Trans. Med. Imaging **35**(9), 2085–2097 (2016)

39. Behzad, M.: Image denoising via collaborative dual-domain patch filtering. arXiv preprint arXiv:1805.00472 (2018)

40. Van Hulle, M.M.: Self-organizing maps. In: Seel, N.M. (ed.) Encyclopedia of the Sciences of Learning, pp. 585–622. Springer, Boston (2012). https://doi.org/10.1007/978-1-4419-1428-6

41. Gersho, A.: On the structure of vector quantizers. IEEE Trans. Inf. Theory **28**(2), 157–166 (1982)

42. Höppner, F.: Fuzzy Cluster Analysis: Methods for Classification, Data Analysis and Image Recognition. Wiley, New York (1999)

43. Jain, A.K., Murty, M.N., Flynn, P.J.: Data clustering: a review. ACM Comput. Surv. (CSUR) **31**(3), 264–323 (1999)

44. Buades, A., Coll, B., Morel, J.-M.: A non-local algorithm for image denoising. In: IEEE Computer Society Conference on Computer Vision and Pattern Recognition, vol. 2, pp. 60–65 (2005)

45. Dabov, K., Foi, A., Katkovnik, V., Egiazarian, K.: Image denoising by sparse 3-D transform-domain collaborative filtering. IEEE Trans. Image Process. **16**(8), 2080–2095 (2007)

46. Liu, G., Zhong, H., Jiao, L.: Comparing noisy patches for image denoising: a double noise similarity model. IEEE Trans. Image Process. **24**(3), 862–872 (2015)

47. Panetta, K., Bao, L., Agaian, S.: Sequence-to-sequence similarity-based filter for image denoising. IEEE Sens. J. **16**(11), 4380–4388 (2016)

48. Behzad, M., Abdullah, M., Hassan, M.T., Ge, Y., Khan, M.A.: Layer-adaptive communication and collaborative transformed-domain representations for performance optimization in wsns. arXiv preprint arXiv:1712.04259 (2017)

49. Behzad, M., Abdullah, M., Hassan, M.T., Ge, Y., Khan, M.A.: Toward performance optimization in IoT-based next-Gen wireless sensor networks. arXiv preprint arXiv:1806.09980 (2018)

Enabling Custom Security Controls as Plugins in Service Oriented Environments

Dimosthenis Kyriazis$^{(\boxtimes)}$

University of Piraeus, Karaoli & Dimitriou 80, 18532 Piraeus, Greece
dimos@unipi.gr

Abstract. Service oriented environments such as cloud computing infrastructures aim at facilitating the requirements of users and enterprises by providing services following an on-demand orientation. While the advantages of such environments are clear and lead to wide adoption, the key concern of the non-adopters refers to privacy and security. Even though providers put in place several measures to minimize security and privacy vulnerabilities, the users are still in many cases reluctant to move their data and applications to clouds. In this paper an approach is presented that proposes the use of security controls as plugins that can be ingested in service-oriented environments. The latter allows users to tailor the corresponding security and privacy levels by utilizing security measures that have been selected and implemented by themselves, thus alleviating their security and privacy concerns. The challenges and an architecture with the corresponding key building blocks that address these challenges are presented. Furthermore, results in the context of trustworthy requirements, i.e. dependability, are presented to evaluate the proposed approach.

Keywords: Cloud computing · Service oriented infrastructures · Security · Privacy · Dependability

1 Introduction

The ever increasing need for data processing, storage, elastic and unbounded scale of computing infrastructure has provided great thrust for shifting the data and computing operations to the cloud. The benefits for both enterprises and single users moving to the cloud (cloud adoption) are clear: greater agility, data availability, and collaboration. According to a survey [1], in 15 months, 80% of all IT budgets will be committed to cloud apps and solutions, while private cloud-only adoption is lowest in services companies (16%) due to concerns over IT security skills. These representative facts highlight that even through there are clear benefits in the use of service-based environments, these are weighed against potential risks [2], as cloud computing comes with its own set of data security issues. Since the cloud is perceived as a "black box", a user has little or no control over the promises set by cloud's Service Level Agreements (SLAs), and as a consequence over the general usage/security of the cloud [3]. Although shifting to cloud technologies exclusively is affordable and fast, doing so undermines important security policies, processes, and best practices. To this end, the CSA (Cloud Security Alliance) has identified "The Treacherous Twelve", the top

© Springer-Verlag GmbH Germany, part of Springer Nature 2019
N. T. Nguyen et al. (Eds.): TCCI XXXIII, LNCS 11610, pp. 32–51, 2019.
https://doi.org/10.1007/978-3-662-59540-4_2

twelve cloud computing threats for 2017 [4], including: (i) data breaches, (ii) data loss, (iii) account hijacking, (iv) insecure APIs, (v) denial of service, (vi) malicious insiders, (vii) abuse and nefarious of cloud services, (viii) insufficient due diligence, (ix) denial of service, (x) advanced persistent threats, (xi) weak identity, credential and access management, and (xii) system and application vulnerabilities. Considering that most of these threats could be characterized as 'security threats', a lot of effort has been put from the research community for finding solutions in the name of 'cloud security'.

Cloud computing consists of several components, such as data centers, servers, network, or Virtual Machines (VMs). Various researches have been implemented focusing on the physical domain (data centers, servers, network, etc.), in order to neutralize the threats that are met day-by-day. What is more, there are plenty approaches that address the topic of security in the field of cloud management. A relevant and interesting approach is presented in [6], aiming at modelling different risks and threats, and according to these models provide the corresponding cloud services. However, due to the fact that virtual domains is one of the core components of a cloud, this poses major security risks. Some examples of these risks are how to ensure that different instances running on the same VM are isolated from each other, or how to control the administrator on host and guest operating systems. Another important asset refers to data and the value of the data. The latter has led technology companies (e.g. IBM, Cisco, SAP, EMC) to create the so called "Open Cloud Manifesto" raising the need for more consistent security and monitoring of cloud services [7]. Thus, cloud users rely on their providers for proper security, posing a set of quality of protection parameters as a prerequisite to exploit cloud computing environments. Towards meeting these requirements, providers are now offering Trusted Virtual Data centers (TVDc) that build on the concept of Trusted Virtual Domains [8]. Amazon already offers such a "product", the virtual private cloud [9] that provides dedicated resources and virtual private networks with guaranteed isolation. As a concept, it is not new, since Multics design (in 1965) has been proposed aiming to allow users to build protected subsystems [10, 11]. However, such environments refer to an offering by the providers as yet another choice for users regarding security levels. It mainly targets infrastructure-related security concerns but in many cases, security problems are not isolated: different issues and threats may combine and lead to different security breaches. Furthermore, virtual private clouds do not allow users to enforce their own security controls and this is of major importance since bronze, silver, gold and even platinum "security contracts" may not be adequate for some users and organizations. Thus, when it comes to critical or personal information, users tend to exploit "in house" infrastructures they have under control in order to overcome security concerns: managing data behind firewalls and putting in place "trusted" security mechanisms is their current choice, reducing the potential for innovative uses of data in value chains, reducing flexibility and increasing cost of multi-stakeholder business processes.

In general, as the users take advantage of the operational and economic benefits of virtualization and the cloud, it is critical to secure the virtualized data centers, cloud deployments, and hybrid environments effectively, as if users and enterprises neglect any aspect of security, these will open the doors to web threats and serious data breaches [5]. Security is a central concern for enterprises of any scale, including Small Medium Enterprises (SMEs), which are increasingly relying on ICT infrastructures to support their business models and deliver their services. SMEs face very much the same security issues as large corporations, without however possessing the knowledge, expertise, staff and equity capital required to successfully prevent, mitigate and confront these challenges. It is no accident that in 2015, over 74% of the SMEs faced at least one cyber-security breach. The rise of managed security solutions (including cloud-based security-as-a-service solutions) provides opportunities for alleviating SMEs limitations in terms of deploying and adopting effective cyber security solutions. Managed Security Solutions alleviate SMEs from the burden of hosting and understanding the details of cyber-security infrastructures. Likewise, Security-as-a-Service models enable SMEs to benefit from security assets provided online as services (e.g., data protection, network protection, intrusion detection, authentication, anti-virus, security incidents detection, vulnerability analysis & management).

This paper introduces an approach that aims at addressing security and privacy concerns, in line with security-as-a-service and managed security solutions. The approach proposes an architecture and reference solution that enables the users and enterprises to manage the levels of security and privacy through their own ingested tools and mechanisms. Given that these tools and mechanisms will be ingested, activated and managed in service oriented environments (e.g. clouds), they can be considered as plugins that follow a management lifecycle as agents do [12]. The remainder of the paper is structured as follows: Sect. 2 discusses related work and the challenges to be addressed in different areas of the targeted domain, while Sect. 3 presents the proposed architecture and the key building blocks of it. Section 4 cites relevant experimentation outcomes to validate the introduced architecture. Section 5 concludes with a discussion on future research and potentials for the current study.

2   Challenges to Be Addressed

Approaches and technologies are required to address security aspects across the complete data and service lifecycle by allowing organizations and users to ingest along with their data and application services, their own security tools and mechanisms as plugins. These mechanisms target several aspects such as authentication, identity management, compliance, and access. The proposed approach allows organizations to bring their own security controls beyond what is available in a public cloud environment. Users will be able to seamlessly align enterprise security policies with cloud service policies, and deploy technical countermeasures they think are not appropriate enough to mitigate threats in public cloud environments and multi-stakeholder value chains.

In a published analysis [13], "Reinventing SaaS" Security as a Service is expected to see significant growth in the next years. The presented approach aims at realizing this vision since it allows users to exploit *Security as a Service* either by selecting security services or by ingesting their own security services – as plugins, in cloud infrastructures. The proposed solution enables security controls (i.e. plugins) for detection capabilities, incident responses, and operational capabilities (e.g. patch management) to be ingested, raising trust and security to the corresponding desired levels (as depicted in the next Fig. 1).

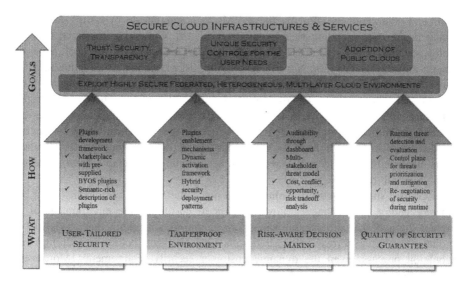

Fig. 1. Key pillars and enabling technologies

One of the key challenges refers to mechanisms for developing plugins or exploiting pre-existing/pre-supplied ones through a repository, as well as tools for describing plugins based on semantic-rich structures are required. These descriptions form the basis for plugins management mechanisms, which enable plugins to be loaded, managed according to their dynamically changing triggering conditions (through the activation framework), and monitored during their execution. However, while cloud customers have better knowledge about their application security requirements, it should be noted that cloud providers potentially have better knowledge about the relevant cloud security issues due to their higher concentration of security expertise. In this context, what is required refers to hybrid solutions combining security controls offered by cloud providers (also in the form of selectable plugins) and plugins ingested by users. The presented approach proposes tools to allow the implementation of such hybrid solutions through enhanced deployment patterns that take into account effectiveness of plugins and combination possibilities. These innovative technologies foster the creation of vertical clouds delivered with regulations and compliance geared towards a particular sector (e.g. finance, automotive, aerospace, media).

Moreover, one needs to consider that there are various security threats in cloud environments, including virtualization/hypervisors security vulnerabilities, sniffing/spoofing in virtual networks, denial of service, etc. Traditional security mechanisms such as digital signatures, encryption (aiming also at privacy as described by the authors in [14]), identity, authentication, and authorization are no longer sufficient for clouds in their current form [15]. Users may be able to control the software executed in their virtual machines but the underlying infrastructure (compute, network, and storage resources) is managed by cloud providers [16]. Thus, various challenges arise regarding multi-tenancy and sharing in cloud environments, which can be exploited to enable a Virtual Machine (VM) - acting as an "attacker node" to target another VM through covert and side channels allowing these VMs to communicate bypassing the rules defined in the corresponding security models [17–19]. Currently, the practice is to employ security policies in order to ensure that data and services are kept separate between different tenants [20]. Nevertheless, in the case of collaborative entities (e.g. in value chain scenarios) such "generic" approaches either limit the required functionality or lead to security vulnerabilities during information and service exchange and usage. Techniques are proposed to evaluate the common ground for the collaborative entities and manage conflicts arising from the usage of different plugins. The information can be provided to all involved entities through a dashboard providing insights to potential threats, deployed plugins as well as providers' security information in order to increase auditability and transparency.

Of course, such non-generic solutions do not come without cost, which may be monetary and/or performance. Allowing users to customize the environment of a provider through the corresponding loadable plugins is something that needs to be negotiated with the corresponding trade-offs [21] analyzed before and during the negotiation process given the dynamic customer security requirements. Moreover, these requirements need to be clarified and captured in contracts and Service Level Agreements (SLAs), which are expected to enforce better risk management [22] and provide the means for enhanced security in cloud environments [23, 24]. Besides negotiation before the use, the presented approach also proposes runtime re-negotiation in an automated way in order to provide quality of security guarantees. Runtime decisions are based on the monitoring data collected and evaluated against the security objectives of users and the enforcement of mitigation plans (triggering the corresponding plugins) through an envisioned control plane.

A key aspect enabling the enforcement and deployment of security measures/plugins refers to the detection of potential anomalies. Anomaly-based solutions try to overcome the inherent limitation of signature-based methods by adopting a more general solution that is not based on a priori knowledge about attacks (e.g. their signature). Anomaly detection aims to find patterns in data that deviates from an expected or normal behavior (i.e. anomalies/outliers). Approaches to anomaly detection can be supervised, semi-supervised or unsupervised. Supervised methods assumed the access to data labelled as normal and abnormal examples. Semi-supervised only assumes one type of label on the training dataset. Unsupervised methods assume no access to labelled data. One can also consider methods that act (learn) online or offline. The majority of methods work offline but some can evolve as data is obtained like in data streams. Supervised methods are based on a classifier like SVM [25]. Unsupervised methods use clustering algorithms like the ones described in [26]. Cluster based method are very popular in practice since it is typically quite common to be very hard to obtain labelled data as deviation and normal behavior. There are several types of studied anomalies: (i) random, when a data object is abnormal in relation to the complete dataset, (ii) contextual anomaly if the data object is abnormal in relation to a context but not against the dataset e.g. a geographical context, and (iii) collective anomalies when a set of data objects with a strong relationship is abnormal in relation to the remain dataset. Anomaly-based solutions look at all the traffic and try to determine deviations between current and reference traffic behavior. A representative example has been followed and applied to identity management and encryption schemes to enhance the latter [27]. In this way, they are also able to overcome the issue that a malicious packet may seem legitimate if analyzed in isolation. Plenty of anomaly-based solutions have been proposed to provide detection or mitigation of multiple types of attacks relying on complex analysis of the traffic features [28], or on partial execution of the content of a packet in an emulated environment for detecting code-injections [29].

An additional security-related challenge emerges from the multi-tenancy support offered by cloud providers. The latter highlights the need for approaches that tackle the conflicting objectives and requirements of the tenants, which range from security mechanisms that are put in place for example for data sharing [30], to allocation of resources to different tenants [31]. To this end, multi-objective optimization techniques are required in order to optimize the corresponding objective functions at the same time. There is no unique solution to multi-objective optimization problems, but instead, a set of good trade-off solutions (Pareto optimal set) [32]. As a primary goal of multi-objective optimization is to model a decision-maker's preferences (ordering or relative importance of objectives and goals), one valid categorization of the methods should be related to the way the decision-maker articulates these preferences. So, a priori artic-ulation of preferences implies that the user indicates the relative importance of the objective functions before running the optimization algorithm. A posteriori articulation of preferences implies the selection of a single solution from a set of mathematically equivalent solutions, while in interactive articulation of preferences the decision-maker is continually providing input throughout the execution of the algorithm [33]. Great progress has been achieved in the field of meta-heuristics especially with the evolu-tionary algorithms that are inspired by evolutionary mechanisms found in biological species. The evolutionary algorithms along with the simulated annealing and Tabu search techniques can be further classified in three main categories: Scalar approaches, Pareto Approaches and non-Pareto and non-scalar approaches. Scalar approaches entail the transformation of the multi-objective optimization problems (MOPs) into a single objective problem. This class of approaches includes algorithms based on aggregation, which combine the various cost functions in only one objective function, generally in a linear way. Scalar approaches are also based on constraint methods and goal pro-gramming. Non-Pareto/non-scalar approaches based on the populations of solutions, use operators to treat the various objectives separately. Only two methods have been studied regarding this approach: parallel selection and lexicographic selection.

Pareto-based approaches use the concept of dominance in the selection process. In this class, ranking, elitism and diversity maintaining methods are included. They can be historically studied as covering two generations. The first generation is characterized by the use of fitness sharing and niching combined with Pareto ranking [34].

Multi-objective optimization using meta-heuristics is an active research field where new techniques are continuously emerging to cope with real settings (such as uncer-tainty and noise, many-objective optimization, and convergence speed). In this context, software frameworks that include state-of-the-art algorithms, commonly accepted benchmark multi-objective optimization problems and quality indicators for perfor-mance assessment are valuable tools for everybody involved in multi-objective opti-mization problems and need assistance in carrying out research studies. For this reason, several frameworks were developed. A well-known framework is PISA [35], a C-based framework for multi-objective optimization, which is based on separating the algorithm specific part of an optimizer from the application-specific part. This is carried out using a shared-file mechanism that enables the communication between the module executing the application and the module running the meta-heuristic. A drawback of PISA is that the internal design hinders to reuse code. EvA2 (an Evolutionary Algorithms framework, revised version 2) is a comprehensive meta-heuristic optimization framework with emphasis on Evolutionary Algorithms (EA) implemented in Java. EvA2 integrates several derivative-free optimization methods, preferably population-based, such as Evolution Strategies, Genetic Algorithms, Differential Evolution, Particle Swarm Optimization and classical techniques such as Simulated Annealing [36]. Other Java-based meta-heuristic optimization frameworks are Opt4J, jMetal and ECJ. Opt4J is an open source Java-based framework for evolutionary computation. It contains a set of (multi-objective) optimization algorithms such as evolutionary algorithms, differential evolution, particle swarm optimization, and simulated annealing [37]. jMetal aims at the development, experimentation and study of meta-heuristics for solving multi-objective optimization problems. jMetal includes a number of classic and modern state-of-the-art optimizers, a wide set of benchmark problems, and a set of well-known quality indicators to assess the performance of the algorithms [38]. ECJ is a general-purpose evolutionary computation framework, which attempts to permit as many valid combinations as possible of individual representation and breeding method, fitness and selection procedure, evolutionary algorithm, and parallelism [39].

3 Proposed Architecture

The presented approach aims at overcoming the current security limitations in cloud environments and providing approaches for increasing their adoption. However, allowing users to bring their own security controls highlights various challenges and research topics that need to be tackled in order to realize this overall vision. A high level conceptual view is presented in the next figure, targeting at the compilation and provisioning of a secure public cloud environment through which users can manage their services and their data (Fig. 2).

Through this architecture, users are able to exploit the plugins development framework to develop security plugins, ingest existing ones or select/trade from the proposed central repository. Plugins along with their descriptions are managed by the enablement mechanisms, while the activation framework provides triggering decisions, linked data, execution rules, temporal information, etc. During the ingestion process, users are able to obtain information through the dashboard, with respect to potential conflicts (from plugins selected in the current deployment) the progress of the ingestion process, the current threat levels (based on the threat detection and evaluation framework), and decision support based on the outcomes of the trade-off analysis. Following the plugins ingestion process, a set of mechanisms is proposed in order to provide quality of security guarantees during runtime according to the security objectives set by the users. Runtime security monitoring information is collected and evaluated against the defined objectives and re-negotiation is triggered in an automated way. The information is also propagated to threat detection and trade-off tools in order to perform

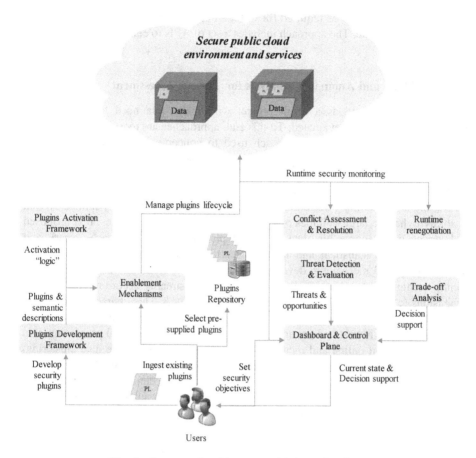

Fig. 2. Conceptual architecture and information flows

the corresponding analysis and inform the user. This information flow is further detailed in the next paragraphs in terms of key concepts and mechanisms being utilized in the proposed architecture.

3.1 Plugins Semantics

A plugin extension that needs to be executed in the Cloud should contain a detailed description, sufficiently detailed so that execution environment can execute it in autonomously, enabling it to communicate with other components if needed and enforcing the cloud to comply with the security plugin. A plugin description can be provided by means of special metadata, custom configuration, parameters, etc. The presented architecture proposes a hierarchical generalized "template" to be used in order to describe the plugin executable, its dependencies, execution environment, external/internal communication pattern, output, data filtering, parameters and more. The aforementioned hierarchical template serves as a generalized template that can be "inherited" and extended as required for different cases: per plugin, per application or per cloud provider site. The approach includes a set of APIs to enable the proper plugin description.

3.2 Workload and Anomalies Analysis for Threats Assessment

To analyze threats and as a result protect workloads, data need to be collected, aggregated and analyzed/evaluated. To this end, approaches are required moving away from the traditional black box approach used to conceptualize infrastructures (e.g. clouds), towards cooperative mechanisms between the cloud provider and the cloud users enabling data security sharing. Many security systems rely on rule-base approaches that are known to be limited to new attacks patterns. While some systems are starting using anomaly detection techniques, still these are typically limited both in of ability to handle large volumes of data and their analytic capabilities. It is proposed to leverage open source big data analytical platforms such as Apache Spark and develop advanced statistical and machine learning anomaly detection analytics on top. The proposed mechanism develops real-time characterizations using online data mining techniques to characterize in real-time data streams according to different dimensions (e.g. source, average traffic, average size, etc.). This characterization also uses a data clustering technique. What is more and since current techniques such as k-means are quadric in cost and not amenable for online and incremental processing, it is proposed to exploit online and incremental techniques for amendable data clustering, which is amenable for doing inexpensive and accurate characterization of massive data. Given that one of the disadvantages of anomaly detection techniques is a high rate of false-positive alerts, it is proposed to introduce techniques for adaptive control of false-positive alerts to manageable levels.

3.3 Multi-tenancy and Multi-stakeholder Security Support

The presented solution addresses security aspects related to multi-tenancy and multi-stakeholder data value chains, by providing technologies enabling users to set their policies and rules with respect to management (and in the case of multi-tenancy separation) of storage, memory, processing and routing. Moreover, a classification framework allows classifying and prioritizing rules that may be conflicting and thus create privacy and security threats. The classification framework takes into account potential conflicts and specific requests posed by tenants in multi-tenancy and value-chain scenarios. Another aspect refers to storage, access and processing of data that are owned and managed by different stakeholders – with potentially different security constraints and profiles. The current solution proposes tools enabling the ingestion of fine-grained dynamic security mechanisms addressing the complete data value chain, thus being active during the "exchange" of information between tenants. Through the current solution, different stakeholders will preserve security and privacy in their own environment (using the corresponding plugins), while posing specific requirements for the "common ground/environment". The latter will be used for storing and processing data emerging from different environments. Given the potential conflicting requirements, the presented approach proposes the use of multi-objective optimization techniques targeting to the selection process and the decision support provided to users and providers with respect to: (i) different tenants in the shared infrastructure that aim at loading plugins with different (conflicting) characteristics, (ii) plugins that are combined towards specific security levels (i.e. hybrid cases). The multi-objective optimization techniques consider these cases along with additional information for the selection of the appropriate plugins according to the users' security objectives. This information refers to the associated cost and performance metrics, as well as the threat model estimations.

Furthermore, a trade-off analysis framework is proposed in order to support selection of security plugins based on the identified security level objectives. The selection of plugins will consider how decisions affect different stakeholders: (i) the user in terms of system security and cost, and (ii) the cloud provider in terms of additional resource management constraints and information disclosure requirements. The analysis framework takes into consideration potential issues that arise from the injection of security plugins provided by the data owner in combination or in contrast with the ones available by the cloud provider. Trade-off analysis is based on assessment of residual threats and opportunities resulting from the aforementioned combinations, whilst also considering the related cost/pricing aspects for cloud provider and consumer.

3.4   Plugins Enablement and Activation Framework

The presented architecture also includes a sub-system, the so-called enablement mechanisms, for the ingestion and execution of the plugins in the cloud infrastructure. These mechanisms aim at managing the plugins lifecycle by addressing also cases of multiple plugins or multiple users, and enforcing the required measures to the target cloud environment since plugins execution may require adaptation of cloud software components. Furthermore, the enablement mechanisms ensure isolation of different plugins by linking them with specific users and data, as well as adherence to policies and regulations according to users' security objectives. The enablement mechanisms are realized through extensions to software-based middleware (e.g. OpenStack Swift) enabling the execution of plugins with a complex flow as well as their operation under dynamically changing rules, policies and conditions.

The proposed solution also proposes an activation framework that provides the "logic" for plugins activation, by utilizing the plugins description semantics to drive decisions regarding: (i) data on which plugins will be executed, (ii) deployment policies – for example in the case of hybrid security, (iii) triggering conditions with respect to spatiotemporal properties, (iv) execution rules such as the duration of execution and non-deterministic execution, and (v) affected software components across different cloud layers.

3.5   Context-Aware Plugins Selection and Deployment

The aforementioned trade-off analysis framework facilitates context-aware selection and deployment. Through the latter the provision of security as a service is extended to fully automated protection "on demand", customized to meet the needs of the users and the applications. In particular, a white box approach is proposed, in which the application provider (e.g. cloud provider) utilizes all security related information in order to deploy and enforce the identified security controls. The latter may involve protection against attacks from external sources, limiting the impact of compromised edge devices, encryption of the data streams travelling between end-points or even ensuring user-friendly management of the end-users' passwords. The proposed sub-system provides the means for collecting and assembling different modules (plugins) available in the repository, through compiling and executing their code on the cloud, ultimately resulting in a deployment of solutions for the end-users. This sub-system also allows the composition of different plugins and their orchestration. The composition will be enabled based on the fact that all security solutions comply with the same guidelines and support the same information and application models (e.g., APIs, metadata), despite the fact that they could be coded in different high-level programming languages (such as Java, JS, Python, Ruby, Go, etc.).

The orchestration and deployment of the security modules into integrated solutions is performed following their selection through the trade-off analysis and the context-aware selection services of the proposed architecture. As already outlined, the selection is driven by the security requirements expressed by end-users and/or collected through probes.

4 Evaluation Results

In this section, a set of experiments is presented that aims at showcasing the added value of brining into a service-oriented environment a specific security solution. The experiments have been conducted for a property of trustworthiness, namely dependability since it is key for users and enterprises. Dependability includes multiple sub-dimensions, such as integrity (i.e. absence of improper system alterations as for example proposed in [40]), availability (i.e. readiness for correct service), reliability (i.e. continuity of correct service), maintainability (i.e. ability to undergo modifications and repairs), safety (i.e. absence of catastrophic consequences on the user(s) and the environment), and performance (i.e. stability over time). While there are several approaches for monitoring and acting accordingly, the experiments have been conducted with a mechanism, namely "Monitoring time interval adaptor", which has been implemented as a plugin being activated in cloud environments as a service: the mechanism is a service that adapts the monitoring time intervals in order to ensure that dependability information is collected on time. Prometheus has been chosen as a monitoring framework. Prometheus gathers monitoring parameters at specified intervals, shows the results, and triggers alerts based on rule expressions. The architecture of the experiment is presented in the following Fig. 3.

The monitoring time interval adaptor follows, adapts and applies a well-established paradigm from the network domain regarding the time at which actions are required: TCP fast recovery in the case of network congestion. In fast recovery, the value of a parameter (congestion window – cwnd) is increased for duplicate ACKs received for the missing segment that caused TCP to enter the fast-recovery state. Eventually, when an ACK arrives for the missing segment, TCP enters the congestion-avoidance state.

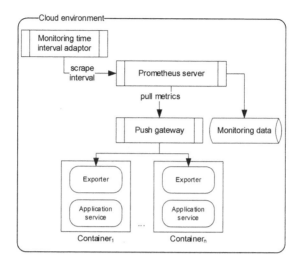

Fig. 3. Experimentation architecture

Two approaches have been proposed for this reason: TCP Reno, in which the congestion window grows linearly and TCP Tahoe, in which the congestion window grows exponentially until it reaches a value after which it grows linearly. In the case of triple ACKs or timeouts Reno halves the rate and continues linearly, while Tahoe starts from the minimum value and grows exponentially. The implemented approach follows the same patterns (evaluating both and switching between them in a hybrid mode) in order to monitor at correct time intervals the VMs/containers of the user. Thus, it adapts the intervals in the case of a failure (similar to congestion cases in the network).

Two scenarios have been studied. The first scenario follows a specific sequence of available/non-available states, while the second one is random. In the first case, the experimentation has been performed for the case of a container as follows: "A-NA-NA-A-NA-NA-A-A-NA-A-NA-NA", where A denotes Available and NA denotes Non-Available. The following tables present the experimentation outcomes and how monitoring time intervals are adapted according to decisions taken for both a Reno- and a Tahoe-based approach (Tables 1 and 2):

Table 1. Scenario 1 – Sequence of available and non-available states of a container: Adaptable monitoring time intervals set by applying a Reno-based approach.

Iteration	Interval (sec)	Actions
0	30	
1	60	
2	90	
3	120	
4	150	
5	180	
6	210	
7	240	

(continued)

Table 1. (*continued*)

Iteration	Interval (sec)	Actions
8	270	
9	300	
10	330	
11	360	
12	390	ACK1
13	420	ACK2
14	450	
15	480	
16	510	
17	540	ACK3
18	270	Interval/2-ACK4
19	300	ACK1
20	330	
21	360	

Table 2. Scenario 1 – Sequence of available and non-available states of a container: Adaptable monitoring time intervals set by applying a Tahoe-based approach.

Iteration	Interval (sec)	Actions
0	30	
1	60	
2	90	
3	120	
4	150	
5	180	
6	210	
7	240	
8	270	
9	300	
10	330	
11	360	
12	390	ACK1
13	420	ACK2
14	450	
15	480	
16	510	
17	540	ACK3-Threshold = 270
18	1	
19	30	ACK1
20	60	ACK2
21	90	ACK3
22	120	ACK4

(*continued*)

Table 2. (*continued*)

Iteration	Interval (sec)	Actions
23	1	Threshold = 60
24	30	
25	60	
26	90	
27	101	90 + 1000/90 = 101
28	111	101 + 1000/101 = 111
29	120	111 + 1000/111 = 120
30	128	120 + 1000/120 = 128
31	136	128 + 1000/128 = 136

The corresponding results are also depicted in the following figures in order to showcase how the custom proposed mechanism allows adaptation of monitoring time intervals and provides the required view to the user (Fig. 4).

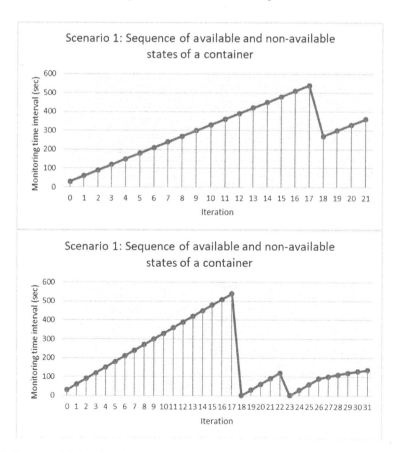

Fig. 4. Reno- and Tahoe-based approaches followed for adapting monitoring time intervals in the case of a container found available/non-available in a specific sequence

The second scenario doesn't follow a specific sequence of available/non-available states, but the order is random to validate the effectiveness of the plugin in this case. The experimentation has been performed for the case of a container as follows: "A-NA-A-A-A-NA-A-NA-A-A-A-NA", where A denotes Available and NA denotes Non-Available. The following tables present the experimentation outcomes and how monitoring time intervals are adapted according to decisions taken for both a Reno- and a Tahoe-based approach (Tables 3 and 4):

Table 3. Scenario 2 – Random available and non-available states of a container: Adaptable monitoring time intervals set by applying a Reno-based approach.

Iteration	Interval (sec)	Actions
0	30	
1	60	
2	90	
3	120	
4	150	
5	180	
6	210	
7	240	
8	270	
9	300	
10	330	ACK1
11	360	ACK2
12	390	ACK3
13	180	ACK4
14	210	ACK1
15	240	ACK2
16	270	ACK3
17	300	ACK4
18	150	
19	180	
20	210	
21	240	
22	270	
23	300	
24	330	
25	360	
26	390	
27	420	
28	450	ACK1
29	480	ACK2

Table 4. Scenario 2 – Random available and non-available states of a container: Adaptable monitoring time intervals set by applying a Tahoe-based approach.

Iteration	Interval (sec)	Actions
0	30	
1	60	
2	90	
3	120	
4	150	
5	180	
6	210	
7	240	
8	270	
9	300	
10	330	ACK1
11	360	ACK2
12	390	ACK3
13	1	ACK4-Threshold = Interval/2
14	30	ACK1
15	60	ACK2
16	90	ACK3
17	1	ACK4-Threshold = Interval/2
18	30	ACK1
19	60	ACK2
20	90	ACK3
21	101	90 + 1000/90 = 101 -ACK4
22	1	
23	30	ACK1
24	60	ACK2
25	90	ACK3
26	101	90 + 1000/90 = 101
27	1	
28	30	
29	60	
30	101	90 + 1000/90 = 101
31	111	101 + 1000/101 = 111
32	120	111 + 1000/111 = 120
33	128	120 + 1000/120 = 128
34	136	128 + 1000/128 = 136
35	143	136 + 1000/136 = 143
36	150	143 + 1000/143 = 150
37	156	150 + 1000/150 = 156
38	162	156 + 1000/156 = 162

(continued)

Table 4. (*continued*)

Iteration	Interval (sec)	Actions
39	168	162 + 1000/162 = 168
40	174	168 + 1000/168 = 174
41	180	
42	186	
43	192	

The corresponding results are also depicted in the following figures in order to showcase how the custom proposed mechanism allows adaptation of monitoring time intervals and provides the required view to the user (Fig. 5).

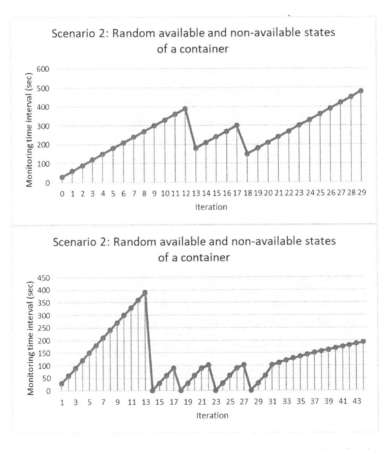

Fig. 5. Reno- and Tahoe-based approaches followed for adapting monitoring time intervals in the case of a container found available/non-available in a random order

5 Conclusions

Cloud security is still a central concern for users and enterprises, which are increasingly relying on ICT infrastructures to support their business models and deliver their services. Moreover, SMEs face very much the same cybersecurity issues as large corporations, without however possessing the knowledge, expertise, staff and equity capital required to successfully prevent, mitigate and confront these challenges. The rise of managed security solutions (including cloud-based security-as-a-service solutions) provides opportunities for alleviating users' limitations in terms of deploying and adopting effective security solutions. The latter also facilitates the emerging need for application portability across different cloud providers [41], given that applications are not coupled with specific security solutions of providers but the application owners can ingest their security plugins to different providers' infrastructures. In this context, an innovative architecture is presented, enabling users to bring their own security mechanisms in cloud environments. The latter obviates the need for on-site security-oriented resources (e.g. hardware, software, personnel), given that these security mechanisms will be offered, managed, selected, activated, deployed and monitored as plugins.

References

1. Cloud Security Alliance: State of Cloud Adoption (2016)
2. Zardari, S., Bahsoon, R.: Cloud adoption: a goal-oriented requirements engineering approach. In: Proceedings of the 2nd International Workshop on Software Engineering for Cloud Computing, pp. 29–35. ACM (2011)
3. Cloud adoption a goal oriented requirements engineering approach.pdf
4. Cloud Security Alliance: The Treacherous Twelve (2017)
5. Hewlett Packard Enterprise: 5 ways cloud security is like data center security and 5 ways it's not. https://www.hpe.com/us/en/insights/articles/5-ways-cloud-security-is-just-like-data-center-security-and-5-ways-its-different-1701.html
6. Kuada, E.: Trust modelling for opportunistic cloud services. Int. J. Grid Util. Comput. 9(4), 289–306 (2018)
7. Open Cloud Manifesto: https://gevaperry.typepad.com/Open%20Cloud%20Manifesto%20v1.0.9.pdf. Accessed 23 July 2018
8. Berger, S., et al.: TVDc: managing security in the trusted virtual datacenter. ACM Oper. Syst. Rev. 42, 40–47 (2008)
9. Amazon Virtual Private Cloud: http://aws.amazon.com/vpc/. Accessed 23 July 2018
10. Corbató, F.J., Vyssotsky, V.A.: Introduction and overview of the multics system. IEEE Ann. Hist. Comput. 2, 12–13 (1992)
11. Saltzer, J.H.: Protection and the control of information sharing in multics. ACM Commun. 17, 388–402 (1978)
12. Lettmann, T., Baumann, M., Eberling, M., Kemmerich, T.: Modeling agents and agent systems. In: Nguyen, N.T. (ed.) Transactions on Computational Collective Intelligence V. LNCS, vol. 6910, pp. 157–181. Springer, Heidelberg (2011). https://doi.org/10.1007/978-3-642-24016-4_9
13. Sentronex Infographic: http://www.sentronex.com/wp-content/uploads/2014/03/Data-Security-Risk-Prevention-for-Financial-Services-in-20141.pdf. Accessed 23 July 2018

14. Wang, X.A., Xhafa, F., Cai, W., Ma, J., Wei, F.: Efficient privacy preserving predicate encryption with fine-grained searchable capability for Cloud storage. Comput. Electr. Eng. **56**, 871–883 (2016)

15. Li, W., Ping, L.: Trust model to enhance security and interoperability of cloud environment. In: Jaatun, M.G., Zhao, G., Rong, C. (eds.) CloudCom 2009. LNCS, vol. 5931, pp. 69–79. Springer, Heidelberg (2009). https://doi.org/10.1007/978-3-642-10665-1_7

16. Jaeger, T., Schiffman, J.: Outlook: cloudy with a chance of security challenges and improvements. IEEE Secur. Priv. **8**(1), 77–80 (2010)

17. Ristenpart, T., Tromer, E., Shacham, H., Savage, S.: Hey, you, get off of my cloud: exploring information leakage in third-party compute clouds. In: 16th ACM Conference on Computer and Communications Security (2009)

18. Song, D.X., Wagner, D., Tian, X.: Timing analysis of keystrokes and timing attacks on SSH. In: 10th Conference on USENIX Security Symposium (2001)

19. Ranjith, P., Chandran, P., Kaleeswaran, S.: On covert channels between virtual machines. J. Comput. Virol. **8**, 85–97 (2012)

20. Bezemer, C-P., Zaidman, A.: Multi-tenant SaaS applications: maintenance dream or nightmare?. In: Joint ERCIM Workshop on Software Evolution (EVOL) and International Workshop on Principles of Software Evolution (IWPSE), Antwerp, Belgium. ACM, New York, USA (2010)

21. Jansen, W.: Cloud hooks: security and privacy issues in cloud computing. In: 44th International Conference on System Sciences, Koloa, Kauai, HI. IEEE Computer Society, Washington, DC, USA, pp. 1–10 (2010)

22. European Network and Information Security Agency: Cloud Computing Benefits, risks and recommendations for information security (2012)

23. Kandukuri, B., Paturi, V., Rakshit, A.: Cloud security issues. In: IEEE International Conference on Services Computing (2009)

24. Casola, V., De Benedictis, A., Modic, J., Rak, M., Villano, U.: Per-service security SLAs for cloud security management: model and implementation. Int. J. Grid Util. Comput. **9**(2), 128–138 (2018)

25. Roth, D., Small, K.: The role of semantic information in learning question classifiers. In: Proceedings of the Conference First International Joint Conference on Natural Language Processing (2004)

26. Varun, C., Banerjee, A., Kumar, V.: Anomaly detection: a survey. ACM Comput. Surv. **41**, 15 (2009)

27. Wang, X.A., Ma, J., Yang, X., Wei, Y.: Security analysis of two identity based proxy re-encryption schemes in multi-user networks. In: Nguyen, N.T., Kowalczyk, R., Xhafa, F. (eds.) Transactions on Computational Collective Intelligence XIX. LNCS, vol. 9380, pp. 69–88. Springer, Heidelberg (2015). https://doi.org/10.1007/978-3-662-49017-4_5

28. Paredes-Oliva, I., Dimitropoulos, X., Molina, M., Barlet-Ros, P., Brauckhoff, D.: Automating root-cause analysis of network anomalies using frequent itemset mining. In: ACM SIGCOMM 2010 Conference, New Delhi, India (2010)

29. Egele, M., Szydlowski, M., Kirda, E., Kruegel, C.: Using static program analysis to aid intrusion detection. In: Büschkes, R., Laskov, P. (eds.) DIMVA 2006. LNCS, vol. 4064. Springer, Heidelberg (2006). https://doi.org/10.1007/11790754_2

30. Wang, X.A., Xhafa, F., Ma, J., Barolli, L., Ge, Y.: PRE+: dual of proxy re-encryption for secure cloud data sharing service. Int. J. Web Grid Serv. **14**(1), 44–69 (2018)

31. Ficco, M., Di Martino, B., Pietrantuono, R., Russo, S.: Optimized task allocation on private cloud for hybrid simulation of large-scale critical systems. Futur. Gener. Comput. Syst. **74**, 104–118 (2017)

32. Coello, C.: Recent trends in evolutionary multiobjective optimization. In: Abraham, A., Jain, L., Goldberg, R. (eds.) Evolutionary Multiobjective Optimization. Advanced Information and Knowledge Processing, pp. 7–32. Springer, London (2005). https://doi.org/10.1007/1-84628-137-7_2

33. Marler, T., Jasbir, A.: Survey of multi-objective optimization methods for engineering. Struct. Multidiscip. Optim. **26**, 369–395 (2004)

34. Talbi, A., Matthieu, B., Nebro, E.: Metaheuristics for Multiobjective Combinatorial Optimization Problems: Review and recent issues (2006)

35. Bleuler, S., Laumanns, M., Thiele, L., Zitzler, E.: PISA—a platform and programming language independent interface for search algorithms. In: Fonseca, Carlos M., Fleming, Peter J., Zitzler, E., Thiele, L., Deb, K. (eds.) EMO 2003. LNCS, vol. 2632, pp. 494–508. Springer, Heidelberg (2003). https://doi.org/10.1007/3-540-36970-8_35

36. Kronfeld, M., Planatscher, H., Zell, A.: The EvA2 optimization framework. In: Blum, C., Battiti, R. (eds.) LION 2010. LNCS, vol. 6073, pp. 247–250. Springer, Heidelberg (2010). https://doi.org/10.1007/978-3-642-13800-3_27

37. Lukasiewycz, M.: Opt4J: a modular framework for meta-heuristic optimization. In: Proceedings of the 13th Annual Conference on Genetic and Evolutionary Computation (2011)

38. Durillo, J., Nebro, A., Alba, E.: The jMetal framework for multi-objective optimization: design and architecture. In: IEEE Congress on Evolutionary Computation (2010)

39. A Java-based Evolutionary Computation Research System: http://cs.gmu.edu/~eclab/projects/ecj. Accessed 23 July 2018

40. Xue, T., Ying, S., Wu, Q., Jia, X., Hu, X., Zhai, X., Zhang, T.: Verifying integrity of exception handling in service-oriented software. Int. J. Grid Util. Comput. **8**(1), 7–21 (2017)

41. Di Martino, B.: Applications portability and services interoperability among multiple clouds. IEEE Cloud Comput. **1**(1), 74–77 (2014)

A Flexible Synchronization Protocol to Learn Hidden Topics in P2PPS Systems

Shigenari Nakamura[1]([✉]), Tomoya Enokido[2], and Makoto Takizawa[3]

[1] Graduate School of Science and Engineering, Hosei University, Tokyo, Japan
`nakamura.shigenari@gmail.com`
[2] Faculty of Business Administration, Rissho University, Tokyo, Japan
`eno@ris.ac.jp`
[3] Faculty of Science and Engineering, Hosei University, Tokyo, Japan
`makoto.takizawa@computer.org`

Abstract. We consider the P2PPS (peer-to-peer type of topic-based publish/subscribe) model where each peer process (peer) can publish and subscribe event messages with no centralized coordinator. Here, hidden topics are topics which a source peer is allowed to subscribe but a target peer is not allowed to subscribe. After receipt of an event message e_1 with hidden topics, if a peer publishes another event message e_2, the event message e_2 may be related with the hidden topics of the event message e_1. Hence, if an event message with hidden topics is received by another target peer which does not subscribe the hidden topics, the target peer can get information on the hidden topics. This means, illegal information flow to the target peer occurs. However, some hidden topics may be related with a subscription topic of a target peer and the target peer just may not know about the hidden topics. In this paper, we newly introduce a learning mechanism where each peer newly obtains hidden topics if the hidden topics are related with subscription topics. In this paper, we newly propose an FS-H (flexible synchronization for hidden topics) protocol. In the evaluation, we show the fewest number of event messages are prohibited from being received in the FS-H protocol compared with the other protocols.

Keywords: Information flow control · P2P (peer-to-peer) model ·
PS (publish/subscribe) systems ·
TBAC (topic-based access control) model ·
FS-H (flexible synchronization for hidden topics) protocol

1 Introduction

A distributed system is composed of peer processes (peers) which are cooperating with one another by manipulating objects and exchanging messages in networks. Through the cooperation among peers, data in objects flows to other objects.

© Springer-Verlag GmbH Germany, part of Springer Nature 2019
N. T. Nguyen et al. (Eds.): TCCI XXXIII, LNCS 11610, pp. 52–70, 2019.
https://doi.org/10.1007/978-3-662-59540-4_3

Even if a peer is not allowed to read data of an object, the peer can obtain the data by reading another object [5]. Here, information in the object is referred to as illegally flow to the peer. Thus, illegal information flow occurs among peers and objects. In secure information systems, it must be guaranteed that only the users allowed to access the data can access the data. In order to secure information systems, various types of methods are proposed, such as user authentication [15], access control [9,10], and so on. Types of synchronization protocols [16–19,21, 22] are proposed based on the role-based access control (RBAC) model [10] to prevent illegal information flow among objects. On the other hand, content-based systems where each peer can get information in which the peer is really interested [2,13] are getting more important. The PS (publish/subscribe) system [4,8,11, 31] which is one of the content-based systems is used in various applications like Google alert [11]. In this paper, we consider a P2PPS (peer-to-peer [33] type of topic-based PS [30]) system [25,26] where each peer can play both publisher and subscriber roles with no centralized coordinator. The *TBAC* (*topic-based access control*) model is proposed as an access control model in topic-based PS systems [24]. Here, only a peer granted an access right to publish and subscribe a topic t is allowed to publish and subscribe the topic t, respectively. The publication $p_i.P$ and subscription $p_i.S$ of a peer p_i are sets of topics which the peer p_i is allowed to publish and subscribe, respectively. An event message e published by a peer p_i is received by a target peer p_j if the subscription $p_j.S$ of the target peer p_j includes at least one common topic with the publication $e.P$ of the event message e. Topics which are carried by an event message e published by a peer p_i but are not in the subscription $p_j.S$ of a target peer p_j are referred to as *hidden* topics of the source peer p_i for the target peer p_j [24]. Here, the target peer p_j can get information on the hidden topics which the peer p_j is not allowed to subscribe. On the other hand, topics in the publication $e.P$ but not in the subscription $p_j.S$ are referred to as *forgotten* topics of a target peer p_j. In our previous studies, the SBS (subscription-based synchronization) [24] and TBS (topic-based synchronization) [20] protocols are proposed to prevent illegal information flow based on the TBAC model. Here, an event message which may cause illegal information flow of the hidden topics is prohibited at each target peer p_i, i.e. event messages are not received by the target peer p_i.

It is difficult, maybe impossible for each peer to know about every topic, especially in a scalable P2PPS system. This means, each peer subscribes only topics which the peer knows by itself. However, an event message e may carry topics which the peer p_i does not know yet but are related with some subscribed topic in $p_i.S$. Hence, we need a learning mechanism for a peer to obtain new topics through communicating with other peers. The FS (flexible synchronization) protocol is proposed with the learning mechanism [23]. In the FS protocol, all the topics are assumed to be classified into classes and the relevance among the topics assumed to be defined. Each peer p_i first subscribes a main topic $p_i.mt$ and then adds topics which the peer knows and are related with the main topic $p_i.mt$ in the subscription topics. On receipt of an event message e including forgotten topics, a peer p_i accepts the event message e with the higher probability if the forgotten topics are more related with the subscribed topics with respect to the topic relevance. In addition, the forgotten topics are added to the subscription

$p_i.S$ with some probability. Thus, each peer obtains new topics, which the peer does not know but are related with subscribed topics, through exchanging event messages with other peers. In the FS protocol, illegal information flow of only forgotten topics are prevented.

In this paper, we newly propose an *FS-H (flexible synchronization for hidden topics)* protocol to prevent illegal information flow of *hidden* topics and to reduce the number of prohibited event messages by introducing the learning mechanism to obtain hidden topics. Similarly to the FS protocol, on receipt of an event message e, a peer p_i adds hidden topics related with subscription topics in the subscription $p_i.S$. If the event message e includes hidden topics which are not related with the subscription topics, the peer p_i prohibits the event message e from being received. In the evaluation, we show the fewest number of event messages are prohibited in the FS-H protocol compared with the other synchronization protocols.

In Sect. 3, we discuss the information flow relation among peers in the TBAC model. In Sect. 4, we propose the FS-H protocol with the learning mechanism of hidden topics using the relevance concept of topics. In Sect. 5, we evaluate the FS-H protocol.

2   Related Studies

An information system is composed of two types of entities, *subjects* and *objects* [5]. Each object is an encapsulation of data and operations for manipulating the data. A subject s manipulates an object o by using operations supported by the object o. Let S, O, and OP be sets of subjects, objects, and operations on the objects in a system, respectively. In this paper, we assume each object o supports a pair of basic operations, read (rd) and write (wr), i.e. $OP = \{rd, wr\}$. An access rule $\langle s, o, op \rangle$ $(\in S \times O \times OP)$ means that a subject s is allowed to manipulate an object o in an operation op in the BAC (basic access control) model [9]. An access right is specified in a pair $\langle o, op \rangle$. A subject s is allowed to manipulate an object o in an operation op only if the subject s is granted the access right $\langle o, op \rangle$. A system is *secure* if and only if (iff) every object o is manipulated by a subject s in an operation op according to an access rule $\langle s, o, op \rangle$.

In the RBAC (role-based access control) model [10,27,29], a role r $(\subseteq O \times OP)$ is a set of access rights. An authorizer grants a role r to a subject while a subject is granted an access right in the BAC model. Each person plays a role r in a society, e.g. a professor role in a university. Each role r shows what can be done by a subject who is granted the role r in a society. Let R be a collection of roles in a system, $R \subseteq 2^{O \times OP}$. A subject s is granted a collection $s.R$ $(\subseteq R)$ of roles in the role set R. Then, the subject s issues a transaction to manipulate objects. A transaction is a sequence of operations on objects. A subject s grants a subset $T.P$ $(\subseteq s.R)$ of the roles $s.R$ to a transaction T. Here, $T.P$ is referred to as *purpose* [6,7] of the transaction T. A transaction T is allowed to issue an operation op on an object o only if an access right $\langle o, op \rangle$ is in the purpose $T.P$.

Illegal information flow to occur in the access control models are discussed as confinement problem [5]. Suppose a subject s_i is granted a pair of a read access right $\langle f, rd \rangle$ on a file object f and a write access right $\langle g, wr \rangle$ on another file object g. Suppose another subject s_j is granted an access right $\langle g, rd \rangle$. Here, suppose the subject s_i reads data d in the file f and then writes the data d to the file g. The subject s_j can obtain the data d in the file f by reading the data d stored in the file g although the subject s_j is not allowed to read data in the file f. That is, information in the file f *illegally flows* into the subject s_j via the subject s_i and the file g.

In order to prevent illegal information flow, the LBAC (lattice-based access control) model [28] is proposed. Here, every entity e, i.e. subject or object, belongs to a security class sc. The relation $sc_1 \rightarrow sc_2$ on a pair of security classes sc_1 and sc_2 shows that information in an entity of the class sc_1 can flow to an entity of the class sc_2. For example, a subject of a class sc_1 can read and write data in an object of a class sc_2 if $sc_2 \rightarrow sc_1$ and $sc_1 \rightarrow sc_2$, respectively.

A transaction *illegally reads* data in an object iff the transaction reads data in the object which includes the data in another object which is not allowed to be read by the transaction [19]. The illegal information flow relation ($r_i \mapsto r_j$) from a role r_i to a role r_j is defined [7,19]. Let $In(r_i)$ and $Out(r_i)$ be sets $\{o \mid \langle o, rd \rangle \in r_i\}$ and $\{o \mid \langle o, wr \rangle \in r_i\}$ of objects whose data are allowed to be read and written by a subject granted a role r_i, respectively. A role r_i *illegally flows* to a role r_j ($r_i \mapsto r_j$) iff $Out(r_i) \cap In(r_j) \neq \phi$ but $In(r_i) \not\subseteq In(r_j)$. Suppose a pair of transactions T_1 and T_2 are granted roles r_1 and r_2, respectively, and $r_1 \mapsto r_2$. If the transaction T_2 is performed after the transaction T_1, the transaction T_2 may illegally read data in an object.

Allowable information flow relation from an object o_1 to an object o_2 is also *a priori* defined by an administrator. A transaction *suspiciously reads* data in an object iff the transaction reads data in the object whose data is not allowed to be brought to other objects [17]. A transaction *illegally writes* data to an object iff the transaction writes data to the object after illegally reading data in another object [17]. A transaction *impossibly writes* data to an object iff the transaction writes the data to the object after suspiciously reading the data in another object [17].

The WA (write-abortion) [17], RWA (read-write-abortion) [18], and FRWA (flexible read-write-abortion) [16] protocols are proposed to prevent illegal information flow. In the WA protocol, a transaction aborts once issuing an illegal or impossible write operation. Even if a transaction illegally reads data in an object, the transaction can commit if the transaction does not issue a write operation. In the RWA protocol, a transaction aborts once issuing an illegal read operation or impossible write operation. In the FRWA protocol, a transaction aborts if the transaction issues an illegal or impossible write operation as well as the WA protocol. Furthermore, the transaction aborts with some probability ap once issuing an illegal read operation.

The concepts of sensitivity of an object and safety of a role in the FRWA-O [21] and FRWA-RS [22] protocols are discussed. In the FRWA-O protocol, the abortion probability ap of a transaction T_t issuing an illegal read operation to an object o_i depends on the sensitivity of the object o_i. Here, the sensitivity of an object o_i just monotonically increases each time a transaction aborts by issuing an illegal read operation to the object even if the transaction commits. Whereas, in the FRWA-RS protocol, the role safety of a role r_i increases and decreases each time a transaction T_t holding the role r_i commits and aborts, respectively, in order to reduce the number of transactions to abort.

A P2P (peer-to-peer) system [3,33] is a distributed system which is composed of peer processes (peers) which are cooperating with one another by exchanging messages in overlay networks. A peer is an autonomous process which makes a decision by itself through communicating with other peers and autonomously leaves and joins the system. There is no centralized coordinator. For a collaborative work among peers, the voting mechanism is needed [14]. For data sharing methods of P2P systems [32], consistency maintenance strategies are discussed [35]. In the large-scale P2P systems where there are a large number of peers, various types of scalability problems occur [12].

In topic-based PS (publish/subscribe) systems [8], a subscriber process specifies a subscription in terms of topics in which the subscriber process is interested. A publisher process publishes an event message with a publication which is also specified in terms of topics. If a publication of an event message and a subscription of the subscriber process include a common topic, the event message is received by the subscriber process. In this paper, we discuss a P2PPS (P2P type of topic-based PS) model [25,26,34]. Here, every peer can publish and receive event messages and there is no centralized coordinator.

The SBS (subscription-based synchronization) [24] and TBS (topic-based synchronization) [20] protocols are proposed to prevent illegal information flow of hidden topics in the P2PPS systems. In the SBS protocol, an event message which may cause an illegal information flow is prohibited. It is checked whether or not an event message causes illegal information flow in terms of access rights granted to each peer. Here, each peer gives all the topics which the peer is allowed to subscribe to an event message even if the peer does not subscribe the topic in reality. Hence, even some legal event messages are unnecessarily prohibited. On the other hand, in the TBS protocol, it is checked whether or not an event message causes illegal information flow in terms of topics which are really manipulated by each peer. Hence, fewer number of event messages are prohibited than the SBS protocol because only and every illegal event messages are prohibited differently from the SBS protocol.

In paper [1], an access control model in the PS system is discussed based on the RBAC model. However, information flow to occur by publishing and subscribing topics in the PS system is not discussed. In this paper, we consider the TBAC (topic-based access control) model of a topic-based PS system based on access rights to publish and subscribe topics. We discuss illegal information flow to occur among peers in terms of publication and subscription rights of the TBAC model in the P2PPS system.

3 Information Flow in TBAC Model

3.1 TBAC Model

In this paper, we consider a P2PPS (P2P (peer-to-peer) type [3,33] of topic-based PS (publish/subscribe) [4,8,11,31]) model [25,26]. Let P be a set of peer processes (peers) $p_1, \ldots, p_{pn}$ ($pn \geq 1$). Here, each peer p_i can play both publisher and subscriber roles and a pair of event messages published by different peers are independently delivered to every common target peer. In this paper, we consider a topic-based PS system [30]. Let T be a set $\{t_1, \ldots, t_{tn}\}$ ($tn \geq 1$) of all topics in a system. A peer p_i publishes an event message e with publication $e.P$ ($\subseteq T$). A peer p_i specifies the subscription $p_i.S$ ($\subseteq T$), which shows topics in which the peer p_i is interested. An event message e is received by a peer p_i if the publication $e.P$ and the subscription $p_i.S$ include at least one common topic, i.e. $e.P \cap p_i.S \neq \phi$. Here, the peer p_i is a *target* peer of the event message e.

In the *TBAC* (*topic-based access control*) model [24], an access right is specified in a pair $\langle t, op \rangle$ of a topic t ($\in T$) and an operation op which is a publish (pb) or subscribe (sb), i.e. $op \in \{pb, sb\}$. A peer p_i is allowed to publish an event message e with publication $e.P$ ($\subseteq T$) only if the peer p_i is granted a publication right $\langle t, pb \rangle$ for every topic t in the publication $e.P$. The subscription $p_i.S$ ($\subseteq T$) of a peer p_i is a subset of topics which the peer p_i is allowed to subscribe. If a peer p_i is a target peer of an event message e, topics which are in the publication $e.P$ but not in the subscription $p_i.S$ are referred to as *forgotten* topics $e.F$ ($\subseteq e.P$) of the event message e. Here, a target peer p_i recognizes an event message e to be related with respect to topics ($\subseteq e.P \cap p_i.S$) in the intersection of $e.P$ and $p_i.S$ but forgets about the forgotten topics ($\subseteq e.P - p_i.S$).

3.2 Information Flow Relations

First, the information flow relation ($p_i \rightarrow p_j$) from a peer p_i to a peer p_j is defined as follows [20,24]:

Definition 1. *A peer p_i precedes a peer p_j with respect to information flow ($p_i \rightarrow p_j$) iff $p_i.P \cap p_j.S \neq \phi$.*

The information flow relation $p_i \rightarrow p_j$ means an event message published by a peer p_i is allowed to be received by a peer p_j. A peer p_i is independent of a peer p_j ($p_i \mid p_j$) iff $p_i \nrightarrow p_j$. The relation $p_i \mid p_j$ means the peer p_j does not receive event messages published by the peer p_i.

The legal and illegal precedent relations among peers are defined as follows [20,24]:

Definition 2

1. *A peer p_i legally precedes a peer p_j with respect to information flow ($p_i \Rightarrow p_j$) iff one of the following conditions holds:*
   (a) *$p_i.S \neq \phi$, $p_i \rightarrow p_j$, and $p_i.S \subseteq p_j.S$.*
   (b) *For some peer p_k, $p_i \Rightarrow p_k$ and $p_k \Rightarrow p_j$.*

2. *A pair of peers p_i and p_j are legally equivalent with each other $(p_i \Leftrightarrow p_j)$ iff $p_i \Rightarrow p_j$ and $p_j \Rightarrow p_i$.*
3. *A peer p_i illegally precedes a peer p_j with respect to information flow $(p_i \mapsto p_j)$ iff $p_i.S \neq \phi$, $p_i \rightarrow p_j$, but $p_i.S \nsubseteq p_j.S$.*

The legal information flow relation $\Rightarrow$ is transitive but not symmetric. If a peer p_i precedes a peer p_j $(p_i \rightarrow p_j)$, i.e. $p_i.P \cap p_j.S \neq \phi$, an event message published by the peer p_i can be received by the peer p_j. Otherwise, i.e. $p_i \mid p_j$, no information from the peer p_i flows into the peer p_j. The condition "$p_i.S \subseteq p_j.S$" means that an event message e from the peer p_i to the peer p_j is related with no hidden topic for the peer p_j, i.e. $e.H = \phi$.

Suppose a peer p_i publishes an event message e_2 with publication $e_2.P$ ($\subseteq p_i.P$) after receiving another event message e_1. Here, the event message e_2 might carry some information in the event message e_1. The event message is characterized by topics in the topic set $p_i.S$.

Definition 3. *Some topics in the subscription $p_i.S$ but not in the subscription $p_j.S$ of a target peer p_j are hidden topics which the event message e carries to the target peer.*

A target peer of the event message e does not know about the hidden topics. Let $e.H$ be a set of hidden topics of an event message e published by a peer p_i with respect to the target peer p_j [20, 24]. Hidden topics of an event message e published by a peer p_i might be related with the topics which the peer p_i so far subscribes but are not included in the subscription $p_j.S$, i.e. $\{t \mid t \in p_i.S \wedge t \notin p_j.S\}$. Here, even if a target peer p_j receives an event message e, the peer p_j does not recognize that the event message e might be related with the hidden topics.

Forgotten topics of an event message are defined as follows [20, 24]:

Definition 4. *Topics in the publication $e.P$ but not in the subscription $p_j.S$, i.e. $\{t \mid t \in e.P \wedge t \notin p_j.S\}$, are forgotten topics $e.F$ $(= e.P - p_j.S)$ of the event message e with respect to the target peer p_j.*

A target peer p_j recognizes an event message e to be only related with topics in $e.P \cap p_j.S$ but forgets that the event message e is related with the forgotten topics in $e.F$.

If an event message e is received by a target peer p_i, the event message e is related with topics in the subscription $p_i.S$. Furthermore, the event message e may be related with not only forgotten topics $e.F$ in the publication $e.P$ but also hidden topics $e.H$. *Implicit* topics of a peer p_i are hidden or forgotten topics of event messages which the peer p_i receives.

Let a variable $p_i.I$ indicate a set of implicit topics of a peer p_i [20, 24]. The variable $p_i.I$ is manipulated by a peer p_i as follows:

[Behavior of a peer p_i]

1. Initially, $p_i.I = \phi$;
2. [Receipt] Each time a peer p_i receives an event message e from a peer p_j,
   $e.F = e.P - p_i.S$; $e.H = p_i.S - p_j.S$; $p_i.I = p_i.I \cup e.H \cup e.F$;
3. [Publication] Let $e.P$ be a set of publication topics of an event message e;
   Then, the peer p_i publishes an event message e;

Thus, implicit topics are accumulated in the peer p_i each time the peer p_i receives an event message.

Example 1. Suppose there are three topics t_1, t_2, and t_3 ($T = \{t_1, t_2, t_3\}$) in a system. We also suppose a peer p_i is granted four access rights $\langle t_2, pb \rangle$, $\langle t_3, pb \rangle$, $\langle t_1, sb \rangle$, and $\langle t_2, sb \rangle$, another peer p_j is granted three access rights $\langle t_1, pb \rangle$, $\langle t_1, sb \rangle$, and $\langle t_2, sb \rangle$, and the other peer p_k is granted three access rights $\langle t_3, pb \rangle$, $\langle t_1, sb \rangle$, and $\langle t_3, sb \rangle$, i.e. $p_i.P$ ($= \{t_2, t_3\}$), $p_i.S$ ($= \{t_1, t_2\}$), $p_j.P$ ($= \{t_1\}$), $p_j.S$ ($= \{t_1, t_2\}$), $p_k.P$ ($= \{t_3\}$), and $p_k.S$ ($= \{t_1, t_3\}$). First, the peer p_i publishes an event message e_i with publication $e_i.P = \{t_2\}$ ($\subseteq p_i.P$). Here, the peer p_i precedes the peer p_j ($p_i \rightarrow p_j$) since $p_i.P$ ($= \{t_2, t_3\}$) $\cap$ $p_j.S$ ($= \{t_1, t_2\}$) $\neq \phi$. $p_i \Rightarrow p_j$ since $p_i.S \neq \phi$, $p_i \rightarrow p_j$, and $p_i.S \subseteq p_j.S$. Hence, the event message e_i is received by the peer p_j.

Next, suppose a peer p_j publishes an event message e_j with publication $e_j.P = \{t_1\}$ ($\subseteq p_j.P$). Here, the peer p_j precedes the peer p_k ($p_j \rightarrow p_k$) since $p_j.P$ ($= \{t_1\}$) $\cap$ $p_j.S$ ($= \{t_1, t_3\}$) $\neq \phi$. However, the peer p_j illegally precedes the peer p_k ($p_j \mapsto p_k$) since $p_j.S$ ($= \{t_1, t_2\}$) $\not\subseteq p_k.S$ ($= \{t_1, t_3\}$). This means, an event message on the topic t_2 which the peer p_k is not allowed to subscribe can be received by the peer p_k because the peer p_j may already get information on the topic t_2 before publishing the event message e_j and may include the information in the event message e_j. In this case, a topic t_2 is a hidden topic of the event message e_j since $t_2 \in p_j.S$ but $t_2 \notin p_k.S$. Here, event information illegally flows to the peer p_k from the peer p_j.

Suppose a peer p_i receives an event message e_1 with publication $e_1.P$ and then publishes an event message e_2. The event message e_2 may bring information, i.e. topics carried by the event message e_1. We introduce the concept of *cone*. A cone $p_i.C$ of a peer p_i is defined to be a subset of topics, i.e. $p_i.C \subseteq T$ which the peer p_i obtains from topics of event messages received. The cone $p_i.C$ is initially empty.

[Cone $p_i.C$]. A topic t is added to the cone $p_i.C$ of a peer p_i each time the peer p_i receives an event message e which satisfies one of the following conditions:

1. A peer p_h whose cone $p_h.C$ includes the topic t publishes the event message e and the peer p_h precedes the peer p_i ($p_h \rightarrow p_i$).
2. A peer p_h whose cone $p_h.C$ is empty publishes the event message e such that the topic t is in intersection of the publication $e.P$ of the event message e and the subscription $p_i.S$ of the peer p_i, i.e. $t \in e.P \cap p_i.S$.

Based on the cone, we define legal and illegal event messages for a target peer.

Definition 5. *Suppose a peer p_h publishes an event message e and a target peer p_i receives the event message e.*

1. *The event message e is legal at the peer p_i ($p_h \overset{e}{\Rightarrow} p_i$) iff $p_h.C \subseteq p_i.S$.*
2. *The event message e is illegal at the peer p_i ($p_h \overset{e}{\mapsto} p_i$) iff the event message e is not legal at the peer p_i.*

Suppose an event message e published by a peer p_h is received by a peer p_i. If the event message e is illegal at the peer p_i ($p_h \overset{e}{\mapsto} p_i$), the peer p_h illegally precedes the peer p_i ($p_h \mapsto p_i$). However, even if $p_h.S \nsubseteq p_i.S$, the cone $p_h.C$ may be included in the subscription $p_i.S$ ($p_h.C \subseteq p_i.S$). Thus, even if $p_h \mapsto p_i$, the event message e may be legal at the peer p_i ($p_h \overset{e}{\Rightarrow} p_i$) depending on the cone $p_h.C$.

4   Synchronization Protocols

4.1   Protocols for Hidden Topics

In our previous studies, the SBS (subscription-based synchronization) [24] and TBS (topic-based synchronization) [20] protocols are proposed to check whether or not an event message is illegal at each target peer. Topics which a peer p_i is allowed to publish and subscribe are in a pair of sets $p_i.P$ and $p_i.S$, respectively.

In the SBS protocol, a topic set $p_i.T$ of each peer p_i is considered, which is composed of topics carried into the peer p_i. If a peer p_i receives an event message e_1 which carries event information on a topic t, the topic t is stored in the topic set $p_i.T$. Here, "a topic t is in the topic set $p_i.T$" means the peer p_i already obtains the information on the topic t. An event message e_2 published by the peer p_i after the peer p_i receives the event message e_1 may include the information on the topic t in the topic set $p_i.T$. Hence, legality feature of each information flow from a source peer p_i to a target peer p_j is decided based on the pair of topic sets $p_i.T$ and $p_j.S$. A topic t such that $\{t \mid t \in p_i.T$ and $t \notin p_j.S\}$ is hidden topic. In the SBS protocol, on receipt of an event message e published by a peer p_i, every topic in the subscription $p_i.S$ is added to the topic set $p_j.T$ of each target peer p_j, i.e. it is checked whether or not an event message is illegal in terms of subscription rights of each peer. If an event message may cause illegal information flow, the event message is prohibited.

[SBS protocol]. A peer p_i publishes an event message e and the peer p_i precedes the peer p_j ($p_i \rightarrow p_j$):

The source peer p_i behaves as follows:

1. $e.T = p_i.T$;
   $e.S = p_i.S$;
   $e.P =$ publication topics of the event message e ($\subseteq p_i.P$);
2. p_i publishes the event message e;

The target peer p_j behaves as follows:

1. If $e.T \subseteq p_j.S$, the event message e is received by the peer p_j and $p_j.T = p_j.T \cup e.S$;
2. Otherwise, the event message e is prohibited at the peer p_j;

In the SBS protocol, each time an event message e published by a peer p_i is received by a peer p_j, the topics in the subscription $p_i.S$ are added to the topic set $p_j.T$ of the peer p_j. Here, $p_i.C \subseteq p_i.S$. This means, even if some event message e is legal, the event message may be unnecessarily prohibited at a peer p_j.

On the other hand, in the TBS protocol, it is checked whether or not an event message is illegal in terms of only topics which are really manipulated by each peer. This means, a cone $p_i.C$ of topics of each peer p_i is stored in the topic set $p_i.T$. Each time an event message e is received by the peer p_j, the topics in the topic set $p_i.T$ of a source peer p_i are added to the topic set $p_j.T$.

[TBS protocol]. A peer p_i publishes an event message e and the peer p_i precedes the peer p_j ($p_i \rightarrow p_j$):

The source peer p_i behaves to publish the event message e as follows:

1. $e.T = p_i.T$;
   $e.P =$ publication topics of the event message e;
2. p_i publishes the event message e;

The target peer p_j behaves to receive the event message e as follows:

1. If $e.T \subseteq p_j.S$, the event message e is received by the peer p_j and
   (a) If $e.T \neq \phi$, $p_j.T = p_j.T \cup e.T$;
   (b) Otherwise, $p_j.T = p_j.T \cup (e.P \cap p_j.S)$;
2. Otherwise, the event message e is prohibited at the peer p_j;

In the SBS protocol, some event information on topics in the subscription of the source peer are considered to flow to the target peer even if the source peer does not have some event information on the topics. Hence, event messages more highly cause illegal information flow than the TBS protocol.

4.2 FS-H (Flexible Synchronization for Hidden Topics) Protocol

In the SBS [24] and TBS [20] protocols, the number of event messages prohibited increases as the number of event messages published increases. In the FS protocol [23], an event message whose forgotten topics may cause illegal information flow is prohibited. In this paper, we propose an FS-H (flexible synchronization for hidden topics) protocol to more reduce the number of event messages prohibited due to hidden topics. Since a P2PPS system is open and scalable, each peer p_i may not know about every topic in the system. This means, there might be topics which a peer p_i does not know but may interest the peer p_i. These topics might be brought to a target peer by an event message as hidden topics of the event message. In this paper, we discuss how to include hidden topics of interest to the subscription $p_i.S$ of the peer p_i. In our previous studies, a *relevance* concept of topics is proposed, which shows how much a pair of topics are related [23]. Here, topics are totally ordered as $t_1, \ldots, t_{tn}$ as follows:

- For three topics t_i, t_j, and t_k, if $|i - j| < |i - k|$, the topic t_j is more related with the topic t_i than the topic t_k.

Then, we define the relevance RbT_{kl} ($0 \leq RbT_{kl} \leq 1$) between a kth topic t_k and an lth topic t_l as follows:

$$RbT_{kl} = e^{-\{(l-k)^2/(2\times\sigma^2)\}}. \tag{1}$$

Here, each peer decides on the membership of topics in its publication and subscription based on the relevance concept. The publication $p_i.P$ and subscription $p_i.S$ of each peer p_i are composed of topics which are related with one another. The publication $e.P$ of each event message e published by a peer p_i is also composed of topics related to the topics in the publication $p_i.P$. On receipt of an event message e, a peer p_i accepts the event message e only if some of hidden topics of the event message e are strongly related with topics in which the peer p_i is interested. The number of topics which each peer is allowed to subscribe increases as the number of event messages which each peer receives increases. That is, each peer p_i learns other topics which the peer p_i should subscribe from event messages and subscribes the topics which the peer cannot subscribe initially. We assume there is a main topic $p_i.mt$ in the subscription of each peer p_i. The main topic t_k $(= p_i.mt)$ of a peer p_i means that the peer p_i subscribes topics related with the topic t_k. That is, every topic in the subscription of a peer p_i is related with the main topic $p_i.mt$.

[**FS-H Protocol**]. A peer p_i publishes an event message e and the peer p_i precedes a peer p_j $(p_i \rightarrow p_j)$ whose main topic $p_j.mt$ is t_k:

The source peer p_i behaves to send the event message e as follows:

1. $e.T = p_i.T$;
   $e.P = $ publication topics of the event message e;
2. p_i publishes the event message e;

The target peer p_j behaves to receive the event message e as follows:

1. If $e.T \subseteq p_j.S$, the event message e is received by the peer p_j and
   (a) If $e.T \neq \phi$, $p_j.T = p_j.T \cup e.T$;
   (b) Otherwise, $p_j.T = p_j.T \cup (e.P \cap p_j.S)$;
2. Else if $PWT(e, p_j) \leq AWT(e, p_j)$, the event message e is received by a peer p_j;
   (a) If $e.T \neq \phi$, $p_j.T = p_j.T \cup e.T$;
   (b) Otherwise, $p_j.T = p_j.T \cup (e.P \cap p_j.S)$;
   Each topic t_l $(\{t_l \mid t_l \in e.T - p_j.S\})$ is added to $p_j.S$ with probability RbT_{kl};
3. Otherwise, the event message e is prohibited at the peer p_j;

Let $AWT(e, p_j)$ be summation of weights of topics in the topic set $p_i.T$ of a peer p_i and subscription $p_j.S$ of a peer p_j ($\{t_m \mid t_m \in p_i.T \cap p_j.S\}$) for acceptance. If t_k is a main topic $p_j.mt$ of the peer p_j, the summation $AWT(e, p_j)$ of weights is given as follows:

$$AWT(e, p_j) = \sum_{t_m \in e.T \cap p_j.S} RbT_{km}. \tag{2}$$

Let $PWT(e, p_j)$ be summation of weights of topics ($\{t_l \mid t_l \in e.T - p_j.S\}$) for prohibition of event messages. If t_k is the main topic $p_j.mt$ of the peer p_j, the summation $PWT(e, p_j)$ of weights is given as follows:

$$PWT(e, p_j) = \sum_{t_l \in e.T - p_j.S} (1 - RbT_{kl}). \tag{3}$$

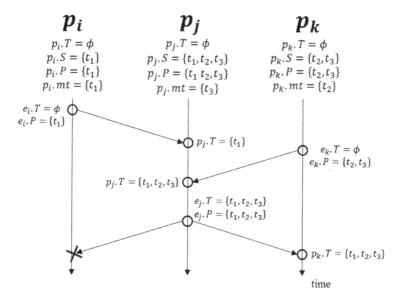

Fig. 1. FS-H protocol.

We consider three peers p_i, p_j, and p_k which are granted publication and subscription rights as shown in Fig. 1. Suppose the value of σ of the relevance RbT_{kl} shown in the formula (1) is 1. Here, the topic sets $p_i.T$, $p_j.T$, and $p_k.T$ are initially empty. First, the peer p_i publishes an event message e_i whose publication $e_i.P = \{t_1\}$. The peer p_j receives the event message e_i since $e_i.P \cap p_j.S$ ($= \{t_1\}$) $\neq \phi$ and $e_i.T$ ($= \phi$) $\subseteq p_j.S$ ($= \{t_1, t_2, t_3\}$). The topic t_1 is added to the topic set $p_j.T$ because $p_j.T = p_j.T \cup (e_i.P \cap p_j.S) = \{t_1\}$. Next, the peer p_k publishes an event message e_k whose publication $e_k.P = \{t_2, t_3\}$. The peer p_j receives the event message e_k since $e_k.P \cap p_j.S$ ($= \{t_2, t_3\}$) $\neq \phi$ and $e_k.T$ ($= \phi$) $\subseteq p_j.S$ ($= \{t_1, t_2, t_3\}$). A pair of the topics t_2 and t_3 are added to the topic set

$p_j.T$ because $p_j.T = p_j.T \cup (e_k.P \cap p_j.S) = \{t_1, t_2, t_3\}$. Then, the peer p_j publishes an event message e_j whose publication $e_j.P$ is $\{t_1, t_2, t_3\}$. $e_j.P \cap p_k.S$ ($= \{t_2, t_3\}$) $\neq \phi$ but $e_j.T$ ($= \{t_1, t_2, t_3\}$) $\not\subseteq p_k.S$ ($= \{t_2, t_3\}$). Here, the summation of acceptance weights $AWT(e_j, p_k)$ is about 1.61 ($= RbT_{22} + RbT_{23} = 1.00 + 0.61$). The summation of prohibition weights $PWT(e_j, p_k)$ is about 0.39 ($= 1 - RbT_{21}$). Since $PWT(e_j, p_k) < AWT(e_j, p_k)$, the peer p_j accepts the event message e_j. The topic t_1 is added to the subscription $p_k.S$ with probability RbT_{21} ($= 0.61$). On the other hand, $e_j.P \cap p_i.S$ ($= \{t_1\}$) $\neq \phi$ but $e_j.T$ ($= \{t_1, t_2, t_3\}$) $\not\subseteq p_i.S$ ($= \{t_1\}$). Here, the summation of acceptance weights $AWT(e_j, p_i)$ is about 1.00 ($= RbT_{11} = 1.00$). The summation of prohibition weights $PWT(e_j, p_i)$ is about 1.25 ($= (1 - RbT_{12}) + (1 - RbT_{13}) = 0.39 + 0.86$). Since $PWT(e_j, p_i) > AWT(e_j, p_i)$, the event message e_j is prohibited at the peer p_i.

5   Evaluation

We evaluate the FS-H protocol on a topic set $T = \{t_1, \ldots, t_{tn}\}$ ($tn \geq 1$) and a peer set $P = \{p_1, \ldots, p_{pn}\}$ ($pn \geq 1$) in terms of the number of event messages prohibited and the number of topics subscribed by each peer compared with the SBS and TBS protocols. In the FS-H protocol, the subscription $p_i.S$ of the target peer p_i is updated each time an event message is received by the peer p_i. We assume an event message can be reliably broadcast to every target peer.

A pair of publish (pb) and subscribe (sb) operations are supported on each topic. Each peer p_i is granted topics in a publication $p_i.P$ and a subscription $p_i.S$, which are related with one another. In the evaluation, each subscription $p_i.S$ is generated based on the relevance concept of topics as follows:

1. The relevance between a kth topic and an lth topic is obtained by the formula (1).
2. First, a topic t_k is randomly selected and included in the subscription $p_i.S$ as a topic which the peer p_i mainly subscribes.
3. Then, each t_n of the other topics ($\{t_n \mid t_n \in T - \{t_k\}\}$) are included in the subscription $p_i.S$ with the probability RbT_{kn}.

On the other hand, each publication $p_i.P$ is generated so that the publication $p_i.P$ includes the main topic t_k of the peer p_i, i.e. $p_i.mt = t_k$ and the publication $p_i.P$ is a subset of the subscription $p_i.S$, i.e. $\{t_k\} \in p_i.P$ and $p_i.P \subseteq p_i.S$.

In the evaluation, we consider one hundred peers ($pn = 100$) and one hundred topics ($tn = 100$). A collection P of pn peers $p_1, \ldots, p_{pn}$ are randomly generated on tn topics $t_1, \ldots, t_{tn}$, i.e. $P = \{p_1, \ldots, p_{100}\}$ and $T = \{t_1, \ldots, t_{100}\}$. The number n of publication events occur in the simulation. We randomly create a peer set P on the topic set T five hundred times for each number n. First, one peer p_i is randomly selected in the peer set P. Then, the peer p_i publishes an event message e with the publication $e.P$ which is composed of some topics randomly selected in the publication $p_i.P$ to every target peer p_j. In the FS-H protocol, if the peer p_j can subscribe all the topics in $e.T$, the event message e is received by the peer p_j and all the topics in $e.T$ are added to $p_j.T$. In addition, even if the peer p_j is not allowed to subscribe all the topics in $e.T$, i.e. $e.H \neq \phi$,

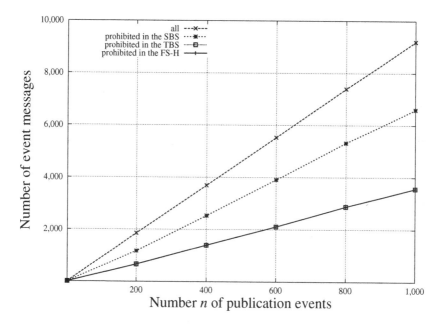

Fig. 2. Number of event messages ($\sigma = 2$).

and all the hidden topics in $e.H$ are strongly related with a main topic $p_j.mt$ of the peer p_j, the event message e is also received by the peer p_j, some topics in $e.H$ are added to the subscription $p_j.S$, and all the topics in $e.T$ are added to $p_j.T$. Otherwise, the event message e is prohibited. These steps are iterated n times. For a given peer set P, n publication events occur five hundred times in the FS-H protocol.

Figure 2 shows the number of event messages for the number n of publication events where the parameter σ of the formula (1) is 2. The total number of event messages published is shown by the dotted line with cross symbols ($\times$). The number of event messages prohibited in the FS-H protocol is not as many as that of the SBS protocol is. On the other hand, the number of event messages prohibited in the FS-H protocol is almost same as that of the TBS protocol.

Figure 3 shows the number of event messages for the number n of publication events where the parameter σ of the formula (1) is 10. The fewest number of event messages are prohibited in the FS-H protocol compared with the other protocols.

Figure 4 shows the number of event messages for the parameter σ of the formula (1) where two hundred events occur ($n = 200$). For $\sigma \leq 4$, the number of event messages prohibited of the FS-H protocol is not as many as that of the SBS protocol is and almost same as that of the TBS protocol. On the other hand, for $\sigma > 4$, the fewest number of event messages are prohibited in the FS-H protocol compared with the other protocols.

Figure 5 shows the number of topics subscribed by each peer for the parameter σ of the formula (1) where two hundred events occur ($n = 200$). In the FS-H

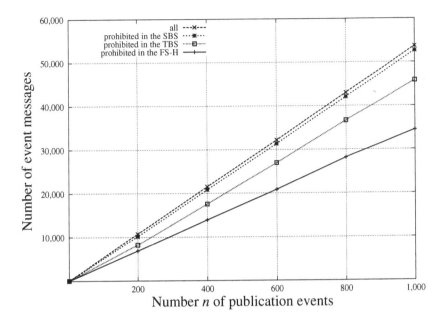

Fig. 3. Number of event messages ($\sigma = 10$).

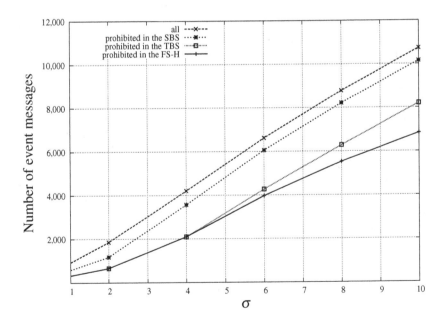

Fig. 4. Number of event messages ($n = 200$).

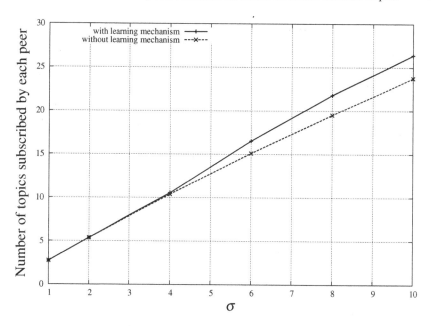

Fig. 5. Number of topics subscribed by each peer ($n = 200$).

protocol, on receipt of an event message with hidden topics, each peer adds the hidden topics to its subscription, i.e. the learning mechanism of topics is supported. The number of topics subscribed by each peer is shown by the solid line with plus symbols (+). On the other hand, the learning mechanism is not supported in the SBS and TBS protocols. The number of topics subscribed by each peer is shown by the dotted line with cross symbols (×). For $\sigma \leq 4$, the number of topics subscribed by each peer in the FS-H protocol is almost same as those in the SBS and TBS protocols. On the other hand, for $\sigma > 4$, the number of topics subscribed in the FS-H protocol is larger than the SBS and TBS protocols. This means, the condition $e.T \subseteq p_i.S$ is likely to be satisfied in the FS-H protocol compared with the SBS and TBS protocols for $\sigma > 4$. Hence, the fewest number of event messages are prohibited in the FS-H protocol compared with the other protocols for $\sigma > 4$ as shown in Fig. 4.

6   Concluding Remarks

In this paper, we newly proposed the FS-H (flexible synchronization for hidden topics) protocol to prevent illegal information flow of hidden topics and to reduce the number of event messages prohibited. In the SBS [24] and TBS [20] protocols, an illegal event message is prohibited at each target peer and some legal event messages are prohibited. In this paper, the FS-H protocol is proposed to more reduce the number of legal event messages prohibited. Here, only if an event message carries hidden topics which are strongly related with some topic in which a target peer is interested, the peer accepts the event message. Then, the peer obtains the hidden topics in the subscription. Thus, even if a peer does not know about all the topics in a system, the peer can obtain new topics which interest the peer through receipt of event messages. The more number of event messages are published, the more number of topics each peer can subscribe. In the evaluation, we showed the number of event messages prohibited in the FS-H protocol is fewest in all the protocols.

In the FS-H protocol, every topic carried into each peer p_i is kept in the peer p_i. Here, the number of topics kept by every peer monotonically increases. However, every topic stored in a peer is not necessarily permanently meaningful such as the topics with time limit. In the new method which we are considering, such meaningless topics are deleted from every peer to more reduce the number of event messages prohibited.

In this paper, we assume every event message is reliably and causally delivered to every peer. We are now discussing how to causally deliver event messages to target peers in the P2PPS system.

Acknowledgement. This work was supported by Japan Society for the Promotion of Science (JSPS) KAKENHI Grant Numbers JP15H0295, JP17J00106.

References

1. Bacon, J., Eyers, D.M., Singh, J., Pietzuch, P.R.: Access control in publish/subscribe systems. In: Proceedings of the 2nd International Conference on Distributed Event-based Systems, pp. 23–34 (2008)
2. Balakrishnan, S.M., Sangaiah, A.K.: Integrated quality of user experience and quality of service approach to service selection in internet of services. Int. J. Grid Util. Comput. **8**(4), 282–298 (2017)
3. Barolli, L., Xhafa, F.: A P2P platform for distributed, collaborative and ubiquitous computing. IEEE Trans. Industr. Electron. **58**(6), 2063–2172 (2011)
4. Blanco, R., Alencar, P.: Event models in distributed event based systems. In: Principles and Applications of Distributed Event-Based Systems, pp. 19–42 (2010)
5. Denning, D.E.R.: Cryptography and Data Security. Addison Wesley, Boston (1982)
6. Enokido, T., Takizawa, M.: A purpose-based synchronization protocol for secure information flow control. Int. J. Comput. Syst. Sci. Eng. **25**(2), 25–32 (2010)
7. Enokido, T., Takizawa, M.: Purpose-based information flow control for cyber engineering. IEEE Trans. Industr. Electron. **58**(6), 2216–2225 (2011)
8. Eugster, P.T., Felber, P.A., Guerraoui, R., Kermarrec, A.M.: The many faces of publish/subscribe. ACM Comput. Surv. **35**(2), 114–131 (2003)
9. Fernandez, E.B., Summers, R.C., Wood, C.: Database Security and Integrity. Addison Wesley, Boston (1980)
10. Ferraiolo, D.F., Kuhn, D.R., Chandramouli, R.: Role-Based Access Control, 2nd edn. Artech, Norwood (2007)
11. Google alert: http://www.google.com/alerts. Accessed 1 Aug 2018
12. Gueye, B., Flauzac, O., Rabat, C., Niang, I.: A self-adaptive structuring for large-scale P2P grid environment: design and simulation analysis. Int. J. Grid Util. Comput. **8**(3), 254–267 (2017)

13. John, P.M., Arockiasamy, S., Thangiah, P.R.J.: A personalised user preference and feature based semantic information retrieval system in semantic web search. Int. J. Grid Util. Comput. **9**(3), 256–267 (2018)
14. Liu, Y., Ozera, K., Matsuo, K., Barolli, L.: An intelligent approach for qualified voting in P2P mobile collaborative team: a comparison study for two fuzzy-based systems. Int. J. Space-Based Situated Comput. **7**(4), 207–216 (2017)
15. Liu, Z., Luo, J., Xu, L.: A fine-grained attribute-based authentication for sensitive data stored in cloud computing. Int. J. Grid Util. Comput. **7**(4), 237–244 (2016)
16. Nakamura, S., Duolikun, D., Enokido, T., Takizawa, M.: A flexible read-write abortion protocol to prevent illegal information flow among objects. J. Mob. Multimed. **11**(3&4), 263–280 (2015)
17. Nakamura, S., Duolikun, D., Enokido, T., Takizawa, M.: A write abortion-based protocol in role-based access control systems. Int. J. Adapt. Innov. Syst. **2**(2), 142–160 (2015)
18. Nakamura, S., Duolikun, D., Enokido, T., Takizawa, M.: A read-write abortion (RWA) protocol to prevent illegal information flow in role-based access control systems. Int. J. Space-Based Situated Comput. **6**(1), 43–53 (2016)
19. Nakamura, S., Duolikun, D., Takizawa, M.: Read-abortion (RA) based synchronization protocols to prevent illegal information flow. J. Comput. Syst. Sci. **81**(8), 1441–1451 (2015)
20. Nakamura, S., Enokido, T., Takizawa, M.: A topic-based synchronisation protocol in peer-to-peer publish/subscribe systems, accepted for publication at International Journal of Communication Networks and Distributed Systems
21. Nakamura, S., Enokido, T., Takizawa, M.: Sensitivity-based synchronisation protocol to prevent illegal information flow among objects. Int. J. Web Grid Serv. **13**(3), 315–333 (2017)
22. Nakamura, S., Enokido, T., Takizawa, M.: A flexible read-write abortion protocol with role safety concept to prevent illegal information flow. J. Ambient. Intell. Hum. Comput. **9**(5), 1415–1425 (2018)
23. Nakamura, S., Ogiela, L., Enokido, T., Takizawa, M.: Flexible synchronization protocol to prevent illegal information flow in peer-to-peer publish/subscribe systems. In: Barolli, L., Terzo, O. (eds.) CISIS 2017. AISC, vol. 611, pp. 82–93. Springer, Cham (2018). https://doi.org/10.1007/978-3-319-61566-0_8
24. Nakamura, S., Ogiela, L., Enokido, T., Takizawa, M.: An information flow control model in a topic-based publish/subscribe system. J. High Speed Netw. **24**(3), 243–257 (2018)
25. Nakayama, H., Duolikun, D., Enokido, T., Takizawa, M.: Selective delivery of event messages in peer-to-peer topic-based publish/subscribe systems. In: Proceedings of the 18th International Conference on Network-Based Information Systems, pp. 379–386 (2015)
26. Nakayama, H., Duolikun, D., Enokido, T., Takizawa, M.: Reduction of unnecessarily ordered event messages in peer-to-peer model of topic-based publish/subscribe systems. In: Proceedings of IEEE the 30th International Conference on Advanced Information Networking and Applications, pp. 1160–1167 (2016)
27. Osborn, S., Sandhu, R.S., Munawer, Q.: Configuring role-based access control to enforce mandatory and discretionary access control policies. ACM Trans. Inf. Syst. Secur. **3**(2), 85–106 (2000)
28. Sandhu, R.S.: Lattice-based access control models. IEEE Comput. **26**(11), 9–19 (1993)
29. Sandhu, R.S., Coyne, E.J., Feinstein, H.L., Youman, C.E.: Role-based access control models. IEEE Comput. **29**(2), 38–47 (1996)

30. Setty, V., Steen, M.V., Vitenberg, R., Voulgaris, S.: Poldercast: fast, robust, and scalable architecture for P2P topic-based pub/sub. In: Proceedings of ACM/IFIP/USENIX 13th International Conference on Middleware, pp. 271–291 (2012)
31. Tarkoma, S.: Publish/Subscribe System: Design and Principles, 1st edn. Wiley, Hoboken (2012)
32. Tomimori, M., Sugawara, S.: Content sharing method using expected acquisition rate in hybrid peer-to-peer networks with cloud storages. Int. J. Space-Based Situated Comput. **7**(4), 187–196 (2017)
33. Waluyo, A.B., Taniar, D., Rahayu, W., Aikebaier, A., Takizawa, M., Srinivasan, B.: Trustworthy-based efficient data broadcast model for P2P interaction in resource-constrained wireless environments. J. Comput. Syst. Sci. **78**(6), 1716–1736 (2012)
34. Yamamoto, Y., Hayashibara, N.: Merging topic groups of a publish/subscribe system in causal order. In: Proceedings of the 31st International Conference on Advanced Information Networking and Applications Workshops, pp. 172–177 (2017)
35. Yoichi, R., Sugawara, S.: Consistency preservation of replicas based on access frequency for content sharing in hybrid peer-to-peer networks. Int. J. Space-Based Situated Comput. **7**(4), 197–206 (2017)

QoS Preservation in Web Service Selection

Adrija Bhattacharya[1]([✉]) and Sankhayan Choudhury[2]

[1] Department of Computer Science and Engineering,
Heritage Institute of Technology, Kolkata, India
`adrija.bhattacharya@acm.org`
[2] Department of Computer Science and Engineering,
University of Calcutta, Kolkata, India
`sccomp@caluniv.ac.in`

Abstract. In cloud computing domain, often service providers offer services with same functionalities, but with varying quality metrics. A suitable service selection method finds the most appropriate solution among the alternatives. The challenge is to deliver a solution satisfying the requirement (quality and other) of a consumer with minimum possible execution time. Many conflicting QoS objectives increase the complexity of the problem. In fact, the problem may be formulated as a multi-objective, NP-hard optimization problem. Most of the existing solutions either satisfies the QoS demands of consumer or only reduces execution time by considering a sub-set of required QoS metrics. Consumer's feedback on the choice of required QoS metrics not only shall help increasing user satisfaction, but also may reduce the complexity effectively. However, this depends on the domain knowledge of a consumer. In this work, we have proposed a goodness measure that replaces all QoS metrics by a single one. The new technique using dimension reduction is proposed to offer significant improvement compared to the existing works in terms of execution time. Moreover, the solution satisfies all the QoS requirements of a consumer in most of the cases. The proposed data driven selection approach has been implemented and the experimental results substantiate the claims as mentioned.

Keywords: QoS · Goodness · Service selection · Factor analysis

1 Introduction

Service Selection from numerous alternative similar services satisfying Quality of Service parameters (QoS) is a well known challenge in service provisioning domain. Service matching based on functional and QoS parameters simultaneously can satisfy the requirement of a consumer in a true sense. Service offerings (both QoS and functionalities) are advertised by the providers through Service Level Agreements (SLA). Consumers have specific requirements with functionalities and in terms of typical QoS parameters. Popular service selection approaches

© Springer-Verlag GmbH Germany, part of Springer Nature 2019
N. T. Nguyen et al. (Eds.): TCCI XXXIII, LNCS 11610, pp. 71–88, 2019.
https://doi.org/10.1007/978-3-662-59540-4_4

consider less number of QoSs (two or three at most) [5, 7, 10] instead of all QoS requirements. It may result dissatisfaction among consumers. Thus an effective service selection process has to be equipped with the ability to choose services with requested level of all QoS metrics without compromising in time complexity.

Service selection problem has a multidimensional solution space and the dimension depends on the number of QoS parameters specified by a consumer. Moreover, some of these QoS parameters are conflicting and makes the problem more critical. For example, minimizing Response Time will increase the cost of other metrics (such as operational cost). Thus there are multiple objectives. Each of the objectives pertains to a single QoS parameter. Optimization of such a complex multi objective function subject to multiple constraints is the intended solution. QoS offering at various levels by multiple (huge) number of providers makes the solution space larger. As a result the selection problem is of NP-hard [10] type and consequently it demands attention of researchers.

Search space reduction is a popular approach for optimization problems [2]. Heuristics can be applied to reduce the search space effectively [13]. Most of the methods target to reduce the execution time of the selection. Often a selected service may satisfy a particular QoS requirement while failing to satisfy another. A negotiation with respect to unsatisfactory QoSs may be the possible solution for seamless provisioning. Feedback from the consumers are helpful for satisfying the quality requirement [18]. Usually preferences about the choices on QoS parameters are collected from consumers to make the selection process simpler but the success highly depends on the domain knowledge of the consumers. These works perform poor in terms of execution time though the quality satisfaction is higher. In contrast solution targeting optimized execution may result a poor performance in terms of QoS satisfaction [18]. A well balance between these two aspects may be the most desirable solution.

In this paper we have addressed the following issues that comes out of the above discussion.

1. Is it possible to make an choice of services without taking preferences from consumers but assuring a satisfactory solution considering all requested QoS metrics?
2. Is it possible to deliver a solution that ensures optimal choices in terms of all QoS (as requested by consumer) without compromising execution time?

We have presented an initial idea in [3] to address the above issues. The idea was to replace all QoS parameters by a single measure, called goodness. The purpose of the approach was to find out a single measure that can be used for satisfying all QoSs. It reduces the multidimensional problem to a single objective one. The problem of service selection is formally defined in Sect. 2. Brief discussion on related works are presented in Sect. 3. The theoretical motivation and outline of the presented work is described in Sect. 4. Section 5 explains the working solution for the problems discussed. Section 6 shows the experimental results pertaining to the methods explained in Sect. 5. The final conclusion is presented in Sect. 7.

2   Problem Formulation

In this section we are stating the problem of service selection in a formal manner. This is primarily a problem of optimization. There is an objective function (O) comprising many QoS metrics (as in Eq. 1).
   Minimize

$$O = \sum_{p} w_p QoS_p^q \tag{1}$$

where w_p is the weight for pth QoS metric (QoS_p) according to requirement. q takes value $+1$ if the QoS QoS_p has to be minimized and -1 if QoS_p has to be maximized. Clearly the objective function may contain many QoS objectives to be optimized at a time while service selection. These QoS metrics often may hold complex relationship which are tough to satisfy simultaneously. Moreover, there are multiple constraint criteria (as described in Eq. 2). These criteria are to be maintained along with achieving the individual QoS objectives. For all j (positive integer)

$$\sum_{i} A_i QoS_i \begin{cases} \leq \\ = & C_j \\ \geq \end{cases} \tag{2}$$

C_j is the constraint value where A_i is the weight signifying importance of ith QoS parameter. QoS_i denotes ith QoS metric. For any positive value of j the above equations represent the problem of service selection as a multi objective multi constraint optimization problem. If each QoS metric is considered as a dimension, the above mathematical problem appears multidimensional. Some of these QoS metrics maintain clear relations among themselves. This is the key criteria to reduce the overall dimension of the problem by process of reduction. Dimension reduction [8] will help in efficient optimization of the complex problem with less overhead involved. In this proposed work a dimension reduction technique along with data driven selection approach is explored for efficient service selection.

3   Related Works

The efficiency of a service selection approach can be measured through two metrics. One is the execution time and the other is how closely it satisfies all required QoSs. The existing works, in general, attempted to optimize the objective function that involves required QoS parameters. The existing works vary in number of QoS parameter considered. In most of the cases the considerable QoS parameters are Response time, Cost and Availability [9,11,14,17,21]. Some other notable works considered other parameters like Latency and Reputation [6], Trust and Maintainability [15]. In one of the approaches [12] a suggestion on considering the non network and network QoS of services separately is followed. A QoS equation is formulated to calculate the network QoS, latency, and transfer rate in [12]. Most of the existing works discussed so far perform selection based on a few QoSs instead of considering all available QoS metrics.

There exist approaches that tried to solve the multi-objective optimization problem of this service domain by several alternatives. In a popular case, previous performance is used to narrow down the solution space [5]. User feedback [10] and recommender based selection [4,22] are also well-known approaches. Cloud Computing Service Composition problem is addressed in [20] and [19]. These are solved by preference-aware QoS evaluation approach based on artificial neural networks. This approach has a QoS value aggregation algorithm for composition. A neural network method is proposed without relying on user's expertise while aggregating the QoS criteria.

The approaches mentioned earlier in this section either satisfy consumer's quality requirement well or gives an efficient selection (execution time for service selection algorithm) time. It is clear from the discussed popular works that the approaches that performs better with respect to execution time have taken fewer number of QoSs. On the other hand the later approaches satisfies large QoS criteria and have longer execution (selection) time. In the proposed work the attempt is to replace all QoS parameters of a service by a single goodness measure and executes the selection based on the new metric. It certainly helps to reduce the execution time significantly as the multi-dimension problem converts to a single dimension. Eventually the other objective is to ensure the performance of the solution in terms of requested QoS parameter satisfaction. It suggests that the solution should not be dependent on the user's feedback. Moreover the

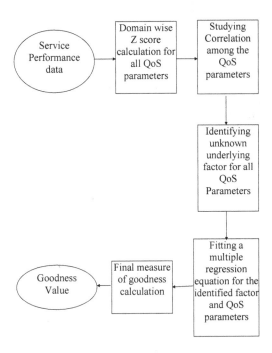

Fig. 1. Outline of solution proposal in [3]

selection process should not be biased to a specific QoS rather to ensure a solution considering all requested QoS of the consumer. Scope of this paper includes a proposal of a data driven approach to find out a single measure (goodness) of all QoSs of a service and execute the selection algorithm based on the new measure. Experiments and subsequent findings are also included within the scope to ensure the effectiveness of the proposed service selection approach.

4   Proposal in Brief

The idea behind the solution proposal is presented in one previous work [3]. Figure 1 depicts the steps used in the said approach. A large number of QoS parameters are associated to each service as per the dataset under experiment. The attempt was to find out the hidden common factors having influence on service performance. The underlying factors are certainly less in number compared to the associated QoSs. The existence of common factors is also substantiated by the correlation measurement among QoSs. The objective is to make the problem simpler for getting feasible solution with less execution time. An attempt had been made to express the QoS metrics through fewer unobserved factors and to offer a combined measure, called goodness, in terms of the said factors.

A complex system may have a number of potentially influential factors (x) that have effect on the predicted variable (Y). The relative importance of each factor is considered and the well known method of Multiple linear regression is used to address this. The general form of the multiple linear regression is:

$$y = a + b_1 x_1 + b_2 x_2 + \ldots + b_k x_k \tag{3}$$

There may exist partial regression also. So, $(bi's)$ i.e. the coefficient for each x term is affected by the presence of the partial regression coefficients for each of the other x variables. The final goodness measure of a service was calculated by combining the identified uncorrelated factor scores. Let the individual factor scores are denoted by Fi as ith factor. Thus the overall goodness measure of a service (for n identified factors) is denoted by,

$$G = \frac{\sum_{i=1}^{n} F_i}{n} \tag{4}$$

Goodness measure for replacing all associated QoS parameters was primarily introduced in [3]. It reduces the complexity of the multi objective multi constraint optimization problem. In this said data driven approach the correlations among QoSs were measured. But the correlation coefficients alone cannot determine the true level of association and dependencies among QoSs. The said situation raises the following research questions:

– R1: How to increase the accuracy in determining the association among QoSs?

In [3] Exploratory Factor Analysis (EFA) was used to describe factors by QoSs. EFA deliberately includes all QoSs into factor determination. As a consequence the actual effect of a particular QoS on a typical factor was disrupted by the mixed effect of other QoSs. The corresponding gap leads to the issue as mentioned in R2.

– R2: How to effectively enhance the factor determination by readjusting the involved QoSs using their mutual association?

In the final steps Multiple Regression was used to predict the factors in terms of underlying QoSs. The motivation behind choosing the method is missing in the scope of [3]. Moreover the proper validation of the used methodology is not fully addressed in [3]. So the research questions arise here are

– R3: What are the alternate regression procedures that could be used to improve the precision of the goodness measure?
– R4: How the alternate regression based solutions can be validate by exhaustive data driven experimental results?

Thus the previously proposed sketchy approach of goodness measure need improvements in context of the above said issues. Moreover the rigorous experiments and analyses are also required for validation of the proposed methodology. In Sect. 5 the improvements with respect to above issues are discussed in detail.

5   Solution Proposal and Experimental Findings

The objective in this proposed work is to enhance the process of finding Goodness measure by improving underlying statistical tools and techniques. Moreover proper validation of the techniques is also another issue in the purview. The enhancement certainly increases the efficiency of the selection algorithm in terms of QoS satisfaction and execution time both.

At first the most appropriate option for finding association among the QoSs is decided. Causal Relationships among QoSs along with the data driven correlation analysis is used for this purpose. The next improvement strategy is to select proper methodology for hidden factor identification. The causal effects of QoSs are also considered while selecting QoSs for constructing certain factor. A conceptual comparison has to be done on the feasibility of using several available regression techniques. Experimental findings drive the decision while validating several techniques suitable in the situation. Tasks for achieving the above objectives are as follows.

– To select the appropriate option for enhancing the accuracy within association finding among QoSs
– To select the ideal hidden factor identification process
– To select the appropriate regression technique
– To execute rigorous experiment for substantiating the above selections that in turn ensures the effectiveness of overall selection process.

5.1   Correlation Among QoSs

Cumulative effects of a group of QoSs are not always reflected by correlation. These effects are essentially causal. Ignoring such causal effect the solution may exhibit biased result. This approach typically works simultaneously in data driven and causal manner. We have the data set of 2500 services as given in [1]. There is nine QoS parameters associated to each service in the said dataset. Association (both causal and data driven) found in the data is noted after removing some outliers and domain wise mapping and the further factor analysis is designed based on the results of identified association.

5.1.1   Analyses of Results Related to QoS Correlations

There are bivariate correlations between pair of QoSs from the given data set shown in Table 1.

Table 1. Correlation coefficients among considered QoSs

Parameter	Availability	Throughput	Successability	Reliability	Compliance	Best Practices	Latency	Documentation
Response Time	−.66	−.253	−.77	.47	−.83	.33	.391	−.40
Availability		.201	.989	.129	.244	.57	−.99	−.6
Throughput			.201	.256	.060	.168	−.145	−.031
Successability				.121	.261	.055	−.011	.004
Reliability					−.030	.689	−.024	.061
Compliance						.34	−.77	−.180
Best Practices							−.008	−.037
Latency								−.40

Some inferences about the possible causal relationships identified. It clearly shows that the Response time, Throughput and Availability have higher association among them. These parameters also have highly positive correlations with Successability, Reliability and Best Practices. These could be a possible group of QoSs constructing one Factor. Another set of parameters for second factor could be Response time, Availability, Latency, Compliance and Documentation. It is also visible that Latency, Compliance and Documentation posses poor association with that of Successability, Reliability and Best Practices. Thus the said two sets of parameters may be kept in different factors to make them un-correlated. Some causal information enhances the understanding of association more accurately. Such as Response Time and Availability are two factors that have inversely proportional relationship. Secondly Latency and Reliability are the two factors that are strongly causally connected with Response Time.

5.2 Factor Identification and Factor Analysis

In this solution phase, some hidden unidentified factors are revealed through necessary analysis. In [3] EFA identified factors that are based only on the dependency on the correlated QoS metrics. EFA involves all QoSs into account even if the impact of the QoS with the factor happened to be least. This may result in poor goodness of fit in the regression fitting that in turn could be the cause of reduced precision of the solution. Here a confirmatory factor analysis is used. The affections among the QoS are measured in terms of correlations and causality as mentioned in Sect. 5.1. The factors are determined based on these associations and the existing knowledge about the causal relationships. Highly correlated QoS parameters are put together into one factor; so that the factors remain uncorrelated or negligibly correlated. In this work, the confirmatory factor analysis is used first with two factors and again it is restructured using three factors.

5.2.1 Factor Analysis Results

The decision regarding number of factor and possible determinant QoSs of each factor is determined mainly from the inferences drawn in earlier Subsect. 5.1. Moreover, some causal information that is often overlooked by the exploratory factor analysis is revisited and included within this proposed work using Confirmatory Factor Analysis (CFA). Response time and Availability are main determinants here as both of them possess higher and significant correlations with other QoSs. Throughput alone has biased relation with a smaller set of QoSs. We have agreed with the decision through causal analysis that availability and response time both have impact on each other. So, these two can be included in a single factor. After revisiting so many such issues a 2 factor and a 3 factor analysis are being done. Component QoSs for each of these analyses are described in Table 2.

Table 2. Factor and component identification

Factors	2 factor CFA	3 factor CFA
F1	Response Time, Throughput, Availability, Successability, Reliability, Best practice	Response Time, Throughput, Availability, Successability, Reliability, Best practice
F2	Response Time, Availability, Latency, Compliance, Documentation	Response Time, Compliance, Latency, Documentation
F3		Compliance, Best Practice Documentation

5.3   Regression Approaches Considered

There are several options in statistical methods that can be used to find out the factors using multiple QoSs at a time. Principal Component analysis is one of the possible tools. It has the required multivariate support as in this case each factor corresponds to several numbers of QoSs. There exist correlations among the participating QoSs within a factor. Partial least Square is a similar option that can be used. Logistic regression, another popular choice, works on categorical data and not suitable for quantitative data set (QWS) as considered. Cox Proportional and Canonical regression techniques also work on categorical data and as a result not to be considered as suitable. Multiple linear Regression and the Polynomial regression could be the approaches that support the features of this data set. Discrete regression procedure is also not acceptable as it needs the regressors to be independent of each other. In this data driven analysis method, factors have highly correlated QoS components and thus the discrete regression is also discarded. The above discussion has been summarized in Table 3. It is inferred from the table that there are four possible alternate regression approaches suitable for the considered data set. These are Principal Component Analysis, Partial least Square, Multiple and Polynomial. The comparative results of the suitable regression techniques are discussed in Sect. 5.3.1.

Table 3. Regression techniques

Method	Properties	Comment
Principal Component Analysis	Supported	Can be used
Partial least Square	Supported	Can be used
Logistic	Suitable for categorical data	Cannot be used
Multiple	Supported	Can be used
Cox proportional	Suitable for categorical data	Cannot be used
Discrete	No correlation in regressor	Cannot be used
Polynomial	Supported	Can be used
Canonical	Suitable for categorical data	Cannot be used

Table 4. Regression techniques efficiencies

Method	Exploratory	2 factor CFA	3 factor CFA
Principal Component Analysis	0.26134	0.36420	0.54143
Partial least Square	0.44436	0.75197	0.78496
Multiple	1.00	0.95998	0.93002
Polynomial	0.35117	0.221086	0.19134

5.3.1   Regression Comparison Results

We have used four regression techniques identified in Table 3. The corresponding R^2 values are compared. We have used each of the four regression techniques on EFA, 2 factor CFA and 3 factor CFA. Table 4 summarizes the results.

It is shown that the Multiple regression model is the most accepted one for all of the three factor analyses. Moreover Partial least square works well for confirmatory factor analysis. One possible reason behind it could be that exploratory factor analysis even includes smallest association (even up to three or four decimal places) of QoS. So the variation of those QoSs is less compared to other more significant QoSs. Polynomial Regression has also been included. It has shown only exponent of two for one QoS (Response Time) have significant regression coefficient. The result shows that the Exponents of other QoSs have negligible coefficients. Finally, we have applied the multiple regression method and found the factor equation for three distinct analyses.

Exploratory Factor Analysis. The equations extracted in Exploratory factor analysis are

$$ZFACT1 = 0.521 * ZResponseTime - 0.229 * ZThroughput$$
$$-0.064 * ZAvailability - 0.073 * ZSuccessability + 0.178 * ZReliability$$
$$-0.109 * ZCompliance + 0.188 * ZBestPractices \tag{5}$$
$$+0.469 * ZLatency - 0.004 * ZDocumentation$$

$$ZFACT2 = -0.01173 * ZResponseTime + 0.23392$$
$$*ZThroughput + 0.17726 * ZAvailability$$
$$+0.17478 * ZSuccessability + 0.44229 * ZReliability \tag{6}$$
$$+0.03414 * ZCompliance + 0.42207 * ZBestPractices$$
$$-0.038118 * ZLatency - 0.00556 * ZDocumentation$$

Confirmatory Factor Analyses with Two Factors. Equations identified with two factor CFA are as follows.

$$ZFACT1 = -0.020043 * ZResponseTime + 0.20393 * ZThroughput$$
$$+ZAvailability + 0.90001 * ZSuccessability + 0.12475 * ZReliability \tag{7}$$
$$+0.05421 * ZBestPractices$$

$$ZFACT2 = 0.68775 * ZResponseTime + +0.025139 * ZAvailability$$
$$+0.56221 * ZLatency - 0.12693ZComplince - 0.06854 * ZDocumentation \tag{8}$$

Confirmatory Factor Analyses with Three Factors. Equations identified in three-factor CFA are given by:

$$ZFACT1 = -0.016174 * ZResponseTime + ZAvailability+$$
$$0.20119ZThroughput + 0.98993 * ZSuccessability \tag{9}$$
$$+0.12965 * ZReliability + 0.05217 * ZBestPractices$$

$$ZFACT2 = 0.62913 * ZResponseTime - 0.12493 * ZCompliance$$
$$+0.61259 * ZLatency - 0.06673 * ZDocumentation \tag{10}$$

$$ZFACT3 = 0.24223 * ZCompliance - 0.36665 * ZDocumentation$$
$$+0.09123 * ZBestpreactices \tag{11}$$

In EFA all extracted equations (Eqs. 3 and 4) involve all the QoS parameters, though some of them have negligible coefficients. In case of confirmatory factor analysis, the choice of QoSs (regressors in the regression equation) is based on the association exhibited (in Table 2). Highly correlated QoS parameters are tend to have similar impact on the particular factor. Two factors are identified based on the causal as well as derived (correlation) QoS associations. The regression equations as estimated for two factor CFA determine that Best Practice and Documentation are two factors having least significant coefficients. The dissatisfaction of QoSs after fitting two factors (for small number of cases) are mainly contributed by these two quality parameters. It is also evident from literatures that these two are less significant and less occurring quality factors in most of the consumer requirements. Further a third factor has been introduced to balance the overall scenario. The performance evaluation of these factor analysis results on the basis of QoS satisfaction is empirically studied in Sect. 6.

6 Performance Evaluation

It is evident from the previous discussion that the process of service selection mechanism must perform well with respect to execution time and the satisfaction of quality requirements. A set of hypotheses has been formed and tested for exhibiting consumer's QoS satisfaction. Moreover the claims are substantiated by evaluating goodness value based on selected types of factor analyses and subsequent comparisons have been done.

6.1 Quality Satisfaction

Following three hypotheses are tested for detailed observation on the quality satisfaction of consumers.

H01: Service qualities are preserved even if the selection is based on the goodness alone

H02: Services are satisfactory for all the involved QoS parameters

H03: Even if all QoS not matched, failure in more than one QoS match is negligible. We have done executed 20 queries for each of the selected five domains (Account, Analysis, bank, Map and Scan). Total of 100 random queries were run with varying choices of QoSs. A few experiments were conducted for checking the three hypotheses mentioned.

Experiment 1: In this experiment it is shown that for each of the queries when Goodness based selection mechanism is used how the QoS requirements are satisfied. Two example domains (Account and analysis) are shown in Fig. 2.

Goodness based selection selects services denoted by blue color for services satisfying goodness and all QoSs. Red signifies services which satisfied goodness value but not all QoSs. It is clear from the figure that for both the domains the service qualities are satisfactory (errors are less than 5%). H01 is accepted.

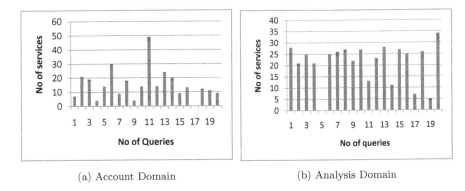

(a) Account Domain   (b) Analysis Domain

Fig. 2. Match and mismatches for two domains

Experiment 2: This experiment is to figure out the mismatches occurred in all queries (varying QoSs for all 100 query we obtained total 500 queries of several functionality and QoS combinations) mostly due to which QoSs. In Fig. 3, the failure occurred for services across the domains are shown. It signifies that Compliance, Best Practices and Documentations are the mostly dissatisfying QoSs.

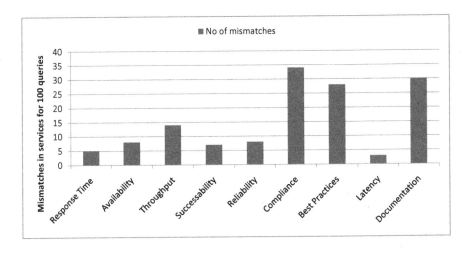

Fig. 3. Failures in QoSs across all domains

Experiment 3: In this experiment domain wise classification of failures is done. Here it is to figure out which domain is more susceptible to which QoS metics. We can summarize the following facts from Fig. 4.

– Account domain is mostly sensitive to Documentation parameter and latency and reliability are the best offered QoSs for Account domain.
– Response Time, throughput and reliability is the best offered QoSs by Analysis domain and it has the poorest Availability performance.
– Compliance is the worst performance metric for banking domain and Throughput, Latency and Documentation works well for Bank Domain.
– Most of the service failures occurred in Map domain is due to unreliability. The Significant portion of the all 100 query related failure for Reliability is contributed by the Domain Map.
– Response Time performs well for the Map services.
– Latency is the best QoS parameters for all domains which is reflected by Fig. 4 also.

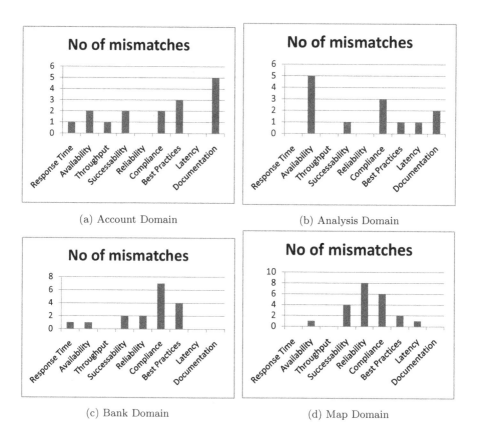

Fig. 4. Mismatches in QoS for different domains

In experiment 3, the second hypothesis (H02) is rejected with reason that the **all** service parameters are not satisfactory for **all** queries. But the fact that Compliance, Best practices and Documentation are less important is also reflected by the coefficient of estimation in the regression analysis as well as from many sources such as [1].

Experiment 4: Here we are interested to see whether the mismatches occurred are acceptable or not with a little negotiation. Alternately it is to show whether the mismatches occurred due to differ in more number of QoSs or fewer. The selection results for all 100 queries are checked thoroughly and the failures along with total matched QoSs in 100 queries are summarized in the Fig. 5 across all the domains. It shows that the numbers of mismatched services compared to total matches are very few. It again accepts H01. Moreover the service mismatched in more than one QoS parameters is even fewer than that of total mismatched. It is considered to be Negligible if number of services with more than one parameter mismatched is compared with respect to that of total matched. Thus H03 is accepted.

Experiment 5: Here goodness values and goodness based selection for all possible alternate methods of factor analyses are compared. It is to find out the most efficient one out of different factor analyses (EFA, 2 factor CFA, and 3 factor CFA)based goodness calculation. All three methods of factor Analysis for measuring goodness based on actual expected outcome of selection are compared. Here the actual outcomes are measure beforehand using brute force technique.

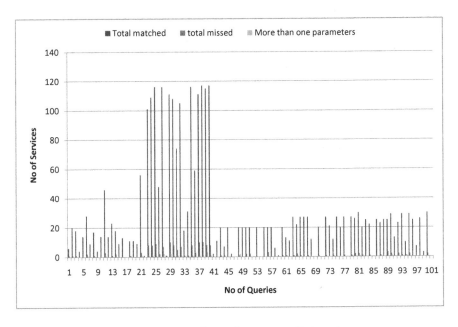

Fig. 5. Misses and matches across all domains

In this regard we have constructed the domain wise chart for selection of number of services and tried to find out which of these three methods results closest to the actual outcome. From Fig. 6, it is evident that the EFA overestimates (red bar) the selection results. i.e. often by exploratory method of goodness tend to include erroneous results that may not be satisfying the services quality requirements. On the other hand three-factor CFA (Green bar) underestimates the selection results. It excludes some of the relevant services. The closest is the two-factor CFA (Blue bar) to the actual matches (purple bar).

Experiment 6: The service quality satisfaction can be measured in terms of number of quality satisfying services. Further the efficiency of the selection mechanism can be measured one step ahead. It will find out how many exact matches (for all quality parameters) actually existed and how many of those have been correctly identified by the selection procedure based on goodness. A comparison among all the three applied analyses method is also done along with all the above tests. In the Fig. 7 goodness values calculated with EFA, two factor CFA and

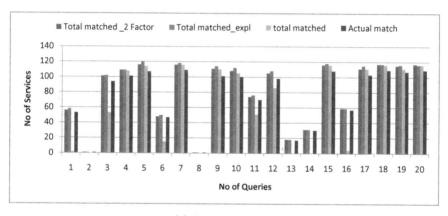

(a) Account Domain

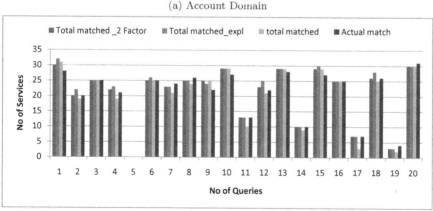

(b) Analysis Domain

Fig. 6. Precision comparison among all factor analyses methods (Color figure online)

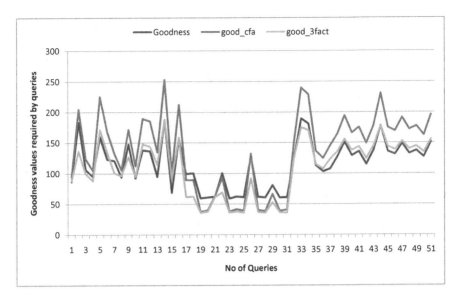

Fig. 7. Goodness for all three factor analyses

three factor CFA are compared. It is clearly shown that all three are estimating the goodness values in the same pattern over all queries. There is an expectation from the correlation measures among the QoS that confirmatory factor analysis would perform better than the exploratory factor analysis which is supported by the curves in Fig. 7. The differences in magnitudes of the curve of EFA and 2-factor CFA may include more services that are excluded when measured using exploratory method. So more accurate selection results are achieved for CFA.

6.2   Complexity Analysis

The service selection algorithm used in this approach is compared with respect execution time with existing selection approaches. The worst case time complexity found for any of the selection approaches in $O(n^3)$ and best case is $O(nlogn)$ for all the considered references [7,11,14–16,21]. Among all these [7] is the best service selection approach that has a best case complexity as $O(nlogn)$. The average as well as worst case complexity in the proposed algorithm is $O(nlogn)$. The proposed measure performs better as it offers equivalent complexity in all cases (even in average and worst) and also considers more QoS metrics at a time (out of which 6 QoSs all satisfied and 9 partially satisfied).

7   Conclusion

Measure of goodness involving all quality parameters associated to a service is the novelty of the proposed work. Use of factor analysis for dimension reduction and getting subsequent successful results are encouraging. Service selection algorithm based on goodness is also implemented and results are used to measure the efficiency of the proposed method. Rigorous inspections have been done and some important hypotheses are proved through the empirical analysis. Efficiency of the selection algorithm is also measured in terms of time complexity. Moreover the QoS requirements are over all satisfactory that is also experimentally proved. Thus the proposed approach works well for an efficient service selection ensuring QoS preservation and reduced execution time as well.

Acknowledgements. This publication is an outcome of the R&D work undertaken in the ITRA project of Media Lab Asia entitled Remote Health: A Framework for Healthcare Services using Mobile and Sensor-Cloud Technologies.

References

1. Al-Masri, E., Mahmoud, Q.H.: QoS-based discovery and ranking of web services. In: Proceedings of 16th International Conference on Computer Communications and Networks. ICCCN 2007, pp. 529–534. IEEE (2007)
2. Barkat Ullah, A.S., Sarker, R., Cornforth, D.: Search space reduction technique for constrained optimization with tiny feasible space. In: Proceedings of the 10th Annual Conference on Genetic and Evolutionary Computation, pp. 881–888. ACM (2008)
3. Bhattacharya, A., Choudhury, S.: An efficient service selection approach through a goodness measure of the participating QoS. In: Proceedings of the International Conference on Informatics and Analytics, ICIA 2016, pp. 94:1–94:6, New York, NY, USA. ACM (2016). https://doi.org/10.1145/2980258.2980451. http://doi.acm.org/10.1145/2980258.2980451
4. Chen, L., Wu, J., Jian, H., Deng, H., Wu, Z.: Instant recommendation for web services composition. IEEE Trans. Serv. Comput. **7**(4), 586–598 (2014)
5. Dastjerdi, A.V., Garg, S.K., Rana, O.F., Buyya, R.: CloudPick: a framework for QoS-aware and ontology-based service deployment across clouds. Softw. Pract. Exp. **45**(2), 197–231 (2015)
6. Dou, W., Zhang, X., Liu, J., Chen, J.: Hiresome-II: towards privacy-aware cross-cloud service composition for big data applications. IEEE Trans. Parallel Distrib. Syst. **26**(2), 455–466 (2015)
7. Elshater, Y., Elgazzar, K., Martin, P.: goDiscovery: web service discovery made efficient. In: 2015 IEEE International Conference on Web Services (ICWS), pp. 711–716. IEEE (2015)
8. Fodor, I.K.: A survey of dimension reduction techniques. Technical report, Lawrence Livermore National Laboratory, CA (US) (2002)
9. Jatoth, C., Gangadharan, G., Fiore, U., Buyya, R.: QoS-aware big service composition using mapreduce based evolutionary algorithm with guided mutation. Future Gener. Comput. Syst. **86**, 1008–1018 (2018)
10. Jurca, R., Faltings, B., Binder, W.: Reliable QoS monitoring based on client feedback. In: Proceedings of the 16th International Conference on World Wide Web, pp. 1003–1012. ACM (2007)
11. Karim, R., Ding, C., Miri, A.: An end-to-end QoS mapping approach for cloud service selection. In: 2013 IEEE Ninth World Congress on Services, pp. 341–348. IEEE (2013)

12. Klein, A., Ishikawa, F., Honiden, S.: Towards network-aware service composition in the cloud. In: Proceedings of the 21st International Conference on World Wide Web, pp. 959–968. ACM (2012)
13. Lee, K.S., Geem, Z.W.: A new meta-heuristic algorithm for continuous engineering optimization: harmony search theory and practice. Comput. Methods Appl. Mech. Eng. **194**(36), 3902–3933 (2005)
14. Ludwig, S.A.: Clonal selection based genetic algorithm for workflow service selection. In: 2012 IEEE Congress on Evolutionary Computation, pp. 1–7. IEEE (2012)
15. Tao, F., LaiLi, Y., Xu, L., Zhang, L.: FC-PACO-RM: a parallel method for service composition optimal-selection in cloud manufacturing system. IEEE Trans. Ind. Inform. **9**(4), 2023–2033 (2013)
16. Tao, F., Zhao, D., Hu, Y., Zhou, Z.: Resource service composition and its optimal-selection based on particle swarm optimization in manufacturing grid system. IEEE Trans. Ind. Inform. **4**(4), 315–327 (2008)
17. Ye, Z., Zhou, X., Bouguettaya, A.: Genetic algorithm based QoS-aware service compositions in cloud computing. In: Yu, J.X., Kim, M.H., Unland, R. (eds.) DASFAA 2011. LNCS, vol. 6588, pp. 321–334. Springer, Heidelberg (2011). https://doi.org/10.1007/978-3-642-20152-3_24
18. Yu, Q., Bouguettaya, A.: Computing service skyline from uncertain QoWS. IEEE Trans. Serv. Comput. **3**(1), 16–29 (2010)
19. Zhang, J., Liu, X.: Evaluation and optimization of QoS-aware network management framework based on process synergy and resource allocation. J. Ambient Intell. Hum. Comput., 1–9 (2018)
20. Zhang, X., Dou, W.: Preference-aware QoS evaluation for cloud web service composition based on artificial neural networks. In: Wang, F.L., Gong, Z., Luo, X., Lei, J. (eds.) WISM 2010. LNCS, vol. 6318, pp. 410–417. Springer, Heidelberg (2010). https://doi.org/10.1007/978-3-642-16515-3_51
21. Zhao, X., Wen, Z., Li, X.: QoS-aware web service selection with negative selection algorithm. Knowl. Inf. Syst. **40**(2), 349–373 (2014)
22. Zheng, Z., Ma, H., Lyu, M.R., King, I.: QoS-aware web service recommendation by collaborative filtering. IEEE Trans. Serv. Comput. **4**(2), 140–152 (2011)

File Assignment Control for a Web System of Contents Categorization

Masaki Kohana[1]([✉]), Hiroki Sakaji[2], Akio Kobayashi[3], and Shusuke Okamoto[4]

[1] Faculty of Engineering, Ibaraki University, Hitachi, Ibaraki, Japan
`masaki.kohana.gopher@vc.ibaraki.ac.jp`
[2] The University of Tokyo, Bunkyo, Tokyo, Japan
`sakaji@sys.t.u-tokyo.ac.jp`
[3] RIKEN Center for Advanced Intelligence Project, Chuo, Tokyo, Japan
`akio.kobayashi@riken.jp`
[4] Seikei University, Musashino, Tokyo, Japan
`okam@seikei.ac.jp`

Abstract. This paper shows the effect of the controlling file assignment on the file transfer time for a Web-based content categorization system. Our proposed algorithm estimates categories of contents based on the terms and the content categories already added. However, our algorithm uses a large table that consists of the scores that represent the relationship between a term and a category. To address the large table size and longer calculation time, we proposed a distributed Web system that uses multiple calculation machines. This Web system runs preprocessors on a Web browser and calculation machines. In this Web system, the file transfer time becomes a problem when a user sends larger files. In this paper, we propose a way to resolve the issue of longer file transfer time by controlling the file assignment. We assign the large files to the Web browser process, and we assign the smaller files to the calculation machines over the network.

Keywords: Content categorization · Parallel computing · Distributed computing · Web application · Web browser computing

1 Introduction

There is a large amount of content on the Internet, such as text, images, videos, and music. Blogs, for example, have much text content. Furthermore, social networking services contain many images and videos that have been uploaded by the users. However, it is difficult to find target content because the amount of content increases day by day. A content owner categorizes content in several ways. In most cases, the owner categorizes content using keywords and tags. For instance, some messages on Twitter have hashtags, which are a kind of tag. An article on a blog has keywords, and a video on YouTube also has categories. However, in some cases, the tags and the keywords are insufficient. One reasons

© Springer-Verlag GmbH Germany, part of Springer Nature 2019
N. T. Nguyen et al. (Eds.): TCCI XXXIII, LNCS 11610, pp. 89–102, 2019.
https://doi.org/10.1007/978-3-662-59540-4_5

is limitations on the number of tags and keywords. Another reasons is that users select the tags and the keywords. In this case, the tags and the keywords depend on the consideration of the users.

To resolve this problem, we proposed an algorithm to find tags that the contents do not have [14]. Our algorithm uses co-occurrence between a tag and a comment and finds some missing tags. We use tags already added and comments on content as training data. This algorithm estimates a new tag using a score that indicates a relationship between a tag and a term. We determine a co-occurrence frequency as a relationship. To evaluate this algorithm, we used the Nico Nico Dataset [3]. This dataset contains video information on Nico Nico Douga, a popular video sharing service in Japan. A user uploads a video to Nico Nico Douga [4]. Viewers can see the video and can add comments. Furthermore, the owner and the viewers can add tags to the video. The Nico Nico Dataset includes over 13,370,000 videos and 5,023,000,000 comments. The video metadata include the tags and the comments on the video. Dowango Co., Ltd. [2] and Brazil Ltd. [1] provide this dataset, and the National Institute of Informatics publishes it as the Nico Nico Dataset. We handled a video as an item of content, a comment as a term, and a tag as a category.

Furthermore, we also proposed a distributed calculation scheme for our categorization algorithm [10]. Our algorithm takes too much time to train and to calculate a score because the Nico Nico Dataset has many data. Another reason is the memory usage. Our algorithm creates a table of the scores. The size of the table depends on the number of categories and terms. If the dataset has many content items, the table size will become large. As a result, the table size will exceed the memory size, which leads to memory swapping. The memory swap process is a reason for the longer calculation time. To resolve this problem, we divide the data into slots and distribute the slots to multiple machines. The machines calculate the scores for the assigned data and create a table of scores. Therefore, each machine has a part of the table.

In our previous study, we used the computing resource of a Web browser to divide the data into slots [11]. In this scheme, a browser processes one part of the data, while the server processes the other part. We could use the computing resource of a browser and could parallelize a part of our scheme. However, our dataset has many files. Some files are large, and other files are small. Therefore, if our method allocates a large file to the server machine, the file transfer time increases. In the dividing step, our algorithm removes the duplicate data. Therefore, after the dividing step, the quantity of data will become small. Our scheme should allocate large files to the browser process. In this paper, we propose preprocessing of the score calculation on a Web browser. Our process controls the file allocation to a browser process or a server process. As mentioned above, the browser should process the large files. Therefore, we allocate the large files to the browser, and we allocate the small files to the server.

This paper consists of the following sections. Section 2 introduces some studies related to our study. Section 3 describes the category estimation algorithm. Section 4 gives an overview of our distributed calculation scheme. Section 5 introduces a way to determine whether a file is large or small. Section 6 shows our experimental results. Section 7 concludes the paper.

2   Literature Survey

This section introduces several studies that relate to our study.

Machova focused on automatic opinion analysis of a discussion on the Web [12]. This paper introduced a way to extract the text of the discussions from a Web forum and a way to filter out irrelevant and nonsensical information.

Balkir et al. proposed a distributed lookup architecture [5]. This paper shows an algorithm for text analysis. They implemented this algorithm using Bloom filters, in-memory caches, and an HBase cluster. This method resolves the problems of latency and storage space.

Wang et al. mentioned a problem with semi-supervised clustering [16]. To resolve this problem, they introduced a soft-constrained optimization problem. They used the remarkable degree to help the search for an optimal solution.

Okamoto and Kohana proposed a parallel calculation using JavaScript Web Workers for Web-based online games [13]. A video game needs several computations, such as for collisions. Generally, the game server is responsible for computing. In this study, they used Web Workers. The worker calculates collisions and other such computations.

Urakawa et al. proposed a way to broadcast video clips with other content such as from Wikipedia [15]. In this study, the Resource Description Framework (RDF) was used to describe various pieces of information about video clips. This method uses natural language processing and a dictionary to construct the RDF store and to combine video clips with other Web services.

Bouramoul improved the search process for the information retrieval and evaluated the tools [6]. The experimental results show that document noise and silence can be reduced by taking context into account the context in the information retrieval.

Bouanaka et al. proposed a bio-inspired approach to classify Web services [7]. Using an ant-based clustering algorithm, this method classifies the Web services that share many interaction relations.

John et al. proposed an ontology-based Semantic Supported Information Retrieval System (SIRS) [9]. This system receives a query from a user. The query is determined by the Hypertext Markup Language (HTML) Parser, and then the Probabilistic Latent Semantic Indexing (PLSI) algorithm is utilized. This system concentrates on resolving the Web search issue and on resolving the personalized Web searches.

3   Categorization Algorithm

In this section, we introduce our categorization algorithm. Firstly, we explain the scoring method, and then, we describe the estimation process. Our algorithm uses the co-occurrence between a category and a term. First, the algorithm calculates a score that represents the relationship between a category and a term, which is the co-occurrence. After that, our algorithm estimates the missing category using the score. In this description, we use a tag as a category and use a comment as a term.

3.1 Scoring Method

Our categorization algorithm calculates a score $S(t,c)$ that represents a relationship between a comment (c) and a tag (t). The following formula (1) calculates the score $S(t,c)$.

$$S(t,c) = PMI(t,c) \times ITF(c)$$
$$\times (0.5 + 0.5 \times \frac{tdf(t)}{max_t tdf(t)}) \tag{1}$$

Formula (2) calculates $PMI(t,c)$, which is the pointwise mutual information (PMI) of a pair comprising a t and a c [8]. It commonly indicates a metric for measuring the correlation between two events [8]. In this study, PMI indicates the correlation between a tag t and a comment c.

$$PMI(t,c) = log_2 \frac{p(t,c)}{p(t)p(c)} \tag{2}$$

The expression $p(t,c)$ is the probability of t and c occurring on the same video. The expression $p(t)$ indicates the probability of tag t occurring in a set of videos, and $p(c)$ is the probability of comment c occurring in a set of videos.

In addition to PMI, we use $ITF(c)$, which is given by Formula (3), where $tf(c)$ is the number of tags occurring with a comment c. The value of $ITF(c)$ is high when the comment c occurs with a small number of tags.

$$ITF(c) = log_2 \frac{max_c tf(c)}{tf(c)} \tag{3}$$

Finally, we use a $tdf(t)/max_t tdf(t)$ to prevent getting inappropriate tags. The PMI of a general comment is high because general comments exist in most documents. In this result, the score for pairs comprising this comment with inappropriate tags will also be high. To avoid this problem, we normalize $tdf(t)$ by dividing it by $max_t tdf(t)$.

3.2 Estimation Process

Figure 1 shows the estimation process of our categorization. We have a set of videos that includes a set of comments and a set of tags. We also have two datasets, D_c and D_t. We use D_c for searching tags with high scores $S(t,c)$ when they appear with a comment. On the other hand, we use D_t for searching tags that frequently occur with the entered tag.

In Fig. 1, T_{sc} is an associative array. The key is a tag name and the value is a score. As the first step, we calculate a score for each comment with all the co-occurrence tags and store the scores in T_{sc}. Then, we calculate $Co\text{-}occurrence(t,t')$ for each tag. This function calculates the number of co-occurrences of tags t and t' in a single video that appears in a set of videos. Finally, we use the function $ExtractTags(T_{sc})$, which retrieves tags that have the high scores.

Estimation Process

Input: A video $V = (C, T)$
    C: Comment Set $(c_0, c_1, \ldots, c_n)$
    T: Tag Set $(t_0, t_1, \ldots, t_m)$
Output: New Tag Set T'
1: $T' \leftarrow \emptyset$
2: $T_{sc} \leftarrow \emptyset$
3: **for each** $c \in C$ **do**
4:     **for each** $t \in D_c(c)$ **do**
5:         $T_{sc}[t] \leftarrow Score(t, c) + T_{sc}[t]$
6:     **end for**
7: **end for**
8: **for each** $t \in T$ **do**
9:     **for each** $t' \in D_t(t)$ **do**
10:         **if** $t' \in T_{sc}$ **then**
11:             $T_{sc}[t'] \leftarrow T_{sc}[t'] \times co - occurrence(t, t')$
12:         **end if**
13:     **end for**
14: **end for**
15: $T' \leftarrow ExtractTags(T_{sc})$
16: **return** T'

Fig. 1. Pseudocode

4 Distributed Calculation

This section describes our distributed calculation system. Our categorization algorithm creates a table that contains scores. The number of elements in the table is the number of comments times the number of categories. Therefore, if the number of categories and comments increases, the table size will become large. If the table size exceeds the memory size of the calculation machine, it leads to memory swapping. As a result, the calculation time will become long.

We have the data as a set of files. Our distributed calculation divides the set of files into some small sets and allocates the sets to the calculation nodes. Each node calculates the scores for the allocated data and creates a table of the scores. Therefore, our system has two steps, the dividing step, and the calculation step.

4.1 Dividing Step

Figure 2 shows an overview of our dividing step. There is one master node. The calculation nodes at the bottom are same as those in the upper part. Therefore, there are four calculation nodes. The master node contains the data as many files. The master node distributes the files to the calculation nodes. Each calculation node divides the data into small slots.

Figure 3 shows the reason. The calculation node receives the data as a file. Therefore, each node has different files. However, each file includes several terms.

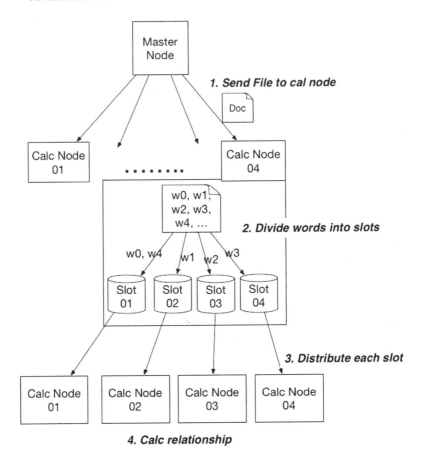

Fig. 2. Distributed calculation

A term may exist in the several files. As a result, a term exists in several tables in some calculation nodes. In this figure, term 1 and term 7 exist in both nodes 1 and 2. At the estimation step, our algorithm estimates a missing tag based on the term included in a document. When we estimate tags related to term 1 and term 2, we need to access node 1 and node 2. Therefore, we expect the score information for a term exists in the one node.

To divide the file into slots, we use the Fowler–Noll–Vo (FNV) hash function. The FNV is a non-cryptographic hash function. We determine the slot by the hash value modulo the number of nodes. Figure 4 shows an example of the division. There are six terms. First, we calculate the FNV hash values of the terms. After that, we would like to divide the terms into four slots. Therefore, we calculate the value modulo the number of slots. Then, the node distributes the slots to the other calculation nodes. In this figure, "system" has slot number 0. The terms "computing," "web," and "mining" have slot number 1. The "distributed"

	cat1	cat2	cat3
term1	0	4	2
term2	3	1	6
term4	0	0	3
term7	1	7	3
term8	6	0	2

| **Node 1** |

	cat1	cat2	cat3
term1	3	8	2
term3	0	1	3
term5	3	4	0
term6	7	6	8
term7	0	1	0

| **Node 2** |

Fig. 3. Duplication problem

and "text" have slot number 2. Thus, we have divided the six terms into three slots. As a result, the score information for a term exists in one calculation node.

After dividing the data into slots, each calculation node distributes the slot to the appropriate node. At this time, the information for one term is in only one calculation node. When the calculation nodes receive files, the master node also sends the tag information for the file. Therefore, all the calculation nodes have the information about the tags. A calculation node can calculate the score of a term using the term information and the tag information. Each calculation node calculates the score for each term and creates a table of scores. Since we have divided the terms into slots and distributed the slots, the term information exists in only one calculation node. As a result, the score information for a term now exists in only one table.

In the estimation step, the master node collects the scores for the terms included in the file. At this time, the master node needs to collect scores from the calculation nodes. The master node also calculates the FNV hash value of each term to find out which node has the score for that term. Then, the master node retrieves the score from the appropriate node.

5   File Size Control

This section describes the parallelization on a Web browser and file size control. Most of the calculation time is used in calculating the score. However, the dividing step also takes some calculation time. As we would like to provide this category estimation process as a Web system, we focus on the computing resource of the Web browser. A user uploads the data file to the master node. Then, the master node and the calculation nodes create the tables with the scores. However, if we can preprocess the dividing step on the user's Web browser, we can use the computing resource of the browser and reduce the quantity of data because the dividing step removes the duplicate terms.

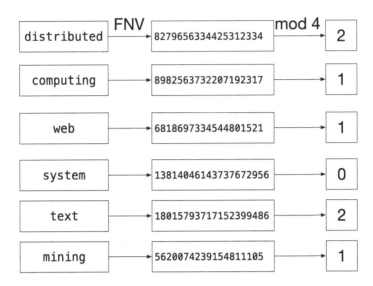

Fig. 4. Fowler–Noll–Vo (FNV) hash example

To achieve the parallelization on a Web browser, we use Web Workers. Web Workers is a way to run JavaScript code in background threads. W3C defines the API specification. A worker thread cannot handle a user interface. However, the thread runs independently of the user interface. In addition, the thread can handle an AJAX (Asynchronous JavaScript + XML) connection. Furthermore, we can use the JavaScript File API. This API can read/write local files using JavaScript.

Our system provides a Web page to upload data. Therefore, the JavaScript code on the page can retrieve the data included in the local files. We assume that a user uploads multiple files. Therefore, our system needs to handle multiple files. Our JavaScript code reads the files. The code sends some of the files to the master node, while the code preprocesses the other files on the Web browser.

Figure 5 shows an overview of our parallelization on a Web browser. The Web page receives the multiple files from the user. The browser calculates scores for some of the files using the Web Workers threads. These threads run the dividing step, which means that the browser reads the contents of the file and divides the set of terms into several slots. On the other hand, the browser sends the other files to the master node. For this, our system uses XMLHttpRequest, which is an AJAX technology. This technology allows the JavaScript code to perform asynchronous communication with the Web server. As AJAX is an asynchronous communication, the communication can run in parallel. The browser can send multiple files to the master node simultaneously.

We understood that we could use the computing resource of a Web browser for the dividing step. However, we also understood that the time needed for file transfer can become a significant problem. Figure 6 shows the average calculation time for the dividing step according to the number of worker threads. This result shows that the calculation time does not decrease despite increasing the number

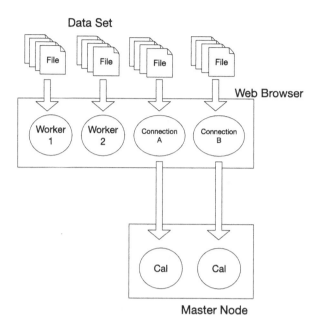

Fig. 5. Web browser parallelization

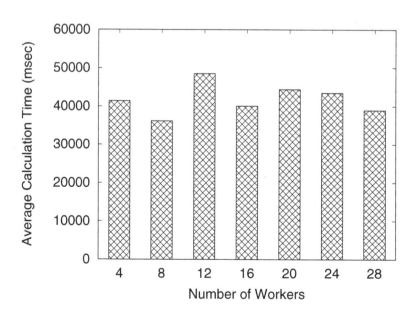

Fig. 6. Calculation time for dividing step

Usage of File API ────────────────────────────────

```
<body>
  <form>
    <input type="file" id="file">
  </form>

<script>
  document.getElementById("file")
        .addEventListener("change", function (e) {
    files = e.target.files;
    console.log(files);
  });
</script>
</body>
```

Fig. 7. Usage of file API

Content of File Object ────────────────────────────────

```
File
lastModified: 1535730620000
name: "sample.txt"
size: 13082
type: "text/plain"
```

Fig. 8. File object

of worker threads. Furthermore, the calculation time is the longest when the number of threads is 12. We consider that one of the reasons for this is the file transfer time. We have many files, and the sizes of the files are inconsistent. If our system sends a large file to the master node, the file transfer time becomes longer. On the other hand, if the browser performs the preprocessing for the large file, the file size decreases because the preprocessing removes the duplicate terms. Therefore, we introduce a way to send small files to the server and perform the preprocessing of the large files on the Web browser.

As mentioned above, we can use the File API. The File API allows JavaScript code to read/write a local file. The API also checks the metadata of the file. Figure 7 shows an example of the File API. This example shows the contents of a FileList object. The FileList object contains a list of the files that were selected in the input element of the HTML code. Figure 8 shows the contents of a file object. The FileList object contains the file information as file objects. The file object contains the file name, the modification time, the file size, the file type, and similar information.

The user uploads the files using the Web page. At this time, the user chooses the files using the input form. Our JavaScript code retrieves the file information as a FileList object. Therefore, we can check the file information by the file object. To control the file assignment, we sort the list of the files by the file size.

We would like to assign the large files to the Web browser and to assign the small files to the master node. Figure 9 shows an overview of the file assignment process. We use the Web Workers to run worker threads on a Web browser and use the XMLHttpRequest (XHR), which is an AJAX communication, to send data to the master node. In this figure, there are four worker threads and three XHR connections. There are also ten files. The larger files are on the left, and the smaller files are on the right. The worker threads choose the files from the left side. The XHR connections choose the files from the right side. When a thread or connection has completed a task, it chooses the next file. Worker 1 picks up file E when the worker has completed the task for file A. On the other hand, XHR 1 picks up file G when it has completed the task for the file J. As a result, the worker threads process the larger files, and the XHR connections process the smaller files. Therefore, the file transfer is needed only for the smaller files, which means that we can reduce the file transfer time.

6   Experimental Results

This section shows our experimental results. To evaluate our file assignment, we measured the calculation time for the dividing step.

We used a part of the Nico Nico Dataset. The dataset includes 1625 files, which have 2,547,980 comments. The minimum file size is 361 bytes and the maximum file size is 24,741,502 bytes. The average file size is 214,358 bytes. Table 1 shows the runtime environment of the client machine, and Table 2 shows the runtime environment of the server machine. The Web browser on the client machine used four worker threads.

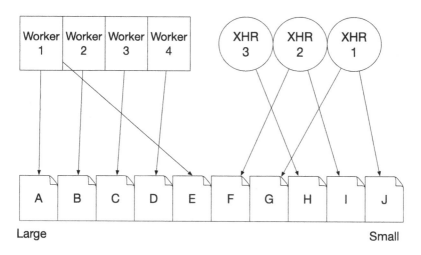

Fig. 9. File trace

Table 1. Client runtime environment

OS	macOS High Sierra 10.13.1
CPU	Intel Core i5 3.2 GHz
RAM	32 GB 1867 MHz DDR3
Web Browser	Safari 11.1.2

Figure 10 shows the average calculation time for the dividing step. We used three patterns of file assignment and ran each pattern ten times. All the patterns already sorted the list of the files. The x-axis indicates the assignment pattern. The y-axis indicates the average calculation time in milliseconds. The random pattern assigns the file randomly. In this pattern, both the worker threads and the XHR connections choose a file from the left side of the list, which means that the system processes the small files, and then, it processes the large files. In the lbss pattern, the worker threads choose a file from the large files located

Table 2. Server runtime environment

OS	Fedora Server 25
CPU	Intel Core i5 2.7 GHz
RAM	8 GB 2400 MHz DDR4
Compiler	Go 1.11

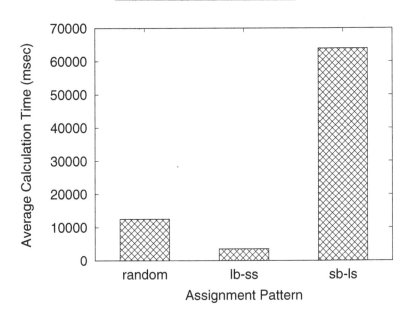

Fig. 10. Average calculation time

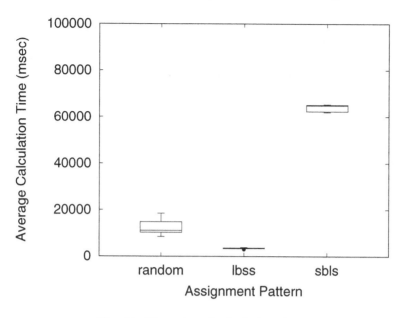

Fig. 11. Dispersion of calculation times

at the left side of the file list, while the XHR connections choose a file from the small files located at the right side of the list. In the sbls pattern, the worker chooses the smaller files, while the XHR connections choose the larger files. Therefore, in this pattern, the master node processes the larger files, and the Web browser processes the smaller files. In the result, the lbss pattern has the shortest calculation time, whereas the sbls pattern has the longest time. This result shows that the file transfer time becomes a significant problem if the Web browser sends the large files to the master node. Therefore, our system should process the large files on the Web browser.

Figure 11 shows the dispersion of the calculation time for each pattern. We used the same patterns as for the average calculation time. In this figure, the random pattern has the most variation. On the other hand, the lbss pattern does not have any variation; the calculation time for lbss is constant. The sbls pattern has a little variation.

7   Conclusion

This paper shows a way to avoid longer file transfer times in a Web application for content categorization. We proposed a system to estimate missing tags of a document using the contents of the document and the categories already added. However, our algorithm uses many memory sizes, which leads to memory swapping. Memory swapping leads to the longer calculation times. Therefore, we proposed a distributed Web system to divide the data into small tables. In this case, the file transfer time becomes a problem. We can reduce the file size using preprocessing on the Web browser. In this study, we controlled the file's assignment to the master node or the Web browser based on the size of the files. According to the experimental results, we should assign the larger files to the Web browser while assigning the smaller files to the master node. By the controlling the file assignment, we can reduce the file transfer time.

References

1. Brazil Ltd. http://razil.jp
2. Dowango Co., Ltd. http://dwango.co.jp/english/index.html
3. Nico Nico Dataset. http://www.nii.ac.jp/dsc/idr/nico/nico.html
4. Nico Nico Douga. http://www.nicovideo.jp
5. Balkir, A.S., Foster, I., Rzhetsky, A.: A distributed look-up architecture for text mining applications using MapReduce. In: The 20th International Symposium on High Performance Distributed Computing (HPDC 2011), pp. 279–280, November 2011
6. Bouanaka, M.A., Benmerzoug, D., Zarour, N.: Bio-inspired-based approach for web services classification. Int. J. Space Based Situated Comput. 6(3), 173–182 (2016)
7. Bouramoul, A.: Contextualisation of information retrieval process and document ranking task in web search tools. Int. J. Space Based Situated Comput. 6(2), 74–89 (2016)
8. Cover, T.M., Thomas, J.A.: Elements of Information Theory. Wiley-Interscience, New York (1991)
9. John, P.M., Arockiasamy, S., Thangiah, P.R.J.: A personalised user preference and feature based semantic information retrieval system in semantic web search. Int. J. Grid Util. Comput. 9(3), 256–267 (2018)
10. Kohana, M., Sakaji, H., Kobayashi, A., Okamoto, S.: A distributed calculation scheme for contents categorization. In: 2017 IEEE 31st International Conference on Advanced Information Networking and Applications (AINA 2017), pp. 614–620, March 2017
11. Kohana, M., Sakaji, H., Kobayashi, A., Okamoto, S.: A parallel calculation method on web browser for contents categorization. In: 2018 IEEE 32nd International Conference on Advanced Information Networking and Applications Workshops (WAINA 2017), pp. 40–44, May 2018
12. Machová, K.: Opinion analysis of texts extracted from the social web contributions. In: Nguyen, N.T. (ed.) Transactions on Computational Collective Intelligence XII. LNCS, vol. 8240, pp. 42–68. Springer, Heidelberg (2013). https://doi.org/10.1007/978-3-642-53878-0_3
13. Okamoto, S., Kohana, M.: Load distribution by using web workers for a real-time web application. Int. J. Web Inf. Syst. 4(7), 381–395 (2011)
14. Sakaji, H., Kohana, M., Kobayashi, A., Sakai, H.: Estimation of tags via comments on Nico Nico Douga. In: The 5th International Workshop on Web Services and Social Media (WSSM 2016), pp. 550–553, September 2016
15. Urakawa, M., Miyazaki, M., Yamada, I., Fujisawa, H., Nakagawa, T.: A study about integrating video contents with web services based on the RDF. Int. J. Space Based Situated Comput. 6(2), 65–73 (2016)
16. Wang, J., Wu, S., Vu, H.Q., Li, G.: Text document clustering with metric learning. In: The 33rd International ACM SIGIR Conference on Research and Development in Information Retrieval, pp. 783–784 (2010)

Byzantine Collision-Fast Consensus Protocols

Rodrigo Saramago[1], Eduardo Alchieri[2], Tuanir Rezende[3],
and Lasaro Camargos[4(✉)]

[1] MonteLabs, Brasília, Brazil
[2] Departamento de Ciência da Computação, Universidade de Brasília, Brasília, Brazil
[3] Telecom SudParis, Évry, France
[4] Faculdade de Computação, Universidade Federal de Uberlândia,
Santa Mônica, Brazil
lasaro@ufu.br

Abstract. Atomic broadcast protocols are fundamental building blocks used in the construction of many reliable distributed systems. Atomic broadcast and consensus are equivalent problems, but the inefficiency of consensus-based atomic broadcast protocols in the presence of collisions (concurrent proposals) harms their adoption in the implementation of reliable systems, as the ones based on state machine replication. In the traditional consensus protocols, proposals that are not decided in some instance of consensus (commands not delivered) must be re-proposed in a new instance, delaying their execution. Moreover, whether different values (commands) are proposed in the same instance (leading to a collision), some of its phases must be restarted, also delaying the execution of these commands involved in the collision. The CFABCast (*Collision-Fast Atomic Broadcast*) algorithm uses m-consensus to decide and deliver multiple values in the same instance. However, CFABCast is not byzantine fault-tolerant, a requirement for many systems. Our first contribution is a modified version of CFABCast to handle byzantine failures. Unfortunately, the resulting protocol is not collision-fast due to the possibility of malicious failures. In fact, our second contribution is to prove that there are no byzantine collision-fast algorithms in an asynchronous model as traditionally extended to solve consensus. Finally, our third contribution is a byzantine collision-fast algorithm that bypasses the stated impossibility by means of a USIG (Unique Sequential Identifier Generator) trusted component.

1 Introduction

Atomic Broadcast (ABCast) is a fundamental building block used in the construction of many modern fault-tolerant distributed systems since it ensures that

This study was financed in part by the Coordenaição de Aperfeiçoamento de Pessoal de Nível Superior - Brasil (CAPES) - Finance Code 001, PVE CAPES 88881.062190/2014-01.

messages broadcast to a set of processes are delivered at these process in the same total order. For example, State Machine Replication (SMR) is a known technique to implement fault-tolerant services [29,35] and can be "easily" implemented by using some ABCast protocol to reliably and totally ordered deliver events to all non-faulty processes in a distributed system, allowing them to execute the same sequence of transitions in their deterministic state machines.

ABCast is equivalent to the consensus problem [14,18,34], which allows a set of process to decide the same value out of a set of proposed values, reaching agreement that is a fundamental property of consensus protocols. ABCast can be reduced to consensus in the following way: let there be a totally ordered set of infinitely many consensus instances; to broadcast a message, propose it in the first instance, w.r.t. such total order, for which a decision is not yet known; the decision of the ith instance is the ith message in the deliver sequence.

Traditional consensus protocols demand three communications steps to decide some value in a system prone to only crash failures [30]. Considering a system subject to byzantine failures, four communication steps are necessary [12]. Trying to improve these protocols allowing the decision to be taken in few communication steps, *fast* consensus protocols for crash [32] and byzantine [40] failure models are able to decide in two communication steps, matching the lower bounds for asynchronous distributed consensus [33]. However, these protocols only maintain optimality in executions without collisions, i.e., when there are not different values being proposed in the consensus instance. Consequently, the previously described reduction of ABCast to consensus is problematic in that only one message proposed in a consensus instance is decided. The remaining ones must be proposed again, in new instances, until successfully delivered, creating a backlog of messages and increasing their delivery latency. Moreover, if different messages are proposed in the same instance, phases of these protocols must be restarted and, consequently, they demand more than two communication steps to finish.

Trying to circumvent this limitation, *collision-fast* protocols [51] allow concurrently different proposed messages (*collision*) to be delivered within the optimum latency of two communication steps (*fast*), without the need for retrying in new consensus instances. However, the known algorithms in this class have drawbacks such as limiting the size of the process set [33], becoming non-fast after a failure and until a restart happens [39], or requiring synchronized clocks in order to be fast [21]. Another important limitation of the previously mentioned collision-fast algorithms is their inability to handle byzantine failures, a limitation studied in a prior version of this work [49]. The difficulty in being fast and byzantine fault-tolerant (BFT) stems from having to trust a process because there is no time to verify whether the information it sent is correct or not. Another important observation regarding these protocols is that they were devised to partially synchronous systems, the minimum level of synchronism need to solve distributed consensus [22].

Contributions. This paper extends these previous results, notably [49], by trying to answer the following question: *"How byzantine collision-fast consensus can be solved in a partially synchronous distributed system?"*. In answering this question, this paper presents the following contributions:

- It proposes and details a byzantine variation of a collision-fast ABCast protocol [51] that tolerates $f < n/5$ failures, out of n processes. We call this protocol as byzantine m-consensus since it is able to handle collisions but it is not fast (and neither collision-fast) demanding three communication steps to finish.
- It presents the full proof that no protocol can be byzantine and collision-fast in an asynchronous model extended with partial synchronism as traditionally done (e.g., with unreliable failure detectors [14]).
- It proposes and details a collision-fast atomic broadcast protocol that tolerates up to $f < n/2$ byzantine failures. We bypass the previously commented impossibility by extending the system model with a trusted Unique Sequential Identifier Generator [54] to constraint malicious actions. The resulting protocol, called USIG based byzantine Collision-Fast protocol or USIG-BCFABCast, is an extension of the crash-stop Collision-Fast Atomic Broadcast protocol [51].

Impact of the Proposed Protocols. The importance of consensus protocols is well-known in the distributed system community and it is expressed both in the theoretical and practical fields. Regarding the theory, a very impressive amount of papers proposed consensus protocols ([1,4,5,12,19,28,43,47,49], just to cite a few recent work). Concerning practical aspects, consensus protocols (or replicated services built over a state machine replication that uses an underlying consensus protocol for atomic requests delivery) has been successfully used in many commercial systems such as Google Spanner [16], Apache Zookeeper [27], Windows Azure Storage [10], MySQL Group Replication [42] and Galera Cluster [25]. Moreover, consensus protocols could be used in many new different contexts such as peer-to-peer systems [2,37,38,44,52,53,56], cloud computing [6,7,20,36,41,45,46,57] and Blockchain [3,9,23,26,48,55].

Paper Organization. The remainder of this work is organized as follows. Section 2 presents some preliminary background, while Sect. 3 discusses the related works. Section 4 presents a byzantine variation of the CFABCast protocol. Section 5 proves that it is impossible to solve byzantine CFABCast in a non-synchronous system. Section 6 presents a collision-fast atomic broadcast protocol that uses USIG to constraints malicious actions. Conclusions are presented in Sect. 7.

2   Background

2.1   System Model

In this paper, as in [30], agreement problems are specified in terms of the roles played by the protocol agents. For example, in consensus there are the following three main roles, which are a constant in multiple agreement problems:

- *proposers* (P), propose values;
- *acceptors* (A), choose a value as the decision; and,
- *learners* (L), learn the chosen value.

The system is asynchronous, i.e., there are no bounds to communication delay and to the time it takes agents to perform computation. Messages can be indefinitely delayed or duplicated, but the communication channels are fair, in the sense that if sender and receiver are correct (non-failed) and the message is repeatedly sent, then it is eventually delivered.

An agent fails by performing arbitrary and unspecified actions (byzantine failures). While any number of *proposers* or *learners* are allowed to fail, only up to f *acceptors* can do so. The value of f varies in our protocols depending on assumptions about the system.

Finally, it is assumed that each agent is assigned a pair of public and private keys used to sign and verify messages and, therefore, messages cannot be undetectably corrupted, forged or repudiated. A message m signed by an agent x is noted $\langle m \rangle_x$. Messages that fail the verification are used as proof of misbehavior to remove an agent from the system; this handling is omitted from the protocols to simplify their presentation. In due time we will further extend the model to overcome the impossibility of an atomic broadcast algorithm to be both collision-fast and byzantine fault tolerant.

2.2 Atomic Broadcast

Algorithms for atomic broadcast ensure that messages broadcast by proposers are eventually delivered by all learners alive, in the same order. As in [31] we phrase the problem as the agreement on an ever-growing sequence of broadcast messages, of which learners learn increasing prefixes. Hence, atomic broadcast can be defined by the following properties, where *delivered*[l] is the sequence of messages delivered by learner $l \in L$, initially empty, and $\sqsubseteq$ represents the prefix operator between sequences.

- *Non-triviality:* $\forall l \in L$, *delivered*[l] contains only broadcast messages and no duplicates.
- *Stability:* $\forall l \in L$, if *delivered*[l] = s at some time, then $s \sqsubseteq$ *delivered*[l] at all later times.
- *Consistency:* $\forall l_1, l_2 \in L$, either *delivered*[l_1] $\sqsubseteq$ *delivered*[l_2] or *delivered*[l_2] $\sqsubseteq$ *delivered*[l_1].

2.3 Fast and Collision-Fast Delivery

Many consensus algorithms take three communication steps from proposal to decision of values. One such protocol, Paxos, was later optimized to reach a decision in two steps in a variant labeled Fast-Paxos. Following this nomenclature, consensus protocols have been called classic and fast if they take three or two steps from proposal to decision, respectively [33].

In (classic) Paxos, proposals are sent to a coordinator agent, from which it takes two communication steps to decision. Hence, from such coordinator's viewpoint, the protocol is fast. In Fast Paxos, proposers bypass the coordinator to reduce the time to decision and, hence, the protocol is fast for all proposers. Such an approach, however, may lead to multiple proposals being issued concurrently and, for not having the coordinator to serialize, to a protocol halt. At this point, recovery measures taking multiple communication steps are required to resume progress. Such concurrent proposals event is called a collision. A protocol is *collision-fast* if it is fast even in the presence of collisions [33]. As atomic broadcast is reducible to consensus [13], with one consensus decision leading to one message deliver, labels fast and collision-fast have also been applied to the time it takes an atomic broadcast protocol to deliver a message.

2.4   M-Consensus

M-Consensus is a variant of consensus in which multiple values get decided within a single instance [51]. Schmidt *et al.* [51] presented a collision-fast M-Consensus algorithm and showed how to reduce atomic broadcast to M-Consensus, exploring the fact that multiple values are decided within a single instance, achieving a collision-fast atomic broadcast [51], that is, one in which multiple messages get delivered within two communication steps, even when proposed concurrently.

The M-Consensus problem is defined in 'terms of a set $CF \subseteq P$ of proposers for which we want collision-fast delivery, value-mappings structures (*v-map*) mutable functions from a subset of $CF \subseteq P$, to the set of proposable values *Cmd* plus *Nil*. Let a v-map whose domain equals the set CF be called *complete* and one whose image equals $\{Nil\}$ be called *trivial*. Let an *append* to a v-map be the inclusion of some process $p \in CF$ to the v-map's domain. Let s be a *prefix* of r (and r be an *extension* of s), denoted by $s \sqsubseteq r$, iff r can be generated from s by a series of append operations. Finally, we say that two v-maps are compatible if they can be extended to a common v-map (they are prefixes to a larger v-map). Then, M-Consensus is defined by the following properties, being *learned*[l] the v-map currently learned by learner l:

- *Nontriviality:* $\forall l \in L$, *learned*[l] is always a nontrivial proposed value-mapping.
- *Stability:* $\forall l \in L$, if *learned*[l] = s at some time, then $s \sqsubseteq$ *learned*[l] at all later times.
- *Consistency:* The set of learned value-mappings is always compatible and nontrivial.
- *Liveness:* For any proposer $p \in P$ and learner $l \in L$, if p, l and a quorum of acceptors are non-faulty and p proposes a value, then eventually *learned*[x] is complete.

At the beginning of the instance, acceptors agree on an empty *v-map* $\perp$, which is a valid prefix for any other v-map. As they receive proposals mapping a single $p \in CF$ to a value, they *append* such proposals to their accepted v-maps and notify the learners, which, in turn, learn about agreed extensions and incorporate them into their learned v-map. Consistency ensures that all currently learned values can be extended to a common *v-map* that satisfies the nontriviality property, even if they differ during the execution of the protocol. Eventually, all correct learners learn the same complete v-map.

It is possible to reduce ABCast to M-Consensus [51], obtaining a protocol in which all messages broadcast by processes in CF are delivered within two communication steps in runs with no failures. Hence, processes in CF are labeled *collision-fast proposers* and, the protocol, collision-fast atomic broadcast. While CF could equal P, we advise that only a subset of trustworthy proposers should be in CF, as proposers in CF will be expected to take part in the protocol and their inability to do so could prevent others from fast delivering.

3   Related Works

In this section we review algorithms that form the basis for our work.

3.1   Paxos

Paxos [30] is a consensus protocol widely used in the industry (e.g., *Chubby Lock Service* [8]). In *Paxos*, proposals are sent by clients (or *proposers*) to an elected *proposer*, the *coordinator*. This agent forwards the proposal to *acceptors*, who accept or refuse them, according to the protocol, and notify the *learners*. Hence, if a regular proposer is proposing, it takes three communication steps to reach a decision; if the coordinator itself is proposing, then it takes two, which is called fast. Paxos tolerates $f < n/2$ acceptor crash failures.

Fast Paxos [32] lets any proposer be a "fast" proposer and propose directly to the acceptors, at the price of decreasing f such that $f < n/3$. If multiple fast proposers do so in parallel, the protocol may get stuck and need recover, not delivering any message due to such collision. *collision-fast* algorithms decide in two steps even under collision [33]. However, in these protocols a single proposal is decided and in the classical reduction from atomic broadcast to consensus, colliding proposals need to be re-proposed, increasing their latency and possibly creating an ever increasing message backlog.

The protocol proposed by [51] (Sect. 3.2) uses M-Consensus instead of consensus in the reduction, allowing multiple proposals to be decided and delivered within a single instance, resulting in collision-fast atomic broadcast that tolerates $f < n/2$ crash failures.

None of these protocols is byzantine fault-tolerant (BFT), but there are variants able to deal with malicious replicas (e.g., BFT Paxos [12] and BFT Fast Paxos [40]). Usually, these protocols need more replicas than their non-byzantine counterparts. The protocol presented in Sect. 6 is the only one we are aware of that tolerates byzantine failures and is collision-fast. Table 1 summarizes several characteristics of the protocols discussed so far.

Table 1. Considering up to f failures, the lines represent: number of communication steps to reach agreement; number of replicas playing the role of acceptors; quorum size; type of failure tolerated; need for secure component; and the indication whether the protocol is fast and/or allows collisions.

	Paxos	Fast Paxos	CFPaxos	BFT Paxos	BFT Fast Paxos	Byz. M-Consensus (Sect. 4)	USIG-BCFPaxos (Sect. 6)
#steps	3	2	2	4	2	3	2
#acceptors	2f + 1	3f + 1	2f + 1	3f + 1	5f + 1	5f + 1	2f + 1
Quorum size	f + 1	2f + 1	f + 1	2f + 1	4f + 1	4f + 1	f + 1
Failure	Crash	Crash	Crash	Byzantine	Byzantine	Byzantine	Byzantine
Component	–	–	–	–	–	–	USIG
Is it fast?	No	Yes	Yes	No	Yes	No	Yes
Allows collisions?	No	No	Yes	No	No	Yes	Yes

Algorithm 1. Collision-fast Atomic Broadcast (CFABCast) [51]

I: the set of all Collision-fast Paxos instances used

$CFP(i)!A$: the action or variable A of Collision-fast Paxos instance i

1:   $Propose(p, V) \triangleq$
2:    $\forall i \in I, CFP(i)!Propose(p, V)$

3:   $NewPhase1a(i, c, r) \triangleq$
4:    **pre-conditions:**
5:     $c = C(r)$
6:     $crnd[c] < r$
7:     c believes itself to be the leader
8:     c heard of a round $r > j > crnd[c]$ for some instance or $CF(crnd[c]) \notin active[c]$
9:    **actions:**
10:     $CFP(i)!Phase1a(c, r)$

11:   $Phase1a(c, r) \triangleq$
12:    $\forall i \in I, CFP(i)!NewPhase1a(i, c, r)$

13:   $Phase1b(a, r) \triangleq$
14:    $\forall i \in I, CFP(i)!Phase1b(a, r)$

15:   $Phase2Start(c, r) \triangleq$
16:    $\forall i \in I, CFP(i)!Phase2Start(c, r)$

17:   $Phase2Prepare(p, r) \triangleq$
18:    $\forall i \in I, CFP(i)!Phase2Prepare(p, r)$

19:   $Phase2a(p, r, V) \triangleq$
20:    **pre-condition:**
21:     p has not yet proposed V
22:    **action:**
23:     LET $i = Min([j : CFP(j)!pval[p] = none])$
24:     $CFP(i)!Phase2a(p, r, V)$

25:   $Phase2b(i, a, r) \triangleq$
26:    $CFP(i)!Phase2b(a, r)$

27:   $Learn(i, l) \triangleq$
28:    $CFP(i)!Learn(l)$

3.2   Collision-Fast Atomic Broadcast

The *Collision-fast Atomic Broadcast* (CFABCast) protocol [51] is reproduced in
Algorithm 1. Similarly to the reduction from atomic broadcast to consensus [13],
CFABCast solves infinitely many M-Consensus instances using *Collision-fast
Paxos* [51] (CFPaxos). Each CFPaxos instance has a unique identifier i and its
actions are prefixed by $CFP(i)$.

   Actions in CFABCast mirror those in the underlying CFPaxos instances;
action $Propose(p, V)$, for example, is executed by process p to broadcast message
V and corresponds to executing action $Propose(p, V)$ in all the M-Consensus
instances. We note that this specification does not imply in infinitely many calls
to *Propose*, because all instances share the variables operated by *Propose*, and
therefore the action is combined. In essence, the algorithm ultimately choses the
M-Consensus instance with smallest identifier that has not yet proposed and
proposes V in it, which can be seen in action *Phase2a*.

   While further details on the workings of this protocol are found in [50] and
[51], here we stress that it solves ABCast in a *collision-fast* way because it
relies on CFPaxos, which is collision-fast. In fact, Algorithm 1 is oblivious to the
underlying M-Consensus protocol and we explore this fact to devise a Byzantine
fault tolerant, in the following section.

4   Byzantine M-Consensus

In this section we introduce a CFPaxos extension to deal with byzantine failures.
Such protocol demands three communications steps to reach a decision and,
therefore, is not collision-fast. Nonetheless, it serves as basis for the collision-
fast variant of CFPaxos, described in Sect. 6.

4.1   Overview

As in other Paxos variants, each instance of byzantine m-consensus runs in
rounds coordinated by some process chosen via leader election. We do not specify a leader election protocol, but alternatives include, for example, rotating the
leader as in PBFT [11]. Figure 1 presents an overview of the protocol normal
case execution, showing the communication steps needed to achieve a complete
v-mapping at the learners. In the presented example, the system is composed by
two collision-fast proposers (CFP_0 and CFP_1), five acceptors (ACC_0 to ACC_4)
and one learner (L_0).

   Whenever a collision-fast proposer wants to propose some value, it must send
a message to the acceptors (to ensure agreement) and to the other collision-fast
proposers that also should make a proposal to ensure termination. In Fig. 1,
CFP_0 proposed a value V and CFP_1 proposed *Nil*, since it did not have any
value to propose, through $2a$ messages in the algorithms below. Acceptors forward these proposals to the learners through messages $2b$. Once a quorum of
such messages is received, for each collision-fast proposer, L_0 achieves a complete
v-mapping, learning these values. Notice that learning V happens after two communication steps from CFP_0 proposing it ($CFP_0 \rightarrow ACC_x$ and $ACC_x \rightarrow L_1$), but

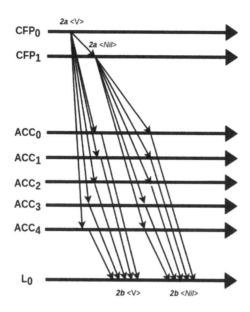

Fig. 1. Byzantine m-consensus normal case execution.

three communication steps are needed to learn *Nil* from CFP_1 ($CFP_0 \rightarrow CFP_1$, $CFP_1 \rightarrow ACC_x$, and $ACC_x \rightarrow L_1$). Consequently, the protocol demands three communication steps, even in the absence of processes misbehaving.

4.2 Protocol

The byzantine m-consensus protocol, split into Algorithms 2, 3 and 4, extend CFPaxos [51] to prevent malicious behavior of agents. The state kept by processes running byzantine m-consensus is described in Algorithm 2. Rounds are

---

Algorithm 2. Byzantine M-Consensus Variables

Pr, A, L: proposers, acceptors and learners sets;
$CF(i)$: round i's collision-fast proposers set;

$C(i)$: round i's coordinator.

$prnd[p]$, $crnd[c]$, $rnd[a]$: current rounds of proposer p, coordinator c, and acceptor a, respectively, initially 0.
$pval[p]$: value p has fast-proposed at $prnd[p]$ or *none* if p has not fast-proposed at $prnd[p]$, initially *none*.
$cval[c]$: initial v-mapping for $crnd[c]$, if c has queried an acceptor quorum or *none* otherwise; initially $\perp$ for coordinator of round 0 and *none* for others.
$vrnd[a]$: round at which a has accepted its latest value.

$vval[a]$: v-mapping a has accepted at $vrnd[a]$ or *none* if no value has been accepted at $vrnd[a]$; initially *none*.
$learned[l]$: v-mapping currently learned by learner l; initially $\perp$.

$m \Leftarrow s$: received message m from source s
$m \Rightarrow d$: send message m to destination d

Algorithm 3. Byzantine M-Consensus Protocol

```
 1:  Propose(p, V) ≜
 2:    pre-condition:
 3:      p ∈ Pr
 4:    action:
 5:      ⟨"propose", V⟩_p ⇒ cf ∈ CF(prnd[p])

 6:  Phase1a(c, r) ≜
 7:    pre-conditions:
 8:      c = C(r)
 9:      crnd[c] < r
10:    actions:
11:      crnd[c] ← r
12:      cval[c] ← none
13:      ⟨"1a", r⟩_c ⇒ A

14:  Phase1b(a, r) ≜
15:    pre-conditions:
16:      a ∈ A
17:      rnd[a] < r
18:      ⟨"1a", r⟩_c ⇐ C(r)
19:    actions:
20:      rnd[a] ← r
21:      ⟨"1b", r, vrnd[a], vval[a]⟩_a ⇒ C(r)

22:  Phase2Start(c, r) ≜
23:    pre-conditions:
24:      c = C(r)
25:      crnd[c] = r
26:      cval[c] = none
27:      ∃Q ⊆ A:
28:        Q is a quorum
29:        ∀a ∈ Q, ⟨"1b", r, vrnd, vval⟩_a ⇐ a
30:    actions:
31:      LET 1bs = [m = ⟨"1b", _, _, _⟩_a : m ⇐ a ∈ Q ]
32:      LET k = Max([vrnd : ⟨"1b", _, vrnd, _⟩_a ∈ 1bs ])
33:      LET A_⟨p,v⟩ = [a : ⟨"1b", r, k, vval⟩_a ∈ 1bs ∧ vval[p] = v]
34:      LET S = [⟨p, v⟩ : |A_⟨p,v⟩| ≥ 2f + 1]
35:      IF S = ∅ THEN
36:        cval[c] ← ⊥
37:        ⟨"2S", r, cval[c], msgs⟩_c ⇒ CF(r)
38:      ELSE
39:        cval[c] ← ⊔S • [⟨p, Nil⟩ : p ∈ CF(r)]
40:        ⟨"2S", r, cval[c], msgs⟩_c ⇒ CF(r) ∪ A
```

divided into two phases: in phase 1 of round r, the coordinator executes action *Phase1a* to query the *acceptors* for previously accepted values; *acceptors* reply in action *Phase1b* and, in action *Phase2Start*, line 22 of Algorithm 3, the coordinator determines if any v-map has possibly been decided in any round $r' < r$, using such replies. If no map v has possibly been decided, the coordinator let the fact be known by the *collision-fast* proposers of the round, *cfproposers* (*CF(r)*, lines 35–37 of Algorithm 3), so they can propose to the *acceptors* by executing action *Phase2Prepare*. Otherwise, if some v has possibly been decided, the coordinator sends v to both collision-fast proposers and *acceptors* (lines 38–40 of

Algorithm 3), so the first will not propose in r and the latter will accept v and inform the *learners*.

Algorithm 4. Byzantine M-Consensus Protocol (Continuation)

1: $Phase2Prepare(p, r) \triangleq$
2: **pre-conditions:**
3:   $p \in CF(r)$
4:   $prnd[p] < r$
5:   $\langle\text{"2S"}, r, v, proofs\rangle_{C(r)} \Leftarrow C(r)$
6:   goodRoundValue(r,v,proofs)
7: **actions:**
8:   $prnd[p] \leftarrow r$
9:   $proof[p] \leftarrow proofs$
10: IF $v = \bot$ THEN $pval[p] \leftarrow none$
11:   ELSE $pval[p] \leftarrow v(p)$

12: $Phase2a(p, r, V) \triangleq$
13: **pre-conditions:**
14:   $p \in CF(r)$
15:   $prnd[p] = r$
16:   $pval[p] = none$
17:   **either** $(V \neq Nil \wedge \langle\text{"propose"}, V\rangle_p \Leftarrow p \in Pr)$
18:   **or** $(V = Nil \wedge \langle\text{"2a"}, r, \langle q, W\rangle, proof\rangle_{\sigma_q} \Leftarrow q \in CF(r) \wedge W \neq Nil)$
19: **actions:**
20:   $pval[p] \leftarrow V$
21:   IF $V \neq Nil$ THEN
22:    $\langle\text{"2a"}, r, \langle p, V\rangle, proof[p]\rangle_p \Rightarrow A \cup CF(r)$
23:    ELSE
24:    $\langle\text{"2a"}, r, \langle p, V\rangle, proof[p]\rangle_p \Rightarrow A$

25: $Phase2b(a, r) \triangleq$
26: LET $Cond1 =$
27:   $vval[a] = none \vee$
28:   $(\langle\text{"2S"}, r, v, proofs\rangle_c \Leftarrow C(r) \wedge \text{goodRoundValue(r, v, proofs)} \wedge v \neq \bot \wedge vrnd[a] < r)$
29: LET $Cond2 =$
30:   $\langle\text{"2a"}, r, \langle p, V\rangle, proofs\rangle_p \Leftarrow p \in CF(r) \wedge V \neq Nil \wedge \text{goodRoundValue(r, V, proofs)}$
31: **pre-conditions:**
32:   $a \in A$
33:   $rnd[a] \leq r$
34:   $Cond1 \vee Cond2$
35: **actions:**
36:   IF $Cond1$
37:   THEN $vval[a] \leftarrow v$
38:   ELSE
39:    IF $Cond2 \wedge (vrnd[a] < r \vee vval[a] = none)$
40:    THEN $vval[a] \leftarrow \bot \bullet \langle p, V\rangle \bullet [\langle p, Nil\rangle : p \in Pr \setminus CF(r)]$
41:    ELSE $vval[a] \leftarrow vval[a] \bullet \langle p, V\rangle$
42:   $rnd[a] \leftarrow vrnd[a] \leftarrow r$
43:   $\langle\text{"2b"}, r, vval[a]\rangle_a \Rightarrow L$

44: $Learn(l) \triangleq$
45: **pre-conditions:**
46:   $l \in learners$
47:   $\exists Q \subseteq A:$
48:    Q is a quorum
49:    $\forall a \in Q, \langle\text{"2b"}, r, \_\rangle_a \Leftarrow a$
50: **actions:**
51:   $Q2bVals = \{v : \langle\text{"2b"}, r, v\rangle_a \Leftarrow a \in Q\}$
52:   $w = \sqcap Q2bVals$
53:   $learned[l] = learned[l] \sqcup w$

To prove that it has calculated v correctly and neither ignored nor forged responses from acceptors, the coordinator includes the responses it got from acceptors as proof in the messages it sends out. Receivers use such proofs to verify the computation in function *goodRoundValue* (lines 6, 28 and 30 of Algorithm 4).

Authorized by the coordinator, a *cfproposer* will forward proposals, from regular *proposers* or itself, in action *Phase2a*. To prove it is allowed to propose, the *cfproposer* forwards to *acceptors* the authorization received from the coordinator.

Upon receiving and validating a proposal in action *Phase2b*, *acceptors* extend the v-maps they have previously accepted with the proposal. The proposed value is associated with the *cfproposer* in the map and, therefore, only one such value is allowed in the map. The newly accepted v-map is then forwarded to the *learners* which, in turn, combine all the accepted v-maps so that any map that has been accepted by a quorum of $n - f$ *acceptors* is *learned*, in action *Learn*.

4.3 Fault Tolerance

A fundamental difference between this protocol and CFPaxos is that it needs more acceptors to tolerate the same number f of failures. This is an intrinsic cost of dealing with malicious agents. Malicious acceptors could impair the system properties, mainly agreement, by forwarding different proposals to different learners or sending incorrect information during a coordinator change, inducing the new coordination to make a proposal inconsistent from values previously learned, breaking agreement. In these cases, it is necessary that the intersections between quorums contain enough non-faulty acceptors to dwarf the influence of malicious ones.

4.4 Latency

In CFPaxos, if all *cfproposers* that have values to propose do so at the same time, then at the end of two communication steps all such values become part of the a decision. If p and q are *cfproposer* and p is the first to propose in a given round and q does not have a proposal to make, then when q hears about p's proposal, it sends a *Nil* directly to the *learners*, informing them that it will not propose any real value. In doing so, it ensures the termination in two communication steps from p's viewpoint. This action is safe because in case of any failures, recovery will ensure that q is mapped to *Nil*.

If q were byzantine, it could send *Nil* to the learners at the same time it proposes some other value w through the *acceptors*. This way, a *learner* that receives the *Nil* proposal and another who receives w in *acceptors'* messages would decide differently, breaking the Consistency property. To avoid such scenarios, byzantine m-consensus (Algorithms 2, 3 and 4) does not allow proposals of *Nil* directly to *learners*. Hence, unless all *cfproposers* have a proposal and put them forward at the same time, decision will take three communication steps.

4.5   Correctness

The correctness of byzantine m-consensus stems directly from that of CFPaxos since the modifications introduced here are of two kinds. First, messages carry extra information, but the original fields are calculated in the same way, and the extra information is used by receivers to verify the computation that resulted in said messages; in case of invalid messages, no change to the state shared with CFPaxos is performed. Second, there is the removal of the *Nil* proposal path, disabling the actions that would be performed based on such messages, possibly preventing progress but not violating any correctness properties. Hence, the changes only restrict the behavior of agents to a smaller set of possible executions, and a refinement mapping from our algorithm to CFPaxos is straightforward. We refer the interested reader to the painstaking detailed proof of CFPaxos [50] for more details.

4.6   Progress

Even though *proposers* can be Byzantine, they are forced to either propose values following the protocol specification, to stay silent and be eventually flagged as uncooperative, or to attempt denial of services attacks, which we do not consider here since the literature already covers this problem well. As for *acceptors*, since they cannot forge messages, they are forced to follow the protocol or stay silent in order to slow down decision. In either case, the system can still progress since the number of faulty acceptors is limited. Under such circumstances, non-faulty learners cannot be prevented from progressing.

5   On the Impossibility of Byzantine Collision-Fast Atomic Broadcast

It is well known as the FLP result that consensus and atomic broadcast cannot be deterministically solved in purely asynchronous systems [24]. To circumvent the impossibility, the model must be extended with some minimum synchronism, equivalent to the Ω leader election oracle [13]. In this section we argue that any atomic broadcast algorithm that tolerates byzantine failures of proposers and concurrent proposals will not be able to decide within two communication steps even when the asynchronous model has been extended with Ω or equivalent mechanisms that would make it possible to ensure the eventual termination in the absence of byzantine failures. This impossibility stems from the need to validate every proposals at the acceptors, before forwarding them to the learners and from the assumption that proposers should be provoked before proposing any value. This is captured by the following theorem.

Theorem 1. *Consider an asynchronous system extended with partial synchronism enough to circumvent FLP (e.g., with Ω, Unreliable Failure Detectors or*

Globally Stabilizing Time). In this system, it is impossible to solve Atomic Broadcast in a quiescent manner and within two communication steps, under the possibility of collisions and of potentially byzantine proposers, even when they do not act as such.

Proof. Assume, for the sake of contradiction, that there exists a BCFABCast (Byzantine Collision-Fast Atomic Broadcast) protocol $\mathcal{A}$ that delivers broadcast messages within two communication steps in the extended asynchronous system model considered. Because multiple messages may be broadcast in parallel, $\mathcal{A}$ must handle collision while remaining fast. We will show that $\mathcal{A}$ admits an execution e that violates *Agreement*.

Let $\mathcal{A}$ have a set of collision-fast proposers, CFP, of minimal size in the execution e, i.e., two; this is without loss of generality since it is enough that $\mathcal{A}$ decides only the concurrent proposals made by the agents in CFP to satisfy collision-fast termination. Since the system is quiescent, there is a time t_q after which no messages will be transmitted in the network unless some proposal is made by agents in CFP.

Now, let process $i \in$ CFP propose at time $t > t_q$. Since i could be byzantine, proposals cannot be send directly to learners and taken at face value, since different values could be sent to different learners, impairing the agreement property of consensus. Instead, the proposal must be sent to acceptors for certification at time $t + 1$ and then forwarded to learners, which receive it at time $t + 2$, hence requiring two communication steps for i's proposal to be learned. However, at $t+2$, learners cannot yet deliver anything since the other process $j \in$ CFP could have issued a concurrent proposal and $\mathcal{A}$ is collision-fast. Hence learners must wait for a proposal from j, i.e., all values are delivered only when they learn one value from each collision-fast proposer.

Since the system is asynchronous, it is not possible do define a common time to be used by i and j to issue their proposals. Consequently, j does not know that i had sent its proposal at time t. Moreover, since the system is quiescent and considering that j did not issued its proposal yet in the execution e and that it does not have anything to propose, j will only send a message (with its abstention from proposing anything) when provoked. Consequently, i must provoke j by sending it some message upon proposing at time t. The provocation can be heard, the earliest, at $t + 1$, so j will send its message at such an instant. Since $\mathcal{A}$ is collision-fast, j must send its proposal directly to the learners, that receive it at $t + 2$ and must take it as the decision value for j in order to be able to finish the consensus instance at $t + 2$, i.e., to complete their *v-mapping* at $t + 2$. Considering that j could be byzantine in the execution e, we have two cases:

– *Case 1 - Learners accept and learn any value proposed directly by j:* clearly, in this case j could send different proposals for different learners, violating the *Agreement* property of consensus. Hence, learners cannot learn the proposed values directly.
– *Case 2 - Learners accept and learn only abstentions (Nil) proposed directly by j:* trying to avoid to fall in the previous case 1, learners could consider only

abstentions received directly from j. In this case, j could send *Nil* directly to some learner l_1 but a value $v \neq Nil$ to the acceptors that forward it to other learners. Considering that v is received at l_1 after the *Nil* proposal, l_1 decides by *Nil* for j while the remaining learners decide by v, violating *Agreement* property of consensus. Hence, learners cannot learn *Nil* proposals directly.

In both cases we reached a contradiction that $\mathcal{A}$ solves BCFABCast: learners cannot trust in the proposals received directly from the collision-fast proposals, but this is necessary to finish in two communication steps. Consequently, we conclude that $\mathcal{A}$ does not exists.   □

The previous argument can be visualized in Fig. 2, which shows the message flow of CFPaxos (Fig. 2(a)) and the supposed correct algorithm $\mathcal{A}$ (Fig. 2(b)). While a consistent collision-fast decision is reached on Fig. 2(a) over the proposal of CFP_0 and the abstention of CFP_1 that proposed *Nil* (both L_0 and L_1 learn the *v-mapping* containing V from CFP_0 and *Nil* from CFP_1), on Fig. 2(b) $\mathcal{A}$ would allow a malicious collision-fast proposer CFP_1 to impair the agreement property if the learners consider a *Nil* proposal received directly from the collision-fast proposers (as argued in Theorem 1, this is necessary to be fast and deliver the broadcast messages in two communication steps).

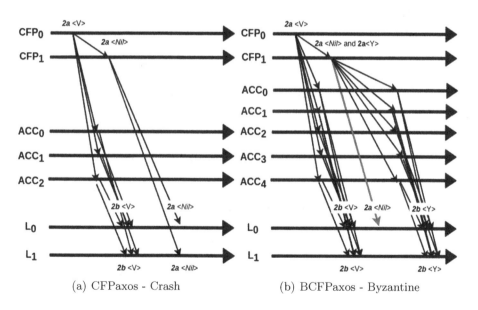

(a) CFPaxos - Crash   (b) BCFPaxos - Byzantine

Fig. 2. Communication steps needed to achieve a complete *v-mapping*.

The *Agreement* property is impaired in the example of Fig. 2(b) in the following way. When CFP_0 proposed some value V, CFP_1 proposes *Nil* to the learner L_0 and Y through the acceptors, that forward this proposal to the learners but it arrives at L_0 after the *Nil* proposal received directly from CFP_1. Consequently, L_0 learns a *v-mapping* containing V for CFP_0 and *Nil* for CFP_1, while L_1 learns a *v-mapping* containing V for CFP_0 and Y for CFP_1, violating the *Agreement* property. Notice that L_0 also received the proposal Y, but it already decided by *Nil* for CFP_1. To prevent this from happening, L_0 can not consider the *Nil* proposal coming directly from CFP_1, only the proposals sent through the acceptors. Consequently, one more communication steps is needed and $\mathcal{A}$ can not reach a fast decision and deliver the messages within two communication steps.

6 USIG Based Byzantine Collision-Fast Atomic Broadcast

In this section we extend the system model with a trusted component to solve collision-fast atomic broadcast in spite of malicious agents (BCFABCast). First, we present the USIG component and then the USIG based byzantine collision-fast Paxos protocol (USIG-BCFPaxos). By using this algorithm instead of CFPaxos as underlining M-Consensus in Algorithm 1, we have a protocol that demands only two communication steps and, consequently, solves BCFABCast.

6.1 Extending the System Model Using a Trusted Component

The byzantine m-consensus algorithms presented at Sect. 4 may be extended using a trusted component to circumvent the impossibility described in Sect. 5. This mechanism ensures a delivery latency of two communication steps instead of the original three in the presence of a byzantine *cfproposer*, and also reduces the number of replicas needed to solves BCFABCast from $5f + 1$ to $2f + 1$. In fact, $2f + 1$ is the same number of replicas needed to solve the non-byzantine version of the protocol (CFABCast) [51].

The trusted components normally used to develop byzantine fault-tolerant protocols have considerable differences in terms of implementation and performance. They can be, mainly, *(i)* implemented in a distributed fashion, like *Trusted Timely Computing Base* (TTCB) [17], *(ii)* use locally available tamper-proof components, like *Attested Append-Only Memory* (A2M) [15]; or *(iii)* use local counter-based algorithms that ensures the uniqueness and authenticity of exchanged messages, like the *Unique Sequential Identifier Generator* (USIG) [54].

Such mechanisms are implemented in a manner that an attacker cannot compromise even if he can compromise the servers hosting them. Thus, it is possible to build protocols that restrict the actions that a malicious process can execute without being discovered. In this work, we chose the USIG trusted component for its simplicity as well as easy of implementation and use in the system [54].

6.2 Unique Sequential Identifier Generator – USIG

The USIG component is a local service present in every agent (process) of the protocol (proposers, acceptors and learners). Its function is to assign a unique identifier to each message and then sign the message. Identifiers are unique, monotonic and sequential, for each agent, and these three properties need to be guaranteed even if the agent is compromised, so this service must be implemented in a tamper-proof module.

The service interface has two functions [54]:

- `createUI(m)`: returns a USIG certificate that contains an unique identifier `UI` and certifies that this identifier was created by this component for message `m`. The `UI` is essentially a reading of the monotonic counter, which is incremented whenever this function is called. The certification step involves encryption and can be based on cryptographic hashes or public-key cryptography.
- `verifyUI(PK,UI,m)`: verifies if the unique identifier `UI` is valid for message `m`.

When using this component, each process stores the identifiers of the last messages it received from each other processes. This way it knows the next expected identifier and constraints the actions of a malicious processes. A malicious process is not able to send different versions of some message at the same step since their identifiers would be different. Hence, either it sends the same message to all processes or it does not send anything at all.

There are two ways to implement this component [54], either using hashes or relying on digital signatures. We adopted the solution with digital signatures because in this approach the verification could be done outside the trusted component by using the associated public key. Moreover, different isolation levels could be used to deploy this service, as the software-based virtual machines and the hardware-based TPM (*Trusted Platform Module*).

6.3   USIG-BCFABCast Protocol

Algorithms 5 and 6 solves the *byzantine collision-fast atomic broadcast* problem by using the USIG component to constraint malicious actions and should be used by Algorithm 1 to solve USIG-BCFABCast (*USIG based Byzantine Collision-fast Atomic Broadcast*). The resulting solution needs $2f+1$ acceptors to tolerate up to f malicious failures and only two communication steps to achieve a complete v-map in runs without failures.

Overview. The main idea is that by appending a unique identifier to the messages, the collision-fast proposers does not need to send their messages through the acceptors in case they are going to propose *Nil* (do not have a value to propose). Learners trust in a *Nil* propose received directly from a collision-fast proposer since it is not able to do a different proposal with the same identifier. Proposals with non *Nil* values are sent through the acceptors to ensure this information is used to configure a new round in case a coordinator change occurs.

Figure 3 presents an overview of the protocol normal case execution, showing the communication steps needed to achieve a complete *v-mapping* at the learners. In the presented example, the system is composed by two collision-fast proposers (CFP_0 and CFP_1), three acceptors (ACC_0, ACC_1 and ACC_2) and one learner (L_0). In this protocol, the proposals from the collision-fast proposers are sent

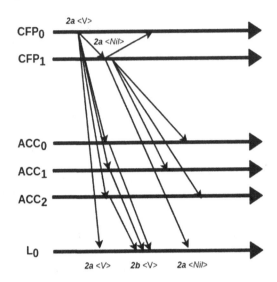

Fig. 3. USIG-BCFABCast normal case execution.

to all other processes, through messages $2a$, allowing all of them to update their counters. Consequently, these processes are able to know the expected next proposal counter for each collision-fast proposer. As commented, the main difference from the previous protocol is related to the *Nil* proposals. In this case, CFP_1 send it directly to L_1 (although it must send to the other process too). L_1 must receive a quorum of $2b$ messages from the acceptors to learn the value V proposed by CFP_0 and the *Nil* proposal from CFP_1 to complete the *v-mapping*. Notice this happens after two communication steps for both CFP_0 ($CFP_0 \rightarrow ACC_x$ and $ACC_x \rightarrow L_1$) and CFP_1 ($CFP_0 \rightarrow CFP_1$ and $CFP_1 \rightarrow L_1$).

Protocol. In the proposed protocol presented at Algorithms 5 and 6, the phases to configure a new round are similar to the crash variant in [51]. Our algorithm, however, needs extra steps to prevent malicious behavior. For example, malicious coordinators cannot send different values for any given round in $1a$ messages, since they cannot produce proof to reconfigure the system by messages $2S$ for both values. It is so because messages $2S$ carry a unique identifier generated by the USIG service of the coordinator. Consequently, the coordinator is not able to send different $2S$ messages to different agents and all of them will receive the same initial configuration for round r.

Each collision-fast proposer also appends a unique identifier to its proposals (messages $2a$). As already commented, this constraint the malicious actions of a process that is not allowed to do different proposals. Although these messages are addressed to all agents ($A \cup CF(r) \cup L$), only the learners execute the proposals with *Nil*. This is necessary to allow acceptors and other collision-fast proposers to increment their counters for the next expected proposal. On the other hand, learners increment their counters for proposals different of *Nil* when they receive

Algorithm 5. USIG *based Byzantine Collision-fast Paxos* (USIG-BCFPaxos)

All variables and sets from Algorithm 3
$USIG^C[c]$, $cnt[c]$: USIG used by coordinator c and expected counter value for msgs received from c, initially 0.
$USIG^A[a]$, $cnt[a]$: USIG used by acceptor a and expected counter value for msgs received from a, initially 0.
$USIG^P[p]$, $cnt[p]$: USIG used by CF proposer p and expected counter value for msgs received from p, initially 0.

1:   $Propose(p, V) \triangleq$ lines 2-5 of Algorithm 3

2:   $Phase1a(c, r) \triangleq$ lines 7-13 of Algorithm 3

3:   $Phase1b(a, r) \triangleq$ lines 15-21 of Algorithm 3

4:   $Phase2Start(c, r) \triangleq$
5:    **pre-conditions:**
6:     $c = C(r)$
7:     $crnd[c] = r$
8:     $cval[c] = none$
9:     $\exists Q \subseteq A$:
10:      Q is a quorum
11:      $\forall a \in Q$, $\langle \text{"1b"}, r, vrnd, vval \rangle_a \Leftarrow a$
12:    **actions:**
13:     LET $msgs = [\, m = \langle \text{"1b"}, r, vrnd, vval \rangle_a : m \Leftarrow a \in Q \,]$
14:     LET $k = Max([vrnd : \langle \text{"1b"}, r, vrnd, vval \rangle_a \in msgs\,])$
15:     LET $S = [vval : \langle \text{"1b"}, r, k, vval \rangle_a \in msgs, \; vval \neq none]$
16:     IF $S = \emptyset$ THEN
17:      $cval[c] \leftarrow \bot$
18:     ELSE
19:      $cval[c] \leftarrow \sqcup S \bullet [\langle p, Nil, Nil \rangle : p \in CF(r)]$
20:     $UI_c \leftarrow USIG^C[c].\text{createUI}(\langle \text{"2S"}, r, cval[c], msgs \rangle)$
21:     $\langle \text{"2S"}, r, cval[c], msgs, UI_c \rangle \Rightarrow CF(r) \cup A$

22:   $Phase2Prepare(p, r) \triangleq$
23:    **pre-conditions:**
24:     $p \in CF(r)$
25:     $prnd[p] < r$
26:     $\langle \text{"2S"}, r, v, proof, UI_{C(r)} \rangle \Leftarrow C(r)$
27:     $goodRoundValue(r,v,proofs)$
28:     $\text{verifyUI}(PK_{C(r)}, UI_{C(r)}, \langle \text{"2S"}, r, v, proofs \rangle)$
29:     $\text{verifyCnt}(UI_{C(r)}, cnt[C(r)])$
30:    **actions:**
31:     $prnd[p] \leftarrow r$
32:     IF $v = \bot$ THEN $pval[p] \leftarrow none$
33:     ELSE $pval[p] \leftarrow v(p)$

34:   $Phase2a(p, r, V) \triangleq$
35:    **pre-conditions:**
36:     $p \in CF(r)$
37:     $prnd[p] = r$
38:     $pval[p] = none$
39:    **either** $(V \neq Nil \wedge \langle \text{"propose"}, V \rangle_{\sigma_p} \Leftarrow p \in Pr)$
40:    **or** $(V = Nil \wedge \langle \text{"2a"}, r, \langle q, W \rangle, UI_q \rangle \Leftarrow q \in CF(r) \wedge$
41:     $\text{verifyUI}(PK_q, UI_q, \langle q, W \rangle) \wedge \text{verifyCnt}(UI_q, cnt[q]) \wedge W \neq Nil)$
42:    **actions:**
43:     $pval[p] \leftarrow V$
44:     $UI_p \leftarrow USIG^P[p].\text{createUI}(\langle p, V \rangle)$
45:     $\langle \text{"2a"}, r, \langle p, V \rangle, UI_p \rangle \Rightarrow A \cup CF(r) \cup L$

Algorithm 6. USIG *based Byzantine Collision-fast Paxos* (USIG-BCFPaxos) (Continuation)

```
1:   Phase2b(a, r) ≜
2:     LET Cond1 =
3:       vval[a] = none ∨ (⟨"2S", r, v, proofs, UI_C(r)⟩ ⇐ C(r)∧
4:       verifyUI(PK_C(r), UI_C(r), ⟨"2S", r, v, proofs⟩) ∧
5:       verifyCnt(UI_C(r), cnt[C(r)]) ∧ goodRoundValue(r,v,proofs) ∧
6:       v ≠ ⊥ ∧ vrnd[a] < r)
7:     LET Cond2 =
8:       ⟨"2a", r, ⟨p, V⟩, UI_p⟩ ⇐ p ∈ CF(r) ∧ V ≠ Nil∧
9:       verifyUI(PK_p, UI_p, ⟨p, V⟩) ∧ verifyCnt(UI_p, cnt[p])
10:    pre-conditions:
11:      a ∈ A
12:      rnd[a] ≤ r
13:      Cond1 ∨ Cond2
14:    actions:
15:      IF Cond1
16:      THEN vval[a] ← v
17:      ELSE
18:        IF Cond2 ∧ (vrnd[a] < r ∨ vval[a] = none)
19:        THEN vval[a] ← ⊥•⟨p, V, UI_p⟩ • [⟨p, Nil, Nil⟩ : p ∈ Pr \ CF(r)]
20:        ELSE vval[a] ← vval[a] • ⟨p, V, UI_p⟩
21:      rnd[a] ← vrnd[a] ← r
22:      UI_a ← USIG^A[a].createUI(⟨"2b", r, vval[a]⟩)
23:      ⟨"2b", r, vval[a], UI_a⟩ ⇒ L

24:   Learn(l) ≜
25:    pre-conditions:
26:      l ∈ learners
27:      ∃Q ⊆ A:
28:        Q is a quorum
29:        ∀a ∈ Q, ⟨"2b", r, _, UI_a⟩ ⇐ a∧
30:        verifyUI(PK_a, UI_a, ⟨"2b", r, _⟩) ∧
31:        verifyCnt(UI_a, cnt[a])
32:    actions:
33:      LET P ⊂ CF(r) : ∀p ∈ P, ⟨"2a", r, ⟨p, Nil⟩, UI_p⟩ ⇐ p∧
                                        verifyUI(PK_p, UI_p, ⟨p, Nil⟩) ∧ verifyCnt(UI_p, cnt[p])
34:      Q2bVals = [v : ⟨"2b", r, v, UI_a⟩ ⇐ a ∈ Q ∧
35:        ∀ ⟨q, W, UI_q⟩ ∈ v: verifyUI(PK_q, UI_q, ⟨p, W⟩) ∧
36:        verifyCnt(UI_q, cnt[q])]
37:      w = ⊓Q2bVals • [⟨u, Nil, UI_u⟩ : u ∈ P]
38:      learned[l] = learned[l] ⊔ w

39:   verifyCnt(UI_x, cnt[x]) ≜
40:     IF (UI_x.cnt = cnt[x]) THEN
41:       cnt[x] ⇐ cnt[x] + 1
42:       return TRUE;
43:     ELSE
44:       return FALSE
```

them from the acceptors. Notice that identifiers are stored together with their proposals and every time a new round must be started, this information is sent to the new coordinator that will send it to the acceptors (messages $2S$). The acceptors forward this information to learners through messages $2b$.

Finally, it is worth noticing that acceptors also add unique identifiers to $2b$ messages sent to the learners. Consequently, a malicious acceptor is not able to send different messages to different learners without being discovered. In fact, learners only process a message with the next expected identifier (see the preconditions for *Learn*).

Correctness. By using the unique sequential identifiers, the proposed protocol constraints the actions of a malicious agent (coordinator, collision-fast proposer or acceptor) since it is not allowed to send different versions of some message. Consequently, the behavior of the agents in the protocol is similar their operation in the crash model [51], i.e., either a agent sends the same message to all other processes or does not send anything.

In this way, each collision-fast proposer is allowed to do a single proposal for some round r. If the proposal is *Nil*, it is sent directly to the learners; otherwise, it is sent to the acceptors that store it since a new round may be needed to finish such consensus instance. Thus, the algorithm needs only two communication steps to decide, being collision-fast despite malicious agents.

Finally, only $2f + 1$ acceptors are necessary since they are not able to modify a proposal coming from a collision-fast proposer or send different version of a message to different learners. Notice the proposal unique identifier always is sent together with the proposal.

7   Conclusion

In this work we studied the problem of providing atomic broadcast primitives in a setup subject to byzantine failures and concurrent proposals (collisions), while delivering messages in only two communications steps (fast). In summary, our contributions are threefold: *(i)* the proposal of an extension to the *Collision-Fast Atomic Broadcast* protocol that tolerates byzantine failures, but needs three communication steps to decide; *(ii)* the proof that it is not possible to solve byzantine collision-fast atomic broadcast problem in an asynchronous system, even when extended in ways that ensure that a decision is achievable in a system subject to crash failures; and, *(iii)* the proposal of a protocol that circumvent this impossibility by enhancing the system model with a trusted USIG service. As future work we intend to evaluate the performance of the proposed solutions.

Finally, it is important to observe that in these protocols all collision-fast proposers must issue a proposal and the decision is the combination of such proposals (the *v-mapping*). Each of these proposals is forwarded by the acceptors to the learners, leading to more messages than in the traditional consensus algorithms, like Paxos, where only the leader is allowed to propose. Fortunately, messages for different proposals from different collision-fast proposers could be sent in parallel and it is necessary fewer communications steps to reach a decision than in a traditional consensus protocol. Moreover, learners decide by a set of values (the *v-mapping*) and not just one, i.e., they deliver a set of broadcast messages per consensus instance (similar to a batch of messages).

References

1. Abd-El-Malek, M., Ganger, G., Goodson, G., Reiter, M., Wylie, J.: Fault-scalable Byzantine fault-tolerant services. In: Proceedings of the ACM Symposium on Operating Systems Principles (2005)
2. Abe, K., Ueda, T., Shikano, M., Ishibashi, H., Matsuura, T.: Toward fault-tolerant P2P systems: constructing a stable virtual peer from multiple unstable peers. In: 2009 First International Conference on Advances in P2P Systems, pp. 104–110 (2009)
3. Abraham, I., Malkhi, D., Nayak, K., Ren, L., Spiegelman, A.: Solida: a blockchain protocol based on reconfigurable byzantine consensus. In: Proceedings of the 21st International Conference on Principles of Distributed Systems (2017)
4. Alchieri, E.A.P., Bessani, A.N., da Silva Fraga, J., Greve, F.: Byzantine consensus with unknown participants. In: Baker, T.P., Bui, A., Tixeuil, S. (eds.) OPODIS 2008. LNCS, vol. 5401, pp. 22–40. Springer, Heidelberg (2008). https://doi.org/10.1007/978-3-540-92221-6_4
5. Alchieri, E.A.P., Bessani, A., Greve, F., da Silva Fraga, J.: Knowledge connectivity requirements for solving byzantine consensus with unknown participants. IEEE Trans. Dependable Secur. Comput. 15(2), 246–259 (2018). https://doi.org/10.1109/TDSC.2016.2548460
6. Benedictis, A.D., Rak, M., Villano, U.: Slas for cloud applications: agreement protocol and rest-based implementation. Int. J. Grid Util. Comput. 8(2), 120–132 (2017). https://doi.org/10.1504/IJGUC.2017.085910
7. Birman, K., Chockler, G., van Renesse, R.: Toward a cloud computing research agenda. SIGACT News 40(2), 68–80 (2009). https://doi.org/10.1145/1556154.1556172
8. Burrows, M.: The chubby lock service for loosely-coupled distributed systems (2006)
9. Cachin, C., Vukolic, M.: Blockchain consensus protocols in the wild. CoRR abs/1707.01873 (2017), http://arxiv.org/abs/1707.01873
10. Calder, B., et al.: Windows azure storage: a highly available cloud storage service with strong consistency. In: Proceedings of the ACM Symposium on Operating Systems Principles (2011)
11. Castro, M., Liskov, B.: Practical byzantine fault tolerance. In: Proceedings of the 3rd Symposium on Operating Systems Design and Implementation, OSDI 1999, pp. 173–186. USENIX Association (1999)
12. Castro, M., Liskov, B.: Practical Byzantine fault-tolerance and proactive recovery. ACM Trans. Comput. Syst. 20(4), 398–461 (2002)
13. Chandra, T.D., Hadzilacos, V., Toueg, S.: The weakest failure detector for solving consensus. J. ACM 43(4), 685–722 (1996). https://doi.org/10.1145/234533.234549
14. Chandra, T.D., Toueg, S.: Unreliable failure detectors for reliable distributed systems. J. ACM 43, 225–267 (1995)
15. Chun, B.G., Maniatis, P., Shenker, S., Kubiatowicz, J.: Attested append-only memory: making adversaries stick to their word. In: Proceedings of Twenty-First ACM SIGOPS Symposium on Operating Systems Principles, SOSP 2007, pp. 189–204. ACM, New York (2007). https://doi.org/10.1145/1294261.1294280
16. Corbett, J., et al.: Spanner: Google's globally-distributed database. In: Proceedings of the USENIX Symposium on Operating Systems Design and Implementation (2012)

17. Correia, M., Neves, N.F., Verissimo, P.: How to tolerate half less one byzantine nodes in practical distributed systems. In: Proceedings of the 23rd IEEE International Symposium on Reliable Distributed Systems, SRDS 2004, pp. 174–183. IEEE Computer Society, Washington, DC (2004)
18. Correia, M., Neves, N.F., Veríssimo, P.: From consensus to atomic broadcast: time-free Byzantine-resistant protocols without signatures. Comput. J. **49**(1), 82–96 (2006)
19. Cowling, J., Myers, D., Liskov, B., Rodrigues, R., Shrira, L.: HQ-replication: a hybrid quorum protocol for Byzantine fault tolerance. In: Proceedings of the USENIX Symposium on Operating Systems Design and Implementation, November 2006
20. DeCandia, G., et al.: Dynamo: Amazon's highly available key-value store. In: Proceedings of Twenty-First ACM SIGOPS Symposium on Operating Systems Principles - SOSP 2007. ACM Press (2007). https://doi.org/10.1145/1294261.1294281
21. Du, J., Sciascia, D., Elnikety, S., Zwaenepoel, W., Pedone, F.: Clock-RSM: low-latency inter-datacenter state machine replication using loosely synchronized physical clocks. In: 44th Annual IEEE/IFIP International Conference on Dependable Systems and Networks, DSN 2014, Atlanta, GA, USA, 23–26 June 2014, pp. 343–354 (2014). https://doi.org/10.1109/DSN.2014.42
22. Dwork, C., Lynch, N., Stockmeyer, L.: Consensus in the presence of partial synchrony. J. ACM **35**(2), 288–323 (1988). http://doi.acm.org/10.1145/42282.42283
23. Eyal, I., Gencer, A.E., Sirer, E.G., Renesse, R.V.: Bitcoin-NG: a scalable blockchain protocol. In: 13th USENIX Symposium on Networked Systems Design and Implementation (NSDI 2016), pp. 45–59. USENIX Association, Santa Clara (2016). https://www.usenix.org/conference/nsdi16/technical-sessions/presentation/eyal
24. Fischer, M.J., Lynch, N.A., Paterson, M.S.: Impossibility of distributed consensus with one faulty process (1985)
25. Galera Cluster: Minimizing downtime and maximizing elasticity with Galera Cluster for MySQL (2018). http://galeracluster.com/products/#white-papers-case-studies
26. Gilad, Y., Hemo, R., Micali, S., Vlachos, G., Zeldovich, N.: Algorand: scaling byzantine agreements for cryptocurrencies. In: Proceedings of the 26th Symposium on Operating Systems Principles, SOSP 2017, pp. 51–68. ACM, New York (2017)
27. Hunt, P., Konar, M., Junqueira, F., Reed, B.: Zookeeper: wait-free coordination for Internet-scale services. In: Proceedings of the USENIX Annual Technical Conference (2010)
28. Kotla, R., Alvisi, L., Dahlin, M., Clement, A., Wong, E.: Zyzzyva: speculative Byzantine fault tolerance. ACM Trans. Comput. Syst. **27**(4), 7:1–7:39 (2009)
29. Lamport, L.: Time, clocks, and the ordering of events in a distributed system. Commun. ACM **21**(7), 558–565 (1978). https://doi.org/10.1145/359545.359563
30. Lamport, L.: The part-time parliament. ACM Trans. Comput. Syst. **16**(2), 133–169 (1998)
31. Lamport, L.: Generalized consensus and Paxos (2005)
32. Lamport, L.: Fast Paxos. Distrib. Comput. **19**(2), 79–103 (2006). https://doi.org/10.1007/s00446-006-0005-x
33. Lamport, L.: Lower bounds for asynchronous consensus. Distrib. Comput. **19**(2), 104–125 (2006). https://doi.org/10.1007/s00446-006-0155-x
34. Lamport, L., Shostak, R., Pease, M.: The byzantine generals problem. ACM Trans. Program. Lang. Syst. **4**(3), 382–401 (1982). https://doi.org/10.1145/357172.357176

35. Lampson, B.W.: How to build a highly available system using consensus. In: Babaoğlu, Ö., Marzullo, K. (eds.) WDAG 1996. LNCS, vol. 1151, pp. 1–17. Springer, Heidelberg (1996). https://doi.org/10.1007/3-540-61769-8_1

36. Li, B., He, Y., Xu, K.: Distributed metadata management scheme in cloud computing. In: 2011 6th International Conference on Pervasive Computing and Applications, pp. 32–38, October 2011. https://doi.org/10.1109/ICPCA.2011.6106475

37. Lin, S.-D., Lian, Q., Chen, M., Zhang, Z.: A practical distributed mutual exclusion protocol in dynamic peer-to-peer systems. In: Voelker, G.M., Shenker, S. (eds.) IPTPS 2004. LNCS, vol. 3279, pp. 11–21. Springer, Heidelberg (2005). https://doi.org/10.1007/978-3-540-30183-7_2

38. Liu, Y., Ozera, K., Matsuo, K., Barolli, L.: An intelligent approach for qualified voting in P2P mobile collaborative team: a comparison study for two fuzzy-based systems. Int. J. Space Based Situated Comput. 7(4), 207–216 (2017). https://doi.org/10.1504/IJSSC.2017.089882

39. Mao, Y., Junqueira, F.P., Marzullo, K.: Mencius: building efficient replicated state machines for WANs. In: Proceedings of the 8th USENIX Conference on Operating Systems Design and Implementation, OSDI 2008pp. 369–384. USENIX Association, Berkeley (2008)

40. Martin, J.P., Alvisi, L.: Fast byzantine consensus. IEEE Trans. Dependable Secur. Comput. 3(3), 202–215 (2006). https://doi.org/10.1109/TDSC.2006.35

41. Messina, F., Pappalardo, G., Santoro, C., Rosaci, D., Sarné, G.M.L.: A multi-agent protocol for service level agreement negotiation in cloud federations. Int. J. Grid Util. Comput. 7(2), 101–112 (2016). https://doi.org/10.1504/IJGUC.2016.077488

42. MySql Group Replication: Chap. 17 group replication (2018). https://dev.mysql.com/doc/refman/5.7/en/group-replication.html

43. Nakagawa, T., Hayashibara, N.: Resource management for raft consensus protocol. Int. J. Space Based Situated Comput. 8(2), 80–87 (2018). https://doi.org/10.1504/IJSSC.2018.094467

44. Nakamura, S., Duolikun, D., Enokido, T., Takizawa, M.: A read-write abortion protocol to prevent illegal information flow in role-based access control systems. Int. J. Space Based Situated Comput. 6(1), 43–53 (2016). https://doi.org/10.1504/IJSSC.2016.076564

45. Netto, H.V., Lung, L.C., Correia, M., Luiz, A.F., de Souza, L.M.S.: State machine replication in containers managed by kubernetes. J. Syst. Archit. 73, 53–59 (2017). https://doi.org/10.1016/j.sysarc.2016.12.007. Special Issue on Reliable Software Technologies for Dependable Distributed Systems

46. Noor, T.H., Sheng, Q.Z.: Trust as a service: a framework for trust management in cloud environments. In: Bouguettaya, A., Hauswirth, M., Liu, L. (eds.) WISE 2011. LNCS, vol. 6997, pp. 314–321. Springer, Heidelberg (2011). https://doi.org/10.1007/978-3-642-24434-6_27

47. Ongaro, D., Ousterhout, J.: In search of an understandable consensus algorithm. In: USENIX Annual Technical Conference, pp. 305–320 (2014)

48. Pass, R., Shi, E.: Hybrid consensus: efficient consensus in the permissionless model. IACR Cryptology ePrint Archive 2016, 917 (2016)

49. Saramago, R., Alchieri, E.A.P., Rezende, T.F., Camargos, L.: On the impossibility of byzantine collision-fast atomic broadcast. In: 2018 IEEE 32nd International Conference on Advanced Information Networking and Applications (AINA). pp. 414–421, May 2018. https://doi.org/10.1109/AINA.2018.00069

50. Schmidt, R., Camargos, L., Pedone, F.: On collision-fast atomic broadcast. Technical report, SemanticScholar (2007)

51. Schmidt, R., Camargos, L., Pedone, F.: Collision-fast atomic broadcast. In: Proceedings of the 2014 IEEE 28th International Conferene on Advanced Information Networking and Applications, AINA 2014, pp. 1065–1072. IEEE Computer Society, Washington, DC (2014)

52. Schütt, T., Schintke, F., Reinefeld, A.: Scalaris: Reliable transactional P2P key/value store. In: Proceedings of the 7th ACM SIGPLAN Workshop on ERLANG, ERLANG 2008, New York, NY, USA, pp. 41–48 (2008)

53. Valduriez, P., Pacitti, E.: Data management in large-scale P2P systems. In: Daydé, M., Dongarra, J., Hernández, V., Palma, J.M.L.M. (eds.) VECPAR 2004. LNCS, vol. 3402, pp. 104–118. Springer, Heidelberg (2005). https://doi.org/10.1007/11403937_9

54. Veronese, G.S., Correia, M., Bessani, A.N., Lung, L.C., Verissimo, P.: Efficient byzantine fault-tolerance. IEEE Trans. Comput. **62**(1), 16–30 (2013). https://doi.org/10.1109/TC.2011.221

55. Vukolić, M.: The quest for scalable blockchain fabric: proof-of-work vs. BFT replication. In: Camenisch, J., Kesdoğan, D. (eds.) iNetSec 2015. LNCS, vol. 9591, pp. 112–125. Springer, Cham (2016). https://doi.org/10.1007/978-3-319-39028-4_9

56. Weiss, S., Urso, P., Molli, P.: Logoot: a scalable optimistic replication algorithm for collaborative editing on P2P networks. In: 2009 29th IEEE International Conference on Distributed Computing Systems, pp. 404–412, June 2009

57. Zhao, W., Melliar-Smith, P.M., Moser, L.E.: Fault tolerance middleware for cloud computing. In: 2010 IEEE 3rd International Conference on Cloud Computing, pp. 67–74, July 2010. https://doi.org/10.1109/CLOUD.2010.26

A Methodological Approach for Time Series Analysis and Forecasting of Web Dynamics

Maria Carla Calzarossa[1]([⊠]), Marco L. Della Vedova[2], Luisa Massari[1], Giuseppe Nebbione[1], and Daniele Tessera[2]

[1] Dipartimento di Ingegneria Industriale e dell'Informazione, Università di Pavia, Pavia, Italy
{mcc,luisa.massari}@unipv.it, giuseppe.nebbione01@ateneopv.it
[2] Dipartimento di Matematica e Fisica, Università Cattolica del Sacro Cuore, Brescia, Italy
{marco.dellavedova,daniele.tessera}@unicatt.it

Abstract. The web is a complex information ecosystem that provides a large variety of content changing over time as a consequence of the combined effects of management policies, user interactions and external events. These highly dynamic scenarios challenge technologies dealing with discovery, management and retrieval of web content. In this paper, we address the problem of modeling and predicting web dynamics in the framework of time series analysis and forecasting. We present a general methodological approach that allows the identification of the patterns describing the behavior of the time series, the formulation of suitable models and the use of these models for predicting the future behavior. Moreover, to improve the forecasts, we propose a method for detecting and modeling the spiky patterns that might be present in a time series. To test our methodological approach, we analyze the temporal patterns of page uploads of the Reuters news agency website over one year. We discover that the upload process is characterized by a diurnal behavior and by a much larger number of uploads during weekdays with respect to weekend days. Moreover, we identify several sudden spikes and a daily periodicity. The overall model of the upload process – obtained as a superposition of the models of its individual components – accurately fits the data, including most of the spikes.

Keywords: Web dynamics · Temporal patterns ·
Time series analysis · Forecasting · Performance modeling ·
Search engines · ARMA models

1 Introduction

The web is a huge repository of information that provides users with an enhanced experience by combining many different content forms, e.g., text, audio, images,

N. T. Nguyen et al. (Eds.): TCCI XXXIII, LNCS 11610, pp. 128–143, 2019.
https://doi.org/10.1007/978-3-662-59540-4_7

video, animations. This complex information ecosystem is regularly updated to keep the content fresh and attract at the same time the interest of the users. New pages are uploaded, existing pages are updated and eventually removed.

All these changes are often the result of combined effects that involve the management policies of the websites, the behavior of the users as well as external events. For example, news websites are generally updated to report the latest news stories and their developments as well as to keep the websites "alive". The changes of social media websites are mainly driven by the activities and interactions of their users who post and share content, add comments and likes. Corporate websites are periodically updated to advertise and promote the companies and their business and improve customer perception and search engine rankings.

These highly dynamic scenarios challenge all technologies aimed at discovery, retrieval and management of web content and in particular search engines. In fact, to avoid wasting resources, reduce bandwidth usage and server load and keep web pages fresh, these technologies need to adjust their crawling policies according to the dynamics of the websites [4,15]. Hence, it is necessary to derive accurate predictions of the frequency and extent of website changes.

The problem of predicting the future behavior of a phenomenon based on its past behavior can be addressed under different perspectives [18]. In this paper we investigate this problem in the framework of time series analysis – a popular method used for modeling and making forecasts of temporal data. More precisely, we present a general methodological approach for studying the dynamics of any phenomenon that can be described by a time series. In fact, even though time series analysis and forecasting techniques are well defined, their application requires particular care. Our approach tries to overcome this issue by addressing time series analysis as a sequence of steps dealing with the characterization of the overall statistical properties of the time series, the identification of the underlying patterns describing its behavior, the formulation of suitable models and finally the use of these models for predicting the future behavior. Moreover, we include in the framework a novel approach for accurately detecting and modeling the spiky patterns that might be present in a time series.

As an application of the proposed approach, we investigate the dynamics of the Reuters news agency website[1]. Nevertheless, we outline that this approach is general enough and can be easily applied to study and predict the dynamics of various types of web services and applications (e.g., content delivery, video streaming, mobile apps and embedded ads) as well as of the traffic they generate.

In this paper we focus on the analysis of the time series representing the patterns of page uploads. In fact, for news websites these patterns are usually characterized by a time-dependent behavior with well defined periodicity and large fluctuations. Hence, to predict future uploads from past uploads, it is critical to identify models that accurately explain these behaviors.

We summarize our contributions as follows:

– definition of a methodological framework for time series analysis and forecasting,

---

[1] http://www.reuters.com

- identification and modeling of spiky/bursty patterns, and
- application of the proposed approach to study the dynamics of the Reuters news agency website.

The layout of this paper is the following: Sect. 2 reviews the state of the art, while Sect. 3 presents the methodological approach proposed for time series analysis and forecasting. The dataset considered in the study and the results of the analysis and prediction of the dynamics of the Reuters website are addressed in Sects. 4 and 5, respectively. Section 6 summarizes the paper and outlines possible research directions.

2   Related Work

The problem of estimating and predicting web dynamics has been studied under different – although complementary – angles. Some works specifically focused on the changes of individual web pages (see, e.g., [1,13,17,20,22]), while others studied the overall evolution of websites (see, e.g., [3,5–10]). These works have important implications on content reuse and caching and more generally on information retrieval technologies.

In the framework of page changes, the extensive analysis presented by Fetterly et al. [13] suggests that changes of web pages are somehow correlated, thus future changes can be easily predicted from past changes. Similarly, Shi et al. [22] outline that within news and e-commerce websites, objects are characterized by different freshness times with most objects that do not change within the timescale of a week and fewer objects that change within the timescale of a day.

Lim et al. [17] analyze and quantify consecutive changes of individual pages by means of two measures, namely, distance and clusteredness measures. Their study shows that in general changes are small and rather clustered. A similar approach has been applied in [5] to assess the extent of page changes and adjust the models of change rates of the websites accordingly. Measures, such as edit distance, cosine coefficient of similarity, are used for this purpose.

Content change prediction is addressed by Radinsky and Bennet [20] through an expert predictive framework that takes into account various features, such as degree and relationships among changes and similarity in the types of changes. A temporal modeling framework that captures the dynamic nature of Web behaviors is presented in [21]. The proposed models include the typical characteristics observed in query and URL click behavior of Web searchers, that is, trend, periodicity and surprise disruptions.

The temporal patterns of the content changes of three major news webites have been studied in [8]. The patterns of each website are represented as periodic time series whose models explain their dynamics and are the basis for the forecasting.

Yang and Leskovec [23] investigate the temporal patterns associated with online textual content by formulating a time series clustering problem that allows the identification of the shapes characterizing different types of media.

The problem of predicting the time between changes of web pages under blind sampling is addressed by Li et al. [16]. A stochastic modeling framework where updates and sampling follow independent point processes is proposed.

An interesting survey on different approaches applied for quantifying changes and predicting their frequency and dynamics is provided by Oita and Senellart [19].

In this work, we address the problem of modeling and predicting the dynamics of web content changes by devising a systematic methodological framework based on time series analysis. This framework is general and can be easily applied for investigating the characteristics of any temporal data and make forecasts.

3   Methodological Framework

A time series is a sequence of discrete or continuous observations collected at equally spaced time intervals, i.e., $\{Y_t\} = \{y_{t_1}, y_{t_2}, ..., y_{t_N}\}$ with $t_1 \leq t_2 \leq ... \leq t_N$ [14]. As already pointed out, although the techniques for time series analysis and forecasting are well defined, for a proper application of these techniques it is necessary to define a systematic methodological approach.

The workflow of Fig. 1 summarizes the methodological framework proposed in this paper. Starting from the background knowledge of the phenomenon being investigated and from the raw data transformed into a time series, it is necessary to gain some preliminary insights into the behavior of this time series through an exploratory data analysis (EDA) of its temporal patterns. In particular, from the statistical properties of the time series it is possible to explain the inherent structure that has to be modeled. These models are then used to make forecasts. The details of each of these steps are presented in what follows.

3.1   Exploratory Data Analysis

The exploratory analysis of the data is an important step for understanding the overall behavior and the statistical properties of the time series under investigation. Visualization and statistical techniques work for this purpose.

More precisely, the exploratory analysis includes the computation of descriptive statistics, such as mean, percentiles, autocorrelations. In particular, the autocorrelation function at varying time lags is particularly useful in the analysis of a time series since it suggests how similar a sequence is to its previous values. Moreover, autocorrelations allow for checking the randomness of the data and assessing the stationarity of the time series.

In addition, visualization techniques are applied to obtain an overview of the temporal patterns of the time series (see Fig. 2). Their visual inspection highlights recognizable patterns, such as trend, seasonal or cyclic. The trend denotes steadily increasing or decreasing patterns over quite long periods of time. The seasonality denotes a behavior that repeats in time on a regular basis over a fixed period, e.g., each month, each year. On the contrary, a cyclic pattern denotes a behavior that repeats over a variable period.

Time series visualization is also very useful for recognizing sudden rises followed by falls in the data. The nature of these spiky or bursty patterns depends on the intrinsic characteristics of the phenomenon described by the time series. They might represent typical behaviors or anomalous behaviors, thus corresponding to potential outliers. We recall that outliers are defined as the observations in the series that are significantly different from the rest of the observations.

Statistical measures, such as median absolute deviation, Z-score, are applied for the identification of outliers and more generally of spiky patterns.

All these patterns must be treated with particular caution since they might affect the time series analysis and have negative effects on its models. In general, once the patterns have been identified, a good practice is to remove the corresponding observations from the data and replace them with observations obtained by interpolation over neighbor observations. Nevertheless, as we will

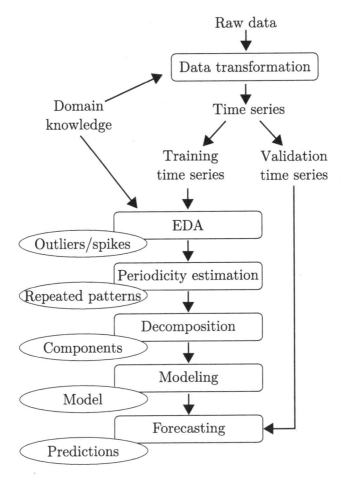

Fig. 1. Methodological framework for time series analysis and forecasting.

discuss in Sect. 3.3, the presence of typical spiky patterns has to be properly included in the final model of the time series.

3.2 Periodicity Estimation

The detection of periodic behaviors in a time series is another important step toward time series modeling. Hence, the periods – usually not known a priori – have to be accurately estimated.

Spectral analysis is a popular method used for this purpose. This is because this method characterizes the frequency representation of a signal. Peaks in the frequency domain will correspond to periods in the time domain. Thus, by analyzing peaks and finding the dominant frequencies, it is possible to estimate the periods of the repeated temporal patterns.

More precisely, the spectral analysis applied to the autocorrelation function of the time series relies on the computation of the discrete Fourier coefficients f_k associated with the k/T frequencies, that is:

$$f_k = \sum_{j=0}^{N-1} y_{t_j} e^{-i2\pi \frac{j}{N}k} , \; k = 0, 1, 2, ..., N-1.$$

The power spectrum density – represented by the absolute value of each Fourier coefficient – highlights the peaks in the spectrum of the autocorrelation function.

3.3 Decomposition

Time series decomposition is primarily applied to better understand its properties, exploring its behavior over time and improve forecasts. In general, a time series exhibits a huge variety of patterns whose classification is at the basis of the decomposition. In fact, the components have to correspond to the underlying pattern categories.

A classical decomposition approach of a time series relies on an additive model that includes deterministic parts, e.g., the trend and seasonal components, and stochastic parts, e.g., the irregular component corresponding to the random noise. Hence, the time series Y_t is given by $Y_t = T_t + S_t + \epsilon_t$, where T_t, S_t and ϵ_t denote the trend, seasonal and irregular components, respectively.

Depending on the characteristics of the time series, smoothing techniques, such as moving average, exponential smoothing, locally weighted polynomial regression, Loess regression, are applied for identifying these components [11].

The estimation of the deterministic components is obtained by fitting appropriate models to the data, while the estimation of the stochastic component – depending on its statistical dependence and random behavior – relies on techniques, such as moving average, auto regressive, Holt-Winters, Box and Jenkins [2].

Another important step proposed in this methodology to improve the forecasts is aimed at including in the final model of the time series the contribution of the spiky patterns identified by the exploratory data analysis (see Sect. 3.1). For this purpose, it is necessary to detect and model the temporal behavior of these patterns. In particular, classifiers (e.g., decision trees, logistic regression) applied to some short term historical data of the time series allow for predicting spikes. By fitting these models, we estimate the probability associated with a future observation being a spike. Moreover, these patterns – depending on their behavior – are described by simple models, such as split, tailing, fronting. The time series final model is then adjusted by adding the contribution of the model chosen to represent the patterns.

3.4   Forecasting

The final step of the methodological framework deals with making forecasts using the models previously identified. This step is rather straightforward. In fact, the predicted value of the time series $\hat{Y}_{t+h}$ at time $t+h$ is obtained by superimposing the values predicted by these models. In detail, for the deterministic components, the new values are extrapolated from the corresponding models computed at time $t+h$. On the contrary, approaches, such as the Box-Jenkins approach, are applied to compute the forecasts of the stochastic component, while the forecasts of the spiky patterns rely on classification techniques applied to short term historical data.

The evaluation of the performance of the forecasts at varying time lags h is based on standard measures of accuracy (e.g., mean error, mean absolute deviation, mean absolute percent error, mean squared error and its square root).

4   Dataset

To test our methodological approach, we analyzed the temporal patterns of the uploads of new pages on the Reuters news agency website over one year. In what follows we describe the dataset considered in this study and its main characteristics.

4.1   Description

The dataset relies on a publicly available unofficial Reuters dataset[2] that stores information about the archival time of the web pages together with their title – referred to as news title in what follows – and the corresponding URL. From this huge dataset – that spans several years from 2007 until 2016 – we extracted the data of 50 weeks since January 4, 2015 that refers to 893,905 pages.

Before applying our methodology, we applied some preliminary transformations to this raw data (see Fig. 1). In particular, since we were interested in modeling and predicting the dynamics of the upload process of new pages rather than their archival process – which is usually of little interest for search engines and similar technologies – it was necessary to adjust the timestamps associated with the pages. For this purpose, we crawled the Reuters website – using the URLs stored in the dataset – to discover the actual publish time of the web

---

[2] https://github.com/philipperemy/Reuters-full-data-set

pages. In detail, to avoid overloading the website, we applied this process to a sample of 13,546 pages, that is, about 1.5% of the pages. For each of them, we extracted the `og:article:published_time` metadata tag[3] used to specify when the page was first published. We discovered that a page is archived on average 19.65 hours after its upload. As expected, the archival process is rather deterministic: the corresponding standard deviation is only 0.47. Hence, by subtracting this average from the archival time, we obtained an accurate estimation of the publish time – used in what follows to describe the upload process.

Another step of the data transformation process deals with approximately 30,000 news titles including the keyword "UPDATE". A manual inspection of a sample of the corresponding pages has shown that these pages were updated once or multiple times after their first upload. Hence, not to mix the upload and update processes, we discarded these observations. The resulting dataset consists of the data of 864,304 pages.

4.2 Characteristics

The exploratory analysis of the data is aimed at gaining some preliminary insights into the time series describing the behavior of the page upload process and into the content of the news titles. We first characterized the dynamics of the website in terms of number of page uploads per day. Figure 2 shows the temporal patterns of this time series over the 50 weeks analyzed in this study. We notice large fluctuations, where the number of uploads per day ranges from 206 up to 4,822 and it is much lower during weekends with respect to weekdays. On average about 3,300 pages are uploaded during a weekday, whereas only about 355 during weekend days (see Table 1 for the details).

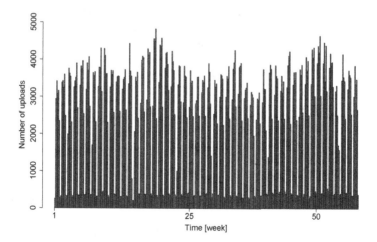

Fig. 2. Temporal patterns of the time series representing the number of uploads per day over 50 weeks.

---

[3] http://ogp.me/

Table 1. Basic statistics of the number of uploads per day broken down for weekdays and weekend days.

	Mean	St. dev	Min	Max
Weekdays	3,315.15	681.9	790	4,822
Weekend days	355.16	53.6	206	540
Overall	2,469.44	1,458	206	4,822

The analysis of the number of uploads at a finer granularity, i.e. per hour, confirms these findings, namely, big differences between weekdays and weekend days (see Fig. 3). This was expected since the Reuters website is mainly focused on business and financial news.

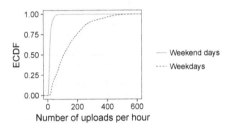

Fig. 3. Cumulative distribution function of the number of page uploads per hour for weekdays and for weekend days. (Color figure online)

An overview of the temporal patterns of the time series over three weeks is shown in Fig. 4. The figure clearly suggests diurnal patterns characterized by sudden spikes with as many as 500 uploads in an hour. We outline that the values of approximately 10% of the observations of the overall time series exceed 250, while only 1% exceed 450.

This spiky behavior is also highlighted in the boxplot of Fig. 5 showing the number of uploads per hour for each day of the week across all weeks. In general, Tuesdays are characterized by the largest variability. Moreover, the website is more active during the mid days of the week.

This characterization, together with the business-oriented focus of the news published on the Reuters website, has suggested that the dynamics of the website is mainly relevant during weekdays. Hence, the time series analysis addresses the page upload dynamics over weekdays only. We analyze the data of 828,788 pages – accounting for approximately 96% of the data.

Another interesting aspect considered in the exploratory data analysis deals with news titles. Although this analysis is not strictly related to the dynamics of the website, it provides some insights in the content of the news. In particular, we analyzed these titles in terms of the words they consist of, i.e., the single units of textual information (tokens).

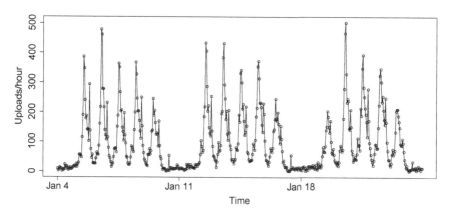

Fig. 4. Temporal patterns of the number of uploads per hour over three weeks.

The number of words per title does not significantly vary: 62% of the titles consist of a number of words between 8 and 13. On average a title includes 10.91 words with a standard deviation of 4.38 words.

To avoid redundancy, inflectional and related forms of a word, we applied Natural Language Processing (NLP) techniques, such as tokenization, stop words removal and stemming [12]. After this process, we obtained 124,914 unique stems (out of 319,165 unique word). The distribution of the popularity of the top 30 stems is shown in Fig. 6. These stems account for 950,736 occurrences, that correspond to 13.4% of the total number of occurrences. In particular, the most popular stem, i.e., *announc* occurs 86,104 times. As expected, most of the stems are related to the financial domain.

Additionally we performed topic modeling in order to extract topics from news titles. For this purpose we applied a graphical probabilistic model, namely, Latent Dirichlet Allocation (LDA) to the titles of the pages uploaded over three weeks – starting May 4, 2015. We labeled each title with the most relevant topic identified by the LDA. For example, it is interesting to point out that by considering three topics, news titles are subdivided into three sets including 32%, 38% and 30% of the pages. The temporal patterns of the number of page uploads per hour subdivided according to these topics is shown in Fig. 7. As can be seen – even though the page published during weekend days mainly refer to one topic – in general the website is characterized by a mix of pages covering different topics that does not depend on the time of the day and the day of the week.

5   Results

In this section, we present the results of the analysis of the time series referring to 250 weekdays, namely, a "training" time series consisting of 5,400 observations

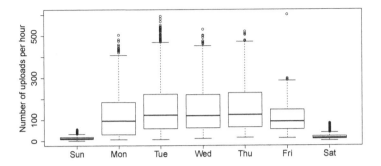

Fig. 5. Boxplot of the number of page uploads per hour for each day of the week.

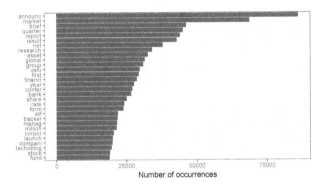

Fig. 6. Popularity of the top 30 stems appearing in the news titles.

– referring to the uploads per hour over 225 consecutive days – and a "validation" time series consisting of 600 observations – referring to the uploads of the
remaining 25 days.

As previously discussed, the upload patterns exhibit large variability across
days, hours and even weeks (see Fig. 4). To further investigate the properties
of these temporal patterns, we analyze in the lag plots of Fig. 8 the overall
behavior of time series to assess whether there is any autocorrelation structure.
The observations tend to group around the diagonal for small time lags, thus
exhibiting a positive autocorrelation. On the contrary, for larger time lags the
observations are more scattered.

The patterns of the autocorrelation function with time lags from one to
120 hours (i.e., five days) – summarized in Fig. 9(a) – clearly suggest a periodic behavior of the uploads. All values fall outside the 95% confidence bands
highlighted in the diagram by dashed lines. Similarly, the power spectrum of the
autocorrelation function shown in Fig. 9(b) confirms that the time series exhibits
a certain periodicity. More precisely, the peak at frequency $24/T$ indicates the
presence of a daily periodicity. This finding will be used for the identification of
the deterministic components of the time series.

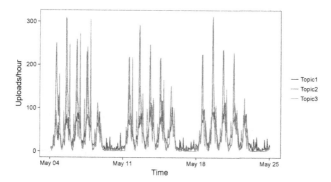

Fig. 7. Temporal patterns of the number of uploads per hour subdivided according to the topics identified by LDA. (Color figure online)

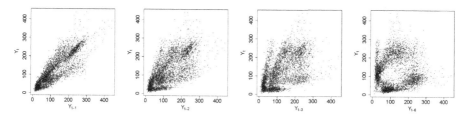

Fig. 8. Lag plots of the time series at varying time lags, i.e., 1, 2, 3 and 6.

As outlined in Sect. 3.3, the decomposition of the time series into deterministic, i.e., trend and seasonal, and stochastic, i.e., irregular, parts relies on an additive approach. In detail, we applied the Loess method to estimate the trend and seasonal components, while the irregular component corresponds to the remainder of the time series.

An example of the decomposition of the time series representing the upload patterns over five days is shown in Fig. 10. Note that we applied the decomposition to the "adjusted" time series where the spikes previously identified have been replaced with observations obtained by interpolation over neighbor observations.

Because of the characteristics of the deterministic components, we selected their models in the family of trigonometric polynomials and we applied least square techniques to fit the models to the data. In details, the model identified for the trend component is a trigonometric polynomial of degree four with eight parameters including the intercept. The seasonal component is modeled by a trigonometric polynomial of degree one with two parameters. On the contrary, the best fit of the irregular component is represented by an ARMA model $(1, 2) \times (1, 0)_{24}$.

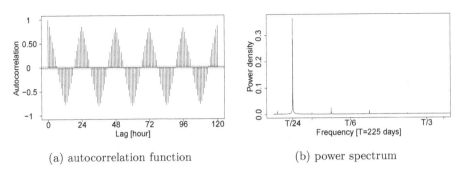

(a) autocorrelation function   (b) power spectrum

Fig. 9. Autocorrelation function of the time series computed for time lags ranging from one to 120 h (a) and corresponding power spectrum (b).

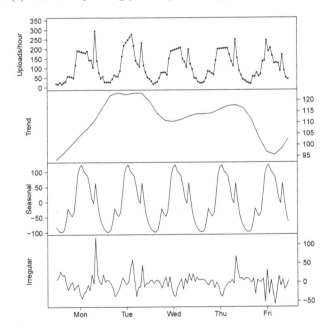

Fig. 10. Temporal patterns of the time series over five days and decomposition into trend, seasonal and irregular components. The labels on the x axis are centered at 12 noon.

Since the final model has to include the contribution of the spiky patterns previously identified, we applied a logistic regression to predict whether the observation y_t corresponds to a spike. In particular, the model takes into account the time t together with y_{t-1} and the difference between y_{t-1} and y_{t-2}.

An example of the overall model of the time series over ten days is shown in Fig. 11. We notice that the model accurately fits the data even though – because of their peculiarities – some of the spikes have not been precisely captured. The root mean squared error computed over the entire "training" time series is equal to 40.1.

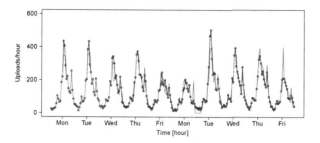

Fig. 11. Overall model (red curve) of the upload patterns (represented by circles) over ten days. The labels on the x axis are centered at 12 noon. (Color figure online)

The final model is used for making forecasts of the future dynamics of the website. For this purpose, we used the "validation" time series consisting of the observations over 25 days. More precisely, we extrapolate the trigonometric polynomials that best fit the trend and seasonal components of the time series, while the predictions of the irregular component rely on the Box-Jenkins approach. The logistic regression model previously identified has been used to predict the spiky patterns. Figure 12 shows an example of the predictions over ten days with a time horizon h equal to one hour.

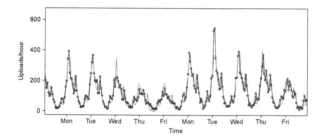

Fig. 12. Predictions of the upload patterns over ten days with a time horizon of one hour. The red curve refers to the predictions, the circles to data. The labels on the x axis are centered at 12 noon. (Color figure online)

We outline that our methodological approach has several advantages with respect to other approaches (e.g., Holt-Winters, Seasonal ARIMA, Recurrent Neural Networks). In details, the periodicity estimation and the identification of the underlying patterns (e.g., spiky patterns) are very useful for understanding and exploring the properties of the time series and improving forecasts. For example, sophisticated methods, such as RNNs, do not provide any insights in the temporal patterns. In addition, their application is usually computationally intensive and requires large training datasets. Similarly, SARIMA models do not break down the contributions of the underlying patterns of the time series. On the contrary, even though Holt-Winters models take into account trend and seasonal components, they describe these components in terms of a sequence of coefficients and smoothing equations.

6   Conclusions

The web is a large information ecosystem where content changes over time as a consequence of combined effects involving the management policies of the websites, the behavior of the users and external events. These dynamics challenge technologies aimed at content management and retrieval.

Time series analysis is a valid and well defined method to model and predict the behavior of temporal data. Nevertheless, its application requires particular care. In this paper we proposed a general methodological framework for time series analysis and forecasting that specifically addresses the estimation of the its periodicity, the detection and modeling of the spikes and the decomposition of the time series into its underlying patterns.

The methodology has been applied to investigate and predict the dynamics of the Reuters news agency website. The page upload process of this website is characterized by a diurnal pattern and a much larger number of uploads during weekdays with respect to weekend days. Moreover, this process exhibits several sudden spikes. From the analysis of the content of the news titles we observed that the pages published on the website cover different topics that do not depend on the time of the day and on day of the week.

The individual components of the time series have been independently modeled and these models have then been used for making forecasts.

We outline that the proposed methodological approach – although tested in this paper in the framework of web dynamics – is general enough and can be applied to model and predict the behavior of any phenomenon represented as a time series.

As a future work, we plan to investigate the dynamics of the access patterns of web robots and identify differences and similarities between the patterns of good and malicious robots. Another possible research direction is in the area of topic modeling to classify pages and assess the relationships between web dynamics and the topics being addressed.

References

1. Adar, E., Teevan, J., Dumais, S.T., Elsas, J.: The web changes everything: understanding the dynamics of web content. In: Proceedings of the 2nd ACM International Conference on Web Search and Data Mining - WSDM 2009, pp. 282–291. ACM (2009)
2. Box, G.E.P., Jenkins, G.M., Reinsel, G.C., Ljung, G.M.: Time Series Analysis: Forecasting and Control, 5th edn. Wiley, Hoboken (2015)
3. Brewington, B., Cybenko, G.: How dynamic is the web? Comput. Netw. **33**(1–6), 257–276 (2000)
4. Calzarossa, M., Massari, L., Tessera, D.: Workload characterization: a survey revisited. ACM Comput. Surv. **48**(3), 48:1–48:43 (2016)

5. Calzarossa, M., Tessera, D.: Characterization of the evolution of a news Web site. J. Syst. Softw. **81**(12), 2236–2344 (2008)
6. Calzarossa, M., Tessera, D.: Time series analysis of the dynamics of news websites. In: Proceedings of the 13th International Conference on Parallel and Distributed Computing, Applications and Technologies - PDCAT 2012, pp. 529–533. IEEE Computer Society Press (2012)
7. Calzarossa, M., Tessera, D.: Multivariate analysis of web content changes. In: Proceedings of the 11th ACS/IEEE International Conference on Computer Systems and Applications - AICCSA 2014, pp. 699–706. IEEE Computer Society Press (2014)
8. Calzarossa, M., Tessera, D.: Modeling and predicting temporal patterns of web content changes. J. Netw. Comput. Appl. **56**, 115–123 (2015)
9. Calzarossa, M., Tessera, D.: Analysis and forecasting of web content dynamics. In: Proceedings of the 32nd International Conference on Advanced Information Networking and Applications Workshops - WAINA 2018, pp. 12–17. IEEE Computer Society Press (2018)
10. Cho, J., Garcia-Molina, H.: Estimating frequency of change. ACM Trans. Internet Technol. **3**(3), 256–290 (2003)
11. Cleveland, R., Cleveland, W., McRae, J., Terpenning, I.: STL: a seasonal-trend decomposition procedure based on loess (with discussion). J. Official Stat. **6**, 3–73 (1990)
12. Collobert, R., Weston, J., Bottou, L., Karlen, M., Kavukcuoglu, K., Kuksa, P.: Natural language processing (almost) from scratch. J. Mach. Learn. Res. **12**, 2493–2537 (2011)
13. Fetterly, D., Manasse, M., Najork, M., Wiener, J.: A large-scale study of the evolution of Web pages. Softw.: Pract. Experience **34**(2), 213–237 (2004)
14. Hamilton, J.D.: Time Series Analysis. Princeton University Press, Princeton (1994)
15. Ke, Y., Deng, L., Ng, W., Lee, D.L.: Web dynamics and their ramifications for the development of web search engines. Comput. Netw. **50**(10), 1430–1447 (2006)
16. Li, X., Cline, D.B.H., Loguinov, D.: Temporal update dynamics under blind sampling. IEEE/ACM Trans. Networking **25**(1), 363–376 (2017)
17. Lim, L., Wang, M., Padmanabhan, S., Vitter, J.S., Agarwal, R.: Characterizing web document change. In: Wang, X.S., Yu, G., Lu, H. (eds.) Advances in Web-Age Information Management - WAIM 2001. LNCS, vol. 2118, pp. 133–144. Springer, Heidelberg (2001). https://doi.org/10.1007/3-540-47714-4_13
18. Makridakis, S., Wheelwright, S.C., Hyndman, R.J.: Forecasting - Methods and Applications, 3rd edn. Wiley, Hoboken (1998)
19. Oita, M., Senellart, P.: Deriving dynamics of web pages: a survey. In: Proceedings of the 1st International Temporal Workshop on Web Archiving - In Conjunction with WWW 2011, pp. 25–32 (2011)
20. Radinsky, K., Bennett, P.: Predicting content change on the web. In: Proceedings of the 6th ACM International Conference on Web Search and Data Mining - WSDM 2013, pp. 415–424. ACM (2013)
21. Radinsky, K., et al.: Behavioral dynamics on the web: learning, modeling, and prediction. ACM Trans. Inf. Syst. **31**(3), 16:1–16:37 (2013)
22. Shi, W., Collins, E., Karamcheti, V.: Modeling object characteristics of dynamic Web content. J. Parallel Distrib. Comput. **63**(10), 963–980 (2003)
23. Yang, J., Leskovec, J.: Patterns of temporal variation in online media. In: Proceedings of the 4th ACM International Conference on Web Search and Data Mining - WSDM 2011, pp. 177–186. ACM (2011)

Static and Dynamic Group Migration Algorithms of Virtual Machines to Reduce Energy Consumption of a Server Cluster

Dilawaer Duolikun[1,3]($\boxtimes$), Tomoya Enokido[2,3], and Makoto Takizawa[1,3]

[1] Graduate School of Science and Engineering, Hosei University, Tokyo, Japan
dilewerdolkun@gmail.com
[2] Faculty of Business Administration, Rissho University, Tokyo, Japan
eno@ris.ac.jp
[3] Faculty of Science and Engineering, Hosei University, Tokyo, Japan
makoto.takizawa@computer.org

Abstract. In prevent global warming, it is critical to reduce electric energy consumed in information systems, especially servers in clusters like cloud computing systems. In this paper, a process migration approach is discussed to reduce the total energy consumption of clusters by using virtual machines. We propose a pair of the static $SM(v)$ and dynamic $DM(v)$ migration algorithms where a group of at most v (≥ 0) virtual machines migrate from a host server to a guest server. A group of virtual machines on a host server to migrate to a guest server are selected so that the total energy to be consumed by the host and guest servers can be reduced. In the $SM(v)$ algorithm, the total number of virtual machines is fixed in a cluster. In the $DM(v)$ algorithm, virtual machines are resumed and suspended so that the number of processes on each virtual machine is kept fewer. In the evaluation, we show the total energy consumption of servers can be mostly reduced in the $DM(v)$ algorithm compared with other algorithms.

Keywords: Energy-efficient computation ·
Dynamic virtual machine migration ·
Static virtual machine migration ·
Group migration of virtual machines · $DM(v)$ algorithm ·
$SM(v)$ algorithm

1 Introduction

In order to prevent global warming, electric energy consumed in information systems has to decrease to reduce carbon dioxide emission [10]. Information systems are getting more scalable like cloud computing systems [23] and IoT (Internet of Things) [20,22] and especially servers consume huge amount of electric energy. In order to discuss how to reduce energy consumption of servers, a formal model is needed to estimate how much electric power [W] a server consumes to perform

© Springer-Verlag GmbH Germany, part of Springer Nature 2019
N. T. Nguyen et al. (Eds.): TCCI XXXIII, LNCS 11610, pp. 144–166, 2019.
https://doi.org/10.1007/978-3-662-59540-4_8

application processes. Power consumption and computation models [11–16] are proposed to estimate the total power consumption of a whole server to perform application processes and the execution time of each application process. Based on the power consumption and computation models, the electric energy to be consumed by a server to perform application processes is able to be estimated. Types of algorithms [12–14, 17] are proposed to select a server to perform an application process issued by a client. In the SLEA (simple locally energy-aware) algorithm [16], a host server is selected, which is expected to consume minimum energy in a cluster. In the SGEA (simple globally energy-aware) algorithm [17], a host server is selected, where total energy to be consumed by not only the host server but also all the other servers is minimum. Total energy consumed by servers is more reduced in the SGEA algorithm than the SLEA algorithm [17]. A process migration approach [2–7, 25] is also proposed where a process on a host server migrates to a guest server if total energy to be consumed by the host and guest servers can be reduced. It is not easy to migrate types of processes among servers, especially heterogeneous servers with different architectures and operating systems. Clusters of servers recently support applications with virtual machines like KVM [1]. Processes can easily migrate among types of servers by migrating a virtual machine where the processes are performed [1].

In our previous studies, static and dynamic migration algorithms are proposed to energy-efficiently migrate virtual machines with application processes among servers [4, 8, 9]. In the static migration algorithm [4], a cluster supports applications with the fixed number of virtual machines. The size of a virtual machine means the number of application processes performed on the virtual machine. If a virtual machine with application processes migrates from a host server to a guest server, the number of application processes on the host and guest servers decreases and increases, respectively. This means, the host and guest servers consume less and more energy, respectively. A virtual machine gets larger as processes are issued. If a virtual machine on the host server gets too large, a guest server may not be found. Hence, each virtual machine has to be kept so small that the virtual machine can migrate to another server any time.

Dynamic migration algorithms [8, 9] are proposed where virtual machines are resumed and suspended as the number of application processes increases and decreases, respectively. In addition, one virtual machine migrates from a host server to a guest server. Each virtual machine can be smaller even if more number of application processes are performed in a cluster. In another dynamic algorithm [9], a group of multiple virtual machines migrate from a host server to a guest server. Here, it is shown the energy consumption of servers and the average execution time of processes can be reduced by migrating virtual machines.

In this paper, a group of multiple virtual machines in parallel migrate from a host server to a guest server. We have to estimate energy to be consumed by servers to perform application processes based on the power consumption and computation models. In order to make the estimation simple, the total amount of computation of each application process is assumed to be the same and to finish. Furthermore, the amount of computation to be performed by each application process is assumed to depend on the number of application processes concurrently performed. That is, the more number of application processes are performed on a server, the more amount of computation to be performed by each application process. We propose an algorithm to estimate energy to be consumed by servers based on the assumption. By using the estimation model, we propose a pair of dynamic DM(v) and static SM(v) group migration algorithms where a group of at most v (≥ 0) virtual machines migrate from a host server to a guest server so that the total energy to be consumed by the host and guest servers can be reduced. In the SM(v) algorithm, a set of virtual machines is fixed in a cluster. On the other hand, a set of virtual machines is dynamically changed by resuming and suspending virtual machines in the DM(v) algorithm. Here, the SM(*) and DM(*) algorithms means, as many number of virtual machines as possible migrate from a host server to a guest server. In the evaluation, the total energy consumption of servers and the average execution time of application processes can be mostly reduced in the DM(*) algorithm compared with other algorithms.

In Sect. 2, we present a system model. In Sect. 3, we discuss the power consumption and computation models. In Sect. 4, we propose the SM(v) and DM(v) algorithms. In Sect. 5, we evaluate the SM(v) and DM(v) algorithms.

2   System Model

2.1   Servers and Virtual Machines in Clusters

An application process is issued to the cluster S of servers $s_1, \ldots, s_m$ ($m \geq 1$). One server s_t is selected and the application process is performed on the server s_t. There are types of application processes like computation, communication, and storage processes [13]. In this paper, a *process* means which is an application process which uses CPU resources.

Each server s_t is equipped with np_t (≥ 1) homogeneous CPUs. Each CPU includes cc_t (≥ 1) cores, each of which supports processes with ct_t (≥ 1) threads. Thus, a server s_t supports the total number nt_t ($= np_t \cdot cc_t \cdot ct_t$) of threads on nc_t ($= np_t \cdot cc_t$) cores. Processes on different threads are performed independently of one another. A thread is *active* if and only if (iff) at least one process is performed, otherwise *idle*. A process performed on a server is *active*. $CP_t(\tau)$ is a set of active processes on a server s_t at time τ.

A cluster supports applications with virtual resources like CPUs and storages on servers through virtual machines. We assume each process is performed on some virtual machine vm_h and no process is directly performed on a server. The size $|vm_h|$ of a virtual machine vm_h shows the number of active processes on the virtual machine vm_h. A virtual machine vm_h is *smaller* than another virtual machine vm_k ($vm_h < vm_k$) iff $|vm_h| < |vm_k|$. A pair of virtual machines vm_h and vm_k are equivalent ($vm_h \equiv vm_k$) iff $|vm_h| = |vm_k|$. $vm_h \leq vm_k$ iff $vm_h < vm_k$ or $vm_h \equiv vm_k$. A virtual machine can migrate on a host server to a guest server in the live migration [1]. In this paper, we assume every virtual machine can migrate to any server anytime, i.e. memory image of each virtual machine *a priori* exits on every server.

We consider four states of a virtual machine, *dormant*, *ready*, *active*, and *idle*. Any process can be neither performed nor issued to a *dormant* virtual machine. Each dormant virtual machine is first created on some server s_t. Here, DVM_t shows a collection of dormant virtual machines on a server s_t. By resuming a dormant virtual machine, the virtual machine transits to *ready* state. Processes can be issued to a ready virtual machine. A ready virtual machine is *active* if a least one process is active. A ready virtual machine which is not active is *idle* where a processes can be issued but no process is active. By suspending an idle virtual machine, the virtual machine transits to dormant. VM_t is a set of ready virtual machines on a server s_t. In this paper, we assume enough number of dormant virtual machines are supported by each server so that a virtual machine can be resumed anytime.

A server is *engaged* iff at least one ready virtual machine resides. A server is *free*, *active*, and *idle* if there are no ready virtual machine, at least one active virtual machine, and only idle virtual machine, respectively.

2.2   Migration of Virtual Machines

A virtual machine vm_h can migrate without terminating processes on the virtual machine vm_h in the live manner [1]. If an instruction of a process is executed on a virtual machine vm_h, the memory pages of the virtual machine vm_h are changed. On issuing a migration command "**virsh** migrate −live *dsvm* qemu+ssh://*destinationURL*/system" [1] to a host server s_t, the memory pages of the virtual machine vm_h are first transferred to the guest server s_u. While the memory pages are transferred to the server s_u, processes are performed on the virtual machine vm_h. This means, some memory pages are changed by performing instructions of the processes, which are referred to as *dirty*. If the transmission of the virtual machine vm_h finishes, the dirty pages changed by the processes are transferred. During the transmission of dirty pages, processes on the virtual machine are suspended. Once the dirty pages are transferred to the server s_u, the processes on the virtual machine vm_h are resumed. The duration the processes are suspended is the *migration time* of the virtual machine vm_h. The migration time depends on the size of dirty pages and the transmission rate of the network.

We measure the migration time of a virtual machine vm_h between a pair of homogeneous servers s_t and s_u. The servers s_t and s_u are homogeneous with the same architectures, i.e. the same CPU Intel Core i5-8400, 8 [GB] memory, and 1 [TB] HDD and the same operating system CentOS 7.4 [21]. The servers s_t and s_u are interconnected in the 100Mbps LAN. A virtual machine vm_h is realized in KVM [1]. We consider a C process which just uses CPU resource. The virtual machine vm_h is first created on the server s_t. We consider two cases, the virtual machine vm_h does not migrate and migrates as shown in Fig. 1 (1) and (2), respectively. In the second case, the virtual machine vm_h migrates between the servers s_t and s_u and finally migrates back to the server s_t. After the process p starts on the virtual machine vm_h at time st, a migration command is issued to the server s_t and the virtual machine vm_h migrates to the server s_u. After some computation of process p is performed on the virtual machine vm_h, a migration command is issued to the server s_u. After the virtual machine vm_h backs to the server s_t, the process p terminates at time et. We measure a pair of the starting time st and ending time et of the process p by using the clock of the server s_t. In Fig. 1, a pair of time st_1 and et_1 and a pair of time st_2 and et_2 show pairs of starting and ending time of the process p in non-migration and migration cases, respectively. Let tt_1 be the execution time $et_1 - st_1$ for non-migration case and tt_2 be $et_2 - st_2$ for the migration case. The migration time mt is given as $(tt_2 - tt_1)/2$. Here, the memory size of the virtual machine vm_h is 1 [GB]. In Fig. 2, the migration time for $l_t = 1$ shows mt, where mt is about 4 [s]. In this paper, the migration time of each virtual machine is assumed to be constant mt for every pair of the servers. This means, each virtual machine has the same size of the virtual memory.

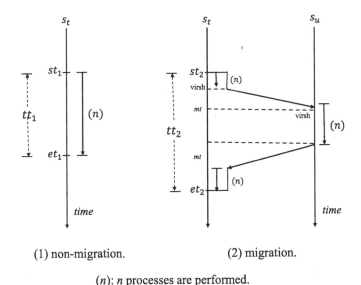

(1) non-migration.   (2) migration.

(n): n processes are performed.

Fig. 1. Measurement of migration time.

Next, we consider case a group GV_t of multiple virtual machines $vm_{t1} \dots vm_{tl_t}$ ($l_t \geq 1$) migrate from the host server s_t to the other guest server s_u. We consider serial and parallel ways to migrate the group GV_t. In the serial migration way, one virtual machine vm_{tk} migrates after a virtual machine $vm_{t,k-1}$ finishes to migrate. One virtual machine at a time migrates. In the parallel migration way, the l_t (≥ 1) virtual machines $vm_{t1} \dots vm_{tl_t}$ in parallel migrate from the server s_t to the server s_u. Figure 2 shows the migration time mt_{tu} for number l_t of virtual machines which migrate from the server s_t to the server s_u. The migration time linearly increases as number l_t of virtual machines increases. The parallel migration time is about 20% shorter than the serial one as shown in Fig. 2. Hence, we take the parallel way to migrate multiple virtual machines

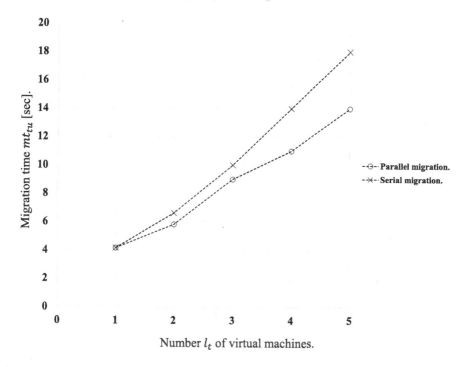

Fig. 2. Migration time of virtual machines.

$vm_{t1}, \ldots, vm_{tl_t}$ on a server s_t to a guest server s_u. Let $mgt(l_t)$ show the migration time [sec] of l_t virtual machines from a host server s_t to a guest server s_u. The migration time $mgt(l_t)$ is given as follows:

$$mgt(l_t) = mt + \beta \cdot (l_t - 1) = (mt - \beta) + \beta \cdot l_t. \tag{1}$$

In Fig. 2, $mt = 4$ and $\beta = 25$. Hence, $mgt(l_t) = 1.5 + 2.5 \cdot l_t$ [sec].

3   Energy Consumption of a Server

3.1   Power Consumption and Computation Models

In our macro-level approach [12], we consider total electric power [W] consumed by a whole server to perform application processes and do not consider how much power each hardware device like CPU consumes. We assume processes are fairly allocated with CPUs, cores, and threads in each server [19]. A power consumption model of a server s_t gives power to be consumed by the server s_t to perform processes. In the SPC (simple power consumption) model [14], the power consumption $NE_t(n)$ [W] of a server s_t to perform n processes is $minE_t + ad_t(n) \cdot sE_t$. Here, $ad_t(n) = 1$ if $n > 0$, else 0. An active and idle server s_t consumes the maximum power $maxE_t = minE_t + sE_t$ [W] and the minimum power $minE_t$ [W], respectively. The SPC model holds for a server with a one-core CPU.

In the MLPCM (multi-level power consumption) model [17,18], the power consumption $NE_t(n)$ is $minE_t + nap_t(n) \cdot bE_t + nac_t(n) \cdot cE_t + nat_t(n) \cdot tE_t$. Here, $nap_t(n) = n$ if $n \leq np_t$, else np_t. $nac_t(n) = n$ if $n \leq nc_t$, else nc_t, and $nat_t(n) = n$ if $n \leq nt_t$, else nt_t. A server s_t consumes the maximum electric power $maxE_t = minE_t + np_t \cdot bE_t + nc_t \cdot cE_t + nt_t \cdot tE_t$ if every thread is active. For example, if two and three processes are performed, $NE_t(2) = minE_t + 2 \cdot bE_t + 2 \cdot nc_t + 2 \cdot tE_t$ and $NE_t(3) = minE_t + 2 \cdot bE_t + 3 \cdot nc_t + 3 \cdot tE_t$, respectively, for a server with dual CPUs. An idle server s_t consumes the minimum power $minE_t$ [W]. The MLPCM model holds for a server with multiple CPUs.

The electric power $E_t(\tau)$ of a server s_t to perform processes at time τ is assumed to be $NE_t(|CP_t(\tau)|)$ in this paper, where $CP_t(\tau)$ is a set of active processes on the server s_t at time τ. Energy consumed by a server s_t from time st [tu (time unit)] to time et is defined to be $\sum_{\tau=st}^{et} NE_t(|CP_t(\tau)|)$ [Wtu].

If only a process p_i is performed on a server s_t without any other process, the execution time T_{ti} [tu] of the process p_i is shortest, $T_{ti} = minT_{ti}$. A *fastest* server s_f is a server where $minT_{fi} \leq minT_{ti}$ for every server s_t. $minT_i$ stands for $minT_{fi}$. One virtual computation step [vs] is assumed to be performed on a thread of the fastest server s_f for one time unit [tu] [14,16]. This means, the thread computation rate TCR_f of a fastest server s_f is one [vs/tu]. For each server s_t, $TCR_t \leq TCR_f$ $(=1)$. The total number VC_i [vs] of virtual computation steps of a process p_i is defined to be $minT_i$ [tu] $\cdot TCR_f$ [vs/tu] $= minT_i$ [vs] since $TCR_f = 1$ for a fastest server s_f. Thus, $minT_i$ shows the total number of virtual computation steps to be performed in a process p_i. If only one process p_i is performed without any other process on a thread of a server s_t, the maximum number $maxPCR_{ti}$ of virtual computation steps of the process p_i are performed for one time unit. The maximum process computation rate $maxPCR_{ti}$ of a process p_i on a server s_t is $VC_i/minT_{ti} = minT_i/minT_{ti}$ [vs/tu] (≤ 1). On a fastest server s_f, $maxPCR_{fi} = TCR_f = 1$. For every pair of processes p_i and p_j on a server s_t, $maxPCR_{ti} = maxPCR_{tj} = TCR_t$ (≤ 1) [16]. The server computation rate $SCR_t(\tau)$ of a server s_t at time τ is $at_t(\tau) \cdot TCR_t$ where $at_t(\tau)$ $(\leq nt_t)$ is the number of active threads. The maximum server computation rate $maxSCR_t$ is $nt_t \cdot TCR_t$. Here, $at_t(\tau)$ is assumed to be $nat_t(n)$ for number n $(=|CP_t(\tau)|)$ of active processes on the server s_t.

In the SC (simple computation) model [14], the server computation rate $NSR_t(n)$ [vs/tu] of a server s_t to perform n current processes is the maximum server computation rate $maxSCR_t$, i.e. TCR_t. The SC model holds for a server with a one-core CPU.

A server with multi-core CPUs follows the MLCM (multi-level computation) model [15]. Here, n processes are performed on a server s_t at the server computation rate $NSR_t(n)$ [vs/tu]:

$$NSR_t(n) = \begin{cases} n \cdot TCR_t & \text{if } n \leq nt_t. \\ maxSCR_t(= nt_t \cdot TCR_t) & \text{if } n > nt_t. \end{cases} \tag{2}$$

Each process p_i is performed at rate $NPR_{ti}(n) = NSR_t(n)/n$ ($\leq TCR_t$) [vs/tu] on a server s_t. Hence, $NPR_{ti}(n) = NPR_{tj}(n) = NPR_t(n)$ for every pair of processes p_i and p_j. In the SC model, $NPR_{ti}(n) = maxSCR_t/n = TCR_t/n$. In the MLCM model, $NPR_t(n) = TCR_t$ for $n \leq nt_t$, $NPR_t(n) = nt_t \cdot TCR_t/n$ for $n > nt_t$.

The server computation rate $SCR_t(\tau)$ [vs/tu] of a server s_t at time τ is assumed to be $NSR_t(n)$ for $n = |CP_t(\tau)|$. The process computation rate $PCR_{ti}(\tau)$ [vs/tu] of each process p_i on the server s_t at time τ is $SCR_t(\tau)/n = NSR_t(n)/n$ ($=NPR_{ti}(n)$).

Suppose a process p_i on a server s_t starts at time st and ends at time et. Here, the total number VC_i of virtual computation steps of the process p_i is given as follows $VC_i = \sum_{\tau=st}^{et} NPR_{ti}(|CP_t(\tau)|) = minT_i$ [vs].

[Computation model of a process p_i]. At each time τ, a process p_i is performed on a server s_t as follows:

1. If the process p_i starts and gets active on the server s_t, the variable plc_i is VC_i [vs].
2. Let n_t be number of active processes on the server s_t, i.e. $n_t = |CP_t(\tau)|$.
3. If the process p_i is active, plc_i is decremented by the process computation rate $NPR_{ti}(|n_t|) = NPR_t(|n_t|)$.
4. Then, the process p_i terminates if $plc_i \leq 0$.

3.2 Estimation Models

In order to select a server where a new process to be performed and where a virtual machine to migrate, the execution time ET_i of each process p_i has to be estimated. It is not easy to *a priori* the total number VC_i of virtual computation steps of each process. Hence, we assume every process p_i has to perform the same number VC_i of virtual computation steps. Then, VC_i is assumed to be one.

The total number of virtual computation steps to be performed by n_t active processes on a server s_t is $\alpha_t(n_t) \cdot n_t$. In this paper, the function $\alpha_t(n_t)$ is given for number nt_t of threads as follows:

$$\alpha_t(n_t) = \begin{cases} 0.5 & \text{for } n_t \leq nt_t. \\ 0.6 & \text{for } nt_t < n_t \leq 2 \cdot nt_t. \\ 0.8 & \text{for } 2 \cdot nt_t < n_t \leq 4 \cdot nt_t. \\ 1 & \text{for } n_t > 4 \cdot nt_t. \end{cases} \tag{3}$$

For example, $\alpha_t(n_t) \cdot n_t = 0.8 \cdot 4 \cdot nt_t = 3.2 \cdot nt_t$ for $n_t = 4 \cdot nt_t$. The more number of active processes, the more number of virtual computation steps each active process has to perform.

Suppose k processes newly start on a server s_t where n_t processes are active. Here, k new processes are composed of k steps according to the assumption. The total number $\alpha_t(n_t) \cdot n_t$ of virtual computation steps are performed by the n_t current processes. It takes $(\alpha_t(n_t) \cdot n_t + k)/NSR_t(n_t + k)$ time units [tu] to perform $(\alpha_t(n_t) \cdot n_t + k)$ virtual computation steps of $(n_t + k)$ processes.

Hence, the expected termination time $SET_t(n_t, k)$ [tu] and expected energy consumption $SEE_t(n_t, k)$ [W tu] of each server s_t to perform both n_t current processes and k new processes are given as follows:

1 $SET_t(n_t, k) = (\alpha_t(n_t) \cdot n_t + k)/NSR_t(n_t + k)$ [tu].

2 $SEE_t(n_t, k) = SET_t(n_t, k) \cdot NE_t(n_t + k)$
   $= (\alpha_t(n_t) \cdot n_t + k) \cdot NE_t(n_t + k)/NSR_t(n_t + k)$ [Wtu].

We consider a pair of servers s_t and s_u where there are n_t (≥ 0) and n_u (≥ 0) processes performed, respectively. A group GV_u of v (≥ 1) virtual machines start migrating from the host server s_u to the server s_t at time τ. Here, totally tnv_u processes are active on the v virtual machines in the group GV_u. The migration time mt_{ut} to migrate v virtual machines is $mgt(v) = mt + \beta \cdot (v - 1)$. Every process on each virtual machine is suspended from time τ to time $\tau + mt_{ut}$. The tnv_u processes on the virtual machines are resumed on the server s_t at time mt_{ut}. As discussed, every current process terminates on the server s_t by time $\tau + ET_t(=SET_t(n_t, 0)) + \tau$ if neither any virtual machine migrates to the server s_t nor a new process starts after time τ. First, suppose $mt_{ut} \leq ET_t$. Here, not only n_t current processes but also tnv_u processes in the group GV_u are performed after time $\tau + mt_{ut}$. The hatched area in Fig. 3(1) shows the energy consumption of the server s_t. Here, $\alpha_t(n_t) \cdot n_t \cdot (mt_{ut}/ET_t)$ and $\alpha_t(n_t) \cdot n_t \cdot (1 - mt_{ut}/ET_t)$ virtual computation steps are so far performed and have to be still performed, respectively, in the n_t current processes. $\alpha_u(n_u) \cdot tnv_u$ virtual computation steps have to be performed in tnv_u processes. Here, it still takes $((1 - mt_{ut}/ET_t) \cdot \alpha_t(n_t) \cdot n_t + \alpha_u(n_u) \cdot tnv_u/NSR_t(n_t + tnv_u)$ [tu] to perform n_t current processes and tnv_u processes on the server s_t. Hence, it takes $NT_t = mt_{ut} + ((1 - mt_{ut}/ET_t) \cdot \alpha_t(n_t) \cdot n_t + \alpha_u(n_u) \cdot tnv_u)/NSR_t(n_t + tnv_u)$ [tu] to migrate the virtual machine group GV_u to the server s_t. Here, the energy $NE_t(n_t) \cdot mt_{ut} + NE_t(n_t + tnv_u) \cdot (NT_t - mt_{ut})$ [Wtu] is consumed by the server s_t.

Next, suppose $mt_{ut} > ET_t$. Here, n_t current processes of the server s_t terminate before tnv_u processes in the group GV_u start on the server s_t at time $\tau + mt_{ut}$. The hatched area in Fig. 3(2) shows energy to be consumed by the server s_t. Only tnv_u processes are performed from time $\tau + mt_{ut}$ to time NT_t $(=mt_{ut} + \alpha_u(n_u) \cdot tnv_u/NSR_t(tnv_u))$. Here, the energy $NE_t(n_t) \cdot ET_t + minE_t \cdot (mt_{ut} - ET_t) + NE_t(tnv_u) \cdot (NT_t - mt_{ut})$ [Wtu] is consumed by the server s_t.

Thus, the expected termination time $MET_t(n_t, tnv_u)$ and expected energy consumption $MEE_t(n_t, tnv_u)$ of a server s_t to which tnv_u processes on a group GV_u of virtual machines migrate from a server s_u are given as follows, where $ET_t = SET_t(n_t, 0)$:

$$MET_t(n_t, tnv_u) = \begin{cases} mt_{ut} + ((1 - mt_{ut}/ET_t) \cdot \alpha_t(n_t) \cdot n_t \\ + \alpha_u(n_u) \cdot tnv_u)/NSR_t(n_t + tnv_u) \text{ if } ET_t > mt_{ut}. \quad (4) \\ mt_{ut} + (\alpha_u(n_u) \cdot tnv_u)/NSR_t(tnv_u) \textbf{ otherwise.} \end{cases}$$

$$MEE_t(n_t, tnv_u) = \begin{cases} mt_{ut} \cdot NE_t(n_t) \\ + (MTE_t(n_t, tnv_u) - mt_{ut}) \cdot NE_t(n_t + tnv_u) \\ \qquad \text{if } ET_t > mt_{ut}. \\ ET_t \cdot NE_t(n_t) + minE_t \cdot (mt_{ut} - ET_t) \\ + (MTE_t(n_t, tnv_u) - ET_t) \cdot NE_t(tnv_u) \text{ otherwise.} \end{cases} \quad (5)$$

Since the $(n_u - tnv_u)$ processes are performed on the server s_u after the group GV_u of virtual machines migrate to the server s_t, the energy $SEE_u(n_u - tnv_u, 0)$ is consumed by the server s_u. It takes $SET_u(n_u - tnv_u, 0)$ time units [tu] to perform $(n_u - tnv_u)$ processes on the server s_u. Let NE_t and NE_u be $MEE_t(n_t, tnv_u)$ and $SEE_u(n_u - tnv_u, 0)$, respectively. Let NT_t and NT_u be $MET_t(n_t, tnv_u)$ and $SET_u(n_t - tnv_u, 0)$, respectively. The total energy $TE_{ut}(n_t, n_u, tnv_u)$ to be consumed by the servers s_t and s_u to perform every current process is given by the following function $TEE(NE_t, NT_t, minE_t, NE_u, NT_u, minE_u)$ [3]:

$$TEE(ET, TT, MT, EU, TU, MU) = \begin{cases} ET + EU + (TT - TU)MU \text{ if } TT \geq TU. \\ ET + EU + (TU - TT)MT \text{ if } TT < TU. \end{cases} \quad (6)$$

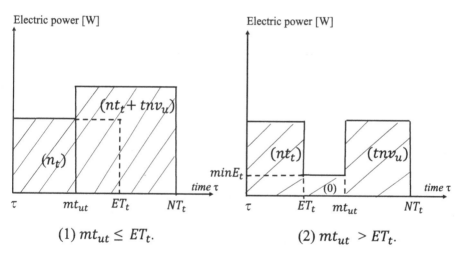

(1) $mt_{ut} \leq ET_t$.   (2) $mt_{ut} > ET_t$.

(n): number n of processes performed.

Fig. 3. Electric energy consumption MEE_t of a server s_t.

4   Group Migration Algorithms

4.1   Selection of a Virtual Machine

We consider a cluster S of servers $s_1, \ldots, s_m$ ($m \geq 1$). Let VM be a set of ready virtual machines in the cluster S. Let VM_t ($\subseteq VM$) show a set of ready virtual machines on each server s_t. $VM_t = VM_1 \cup \ldots \cup VM_m$. Let n_t and nv_h be numbers of active processes on a server s_t and a virtual machine vm_h, respectively. We propose a pair of static and dynamic types of migration algorithms. In the static migration algorithms [24,25], the total number nv (≥ 1) of virtual machines $vm_1, \ldots, vm_{nv}$ is invariant, i.e. $VM = \{vm_1, \ldots, vm_{nv}\}$. Each virtual machine vm_h is deployed on some server s_t. The set VM_t is changed each time a virtual machine migrates to and from the server s_t.

In the dynamic migration algorithms [6,7,9], virtual machines are resumed and suspended as the number of processes increases and decreases, respectively. There is initially no ready virtual machine and every virtual machine is dormant on some server, i.e. $VM_t = \phi$ for every server s_t and $VM = \phi$. DVM_t is a set of dormant virtual machines on each server s_t. If a dormant virtual machine vm_h is resumed on a server s_t, the virtual machine vm_h gets ready and is included in the variable VM_t. If a ready virtual machine vm_h is suspended, the virtual machine vm_h gets dormant. Here, vm_h moves from VM_t to DVM_t. We assume each server s_t supports enough number of dormant virtual machines in the set DVM_t so that dormant virtual machines can be resumed anytime.

Suppose a process p_i is issued to a cluster S. In the static virtual machine migration (SVM) algorithm [Algorithm 1], one ready virtual machine vm_h is selected to perform the new process p_i.

Algorithm 1. Static VM (SVM) selection

Input : p_i = a new process issued by a client;
Output: s_t = server;
           vm_h = a virtual machine on the server s_t;
1 **select** a host server s_t where $SEE_t(n_t, 1)$ is minimum;
2 **select** a smallest virtual machine vm_h in VM_t on the server s_t;

As written in paper [24], the execution time of each process depends on the total number of active processes but is independent of the number of virtual machines on a host sever. In the dynamic virtual machine migration (DVM) algorithm [Algorithm 2], each virtual machine is kept smaller than $maxNVM_t$ even if the number of active processes increases in a cluster. If $nv_h < maxNVM_t$, a smallest ready virtual machine vm_h is selected in the set VM_t. Otherwise, a dormant virtual machine vm_h in the set DVM_t is resumed on the server s_t. Then, the process p_i is issued to the virtual machine vm_h.

In order to reduce the number of idle virtual machines, each engaged server s_t is periodically checked and idle virtual machines are suspended in the VMS algorithm [Algorithm 3].

Algorithm 2. Dynamic virtual machine (DVM) selection

Input : p_i = new process;
Output: s_t = server;
         vm_h = virtual machine on a server s_t;

1 **select** a host server s_t where $SEE_t(n_t, 1)$ is minimum;
2 **if** $VM_t = \phi$, /* the server s_t is not engaged;   */
3 **then**
4 | **resume** a dormant virtual machine vm_h in the pool DVM_t of s_t;
5 **else**
6 | **if** $n_t \, / \, |VM_t| \leq maxNVM_t$; **then**
7 | | **select** a smallest ready virtual machine vm_h in the set VM_t;
8 | **else**
9 | | **resume** a dormant virtual machine vm_h in the pool DVM_t.

Algorithm 3. Virtual machine suspension (VMS)

Input: s_t =a server s_t;

1 **if** $|VM_t| > 1$, **then**
2 | **while** *there is an idle virtual machine and* $n_t/(|VM_t| - 1) < maxNVM_t$
    | **do**
3 | | **select** one idle virtual machine vm_h in VM_t;
4 | | **suspend** the virtual machine vm_h;
5 **else**

4.2   Group Migration of Virtual Machines

Next, we discuss how to migrate a group GV_t of virtual machines on host server s_t to a guest server s_u. Here, active virtual machines in the set $VM_t = \{vm_{t1}, \ldots, vm_{tv_t}\}$ $(v_t \geq 0)$ on the server s_t are ordered in terms of size as $vm_{t1} \leq \ldots \leq vm_{tv_t}$.

At most v $(\leq |VM_t|)$ a active virtual machines on a server s_t and a guest server s_u are selected in a group virtual machine migration $GVM_t(v)$ algorithm [Algorithm 4]. First, suppose no virtual machine on a host server s_t migrates. Here, only n_u active processes are to be performed on each server s_u. For each server s_u $(u = 1, \ldots, m)$, the expected energy consumption $EE_u = SEE_u(n_u, 0)$ and termination time $ET_u = SET_u(n_u, 0)$ are calculated. The total energy CEE_{tu} to be consumed by a pair of the host server s_t and every other server s_u is given by the function TEE (EE_t, ET_t, $minE_t$, EE_u, ET_u, $minE_u$).

Next, suppose a group GV_t of virtual machines on the host server s_t migrate to another server. We have to find a guest server s_u and a group GV_t of virtual machines on the host server s_t. The total energy consumption NEE_{tu} of the host server s_t is obtained for each possible guest server s_u. First, a smallest active virtual machine vm_{t1} is taken on the host server s_t. Here, the number nv $(=nv_{t1})$ of processes migrate as the virtual machine vm_{t1} migrates from the server s_t

---

Algorithm 4. Group virtual machine migration $GVM_t(v)$ on a server s_t

---

Input : s_t = hoset server;
    v = maximum number of virtual machines to migrate from s_t;
Output: s = guest server;
    GV_t = set of virtual machines to migrate from s_t to s;

1 $EE_t = SEE_t(n_t, 0)$; /* energy to perform n_t processes on s_t */
2 $ET_t = SET_t(n_t, 0)$; /* execution time on s_t */
3 **for** each server s_u ($\neq s_t$),
    /* n_u = number of current processes of s_u */
4 **do**
5     $EE_u = SEE_u(n_u, 0)$;
6     $ET_u = SET_u(n_u, 0)$;
7     $CEE_{tu} = TEE(EE_t, ET_t, minE_t, EE_u, ET_u, minE_u)$;
      /* total energy consumption of s_t and s_u */

8 $nv = 0$; $NEE = \infty$; $s = NULL$; $GV_t = \phi$;
9 **if** $v = *$ or $x \geq v_t$ **then**
10    $x = v_t$;
11 **else**
12   **if** $v < v_t$;
13   **then**
14      $x = v$;
15   **else**

16 $i = 0$;
17 **while** $i \leq x$ **do**
18    $i = i + 1$;
19   **if** $nv_{ti} > 0$, /* vm_{ti} is active   */
20   **then**
21      $nv = nv + nv_{ti}$;
      /* total number of processes on vm_{t1}, ..., vm_{ti} */
      /* nv processes migrate from s_t to s_u */
22      $NE_t = SEE_t(n_t - nv, 0)$;
23      $NT_t = SET_t(n_t - nv, 0)$;
24   **else**
25   break;
26   **for** each server s_u ($\neq s_t$) /* vm_{t1}, ..., vm_{ti} to migrate to s_u */
27   **do**
28      $NE_{tu} = MEE_u(n_u, nv)$;
29      $NT_{tu} = MET_u(n_u, nv_h)$;
30      $NEE_{tu} = TEE(NE_t, NT_t, minE_t, NE_u, NT_{tu}, minE_u)$;
31   **if** $NEE_{tu} < CEE_{tu}$ and $NEE_{tu} < NEE$,
      /* energy can be reduced by taking s_u as a guest server   */
32   **then**
33        $NEE = NEE_{tu}$; $s = s_u$;
34        $GV_t = GV_t \cup \{vm_{ti}\}$; /* vm_{ti} is selected   */
35   **else**

36 **if** $s \neq NULL$, /* guest server is found   */
37 **then**
38   **migrate** virtual machines in GV_t from s_t to s;
39 **else**

---

to another server. The host server s_t is expected to consume energy $NE_t = SEE_t(n_t - nv, 0)$ by time $NT_t = SET_t(nt - nv, 0)$. Here, since nv processes leave the host server s_t, the expected energy consumption NE_t is smaller than EE_t and $NT_t < ET_t$. nv processes migrate to a guest server s_u. Here, the server s_u consumes energy $NE_{tu} = MEE_u(n_u, nv)$ by time $NT_{tu} = MTE_u(nv, nv_h)$. Since nv processes on the virtual machine vm_{ti} are additionally performed on the server s_u, $NE_{tu} > EE_u$ and $NT_{tu} > ET_u$. Total energy NEE_{tu}^1 to be consumed by the servers s_t and s_u is $TEE(NE_t, NT_t, minE_t, NE_{tu}, NT_{tu}, minE_u)$. If $CEE_{tu} > NEE_{tu}^1$, the virtual machine vm_{t1} can migrate from the host server s_t to the server s_u because the total energy consumption of the servers s_t and s_u can be reduced. The virtual machine vm_{t1} is included in the set GV_t, i.e. $GV_t = \{vm_{t1}\}$. $NEE = NEE_{tu}^1$ and $s = s_u$. If $CEE_u \leq NEE_{tu}^1$, the $GVM_t(v)$ algorithm terminates, no virtual machine migrates from the server s_t.

Secondly, the virtual machine vm_{t1} and a next smallest active virtual machine vm_{t2} are candidates to migrate from the host server s_t to another guest server s_u. Here, there are totally nv $(=nv_{t1} + nv_{t2})$ processes to migrate. For each server s_u $(s_u \neq s_t)$, $NE_{tu} = MEE_u(n_u, nv_{t1} + nv_{t2})$ and $ET_{tu} = MTE_u(n_u, n_v)$. NEE_{tu}^2 is also calculated by using the function $TEE(NE_t, NT_t, minE_t, NE_{tu}, NT_{tu}, minE_u)$. A guest server s_u to migrate the virtual machines vm_{t1} and vm_{t2} is found where the total energy NEE_{tu}^2 is minimum as discussed in the first virtual machine vm_{t1}. If $CEE_{tu} \leq NEE_{tu}^2$ or $NEE_{tu} \leq NEE_{tu}^2$, the $GVM_t(v)$ algorithm terminates and only one virtual machine vm_{t1} in the set GV_t migrates. Otherwise, $NEE = NEE_{tu}^2$, $GV_t = \{vm_{t1}, vm_{t2}\}$, and $s = s_u$. Then, a third smallest active virtual machine vm_{t3} is a candidate in addition to the virtual machines vm_{t1} and vm_{t2}. Now, nv $(=nv_{t1} + nv_{t2} + nv_{t3})$ processes migrate. For each server s_u, NEE_{tu} is calculated. Unless $NEE_{tu}^3 < CEE_{tu}$ and $NEE_{tu}^3 < NEE_{tu}$ for every server s_u, $GV_t = \{vm_{t1}, vm_{t2}\}$ and a pair of virtual machines vm_{t1} and vm_{t2} migrate to the server s. Otherwise, three virtual machines vm_{t1}, vm_{t2}, and vm_{t3} can migrate. A server s_u whose NEE_{tu}^3 is minimum is a possible guest server, i.e. $s = s_u$, $NE = NEE_{tu}^3$. Here, $GV_t = \{vm_{t1}, vm_{t2}, vm_{t3}\}$.

Thus, these steps are iterated. Then, a group GV_t of the v virtual machines migrate to a guest server s_u. Here, totally nv processes on the active virtual machines in the set GV_t migrate from the host server s_t to the guest server s. In the $GVM_t(*)$ algorithm, as many number of virtual machines as possible migrate from the host server s_t to the guest server s.

4.3   Migration Algorithms

The static $SM(v)$ and dynamic $DM(v)$ migration algorithms are composed of selection and migration procedures. In the first selection procedure, a virtual machine is selected to perform a new process issued by a client. In the $SM(v)$ and $DM(v)$ algorithms, a virtual machine is selected in the SVM and DVM algorithms, respectively. In the $DM(v)$ algorithm, a dormant virtual machine on a server s_t may be resumed and selected depending on the size of each exiting virtual machine.

In the second one, a group GV_t of virtual machines migrate from the host server s_t to another server. The second procedure is periodically performed on each engaged server s_t. For each server s_t, a group GV_t of virtual machines on the server s_t and a host server s_u to which the virtual machines in the set GV_t migrate are selected in the GVM_t algorithm.

The SM(v) and DM(v) algorithms are shown in Algorithms 5 and 6, respectively.

Algorithm 5. Static migration SM(v) algorithm

---

1 A virtual machine vm_h on a host server s_t is selected to perform the process p_i by using the SVM selection algorithm. Then, the process p_i is performed on the virtual machine vm_h.

2 For each server s_t, a group GV_t of active virtual machines on the host server s_t and a guest server s_u are periodically selected in the $GVM_t(v)$ algorithm. The group GV_t of active virtual machines migrate from the host server s_t to the guest server s_u if found.

Algorithm 6. Dynamic migration DM(v) algorithm

---

1 A virtual machine vm_h on a host server s_t is selected to perform the process p_i by using the DVM selection algorithm. The process p_i is performed on the virtual machine vm_h.

2 For each server s_t, a group GV_t of active virtual machines on the host server s_t and a guest server s_u are periodically selected in the $GVM_t(v)$ algorithm. The group GV_t of active virtual machines migrate from the host server s_t to the guest server s_u if found.

3 For each server s_t, the VMS algorithm is periodically performed to suspend idle virtual machines.

---

5   Evaluation

5.1   Environment

In this paper, the static SM(v) and dynamic DM(v) group migration algorithms are proposed. In the simulation, the algorithms are evaluated by measuring the total electric energy consumption TEE [Wtu] and total active time TAT [tu] of servers $s_1, \ldots, s_m$ ($m \geq 1$) and the average execution time AET [tu] of processes $p_1, \ldots, p_n$ ($n \geq 1$). The $SM(v)$ and $DM(v)$ algorithms compared with the non-migration type, random (RD), round robin (RR), and SGEA [16] algorithms. We consider four servers $s_1, \ldots, s_4$ ($m = 4$) in our laboratory, whose parameters on power consumption and performance are shown in Table 2. In the static migration SM(1) and SM(*) algorithms and the non-migration RD, RR, and SGEA algorithms, VM is a set of sixteen virtual machines

$vm_1, \ldots, vm_{16}$ ($nv = 16$). Each server s_t initially provides four virtual machines, i.e. $|VM_t| = |VM|/m = 16/4 = 4$. That is, each server s_t provides four virtual machines vm_t, vm_{t+4}, vm_{t+8}, and vm_{t+12}.

In the RD algorithm, one virtual machine is randomly selected. In the RR algorithm, a virtual machine is selected after a virtual machine vm_{h-1}. In the SGEA algorithm, a host server s_t is selected so that the total energy consumption of all the servers is minimized. Then, the process p_i is performed on a smallest virtual machine of the selected server s_t. In the SM(1), SM(*), DM(1), and DM(*) algorithms, the migration time mt_{tu} of v virtual machines between every pair of servers s_t and s_u is given by the function $mgt(v) = 2.5v - 0.5$. In the dynamic DM(1) and DM(*) algorithms, there is initially no virtual machine on each server s_t, i.e. $VM_t = \phi$. Idle virtual machines are resumed and ready virtual machines are suspended depending on number of active processes on the virtual machines in the VMS algorithm. Here, $maxNVM_t = 10$. In the SM(1) and DM(1) algorithms, only one virtual machine migrates from a host server to a guest server. On the other hand, a group of multiple virtual machines migrate from a host server to a guest server in the SM(*) and DM(*) algorithms. Each engaged server is checked every $\sigma = 5$ time units in the $GVM_t(v)$ algorithm. A group GV_t of virtual machines and a guest server s_u are selected and the group GV_t migrate from the server s_t to the server s_u.

Table 1. Starting time of processes.

$stime_i$	Number of processes
$0 \leq\; < 17 \cdot xtime/80$	$n/8$
$17 \cdot xtime/80 \leq\; < 19 \cdot xtime/80$	$n/8$
$19 \cdot xtime/80 \leq\; < 20 \cdot xtime/80$	$n/2$
$xtime/4 \leq\; < 11 \cdot xtime/40$	$n/8$
$11 \cdot xtime/40 \leq\; < xtime$	$n/8$

One time unit [tu] is assumed to be 100 [ms] in the simulation. Processes $p_1, \ldots, p_n$ ($n \geq 1$) are randomly issued to the cluster S. This means, the total number VC_i of virtual computation steps of each process p_i is randomly taken from 15 to 25 [tu]. The starting time $stime_i$ of each process p_i is also randomly decided between 0 and $xtime - 1$ as shown in Table 1. In the evaluation, $xtime$ is 1,000 [tu]. For example, the half $n/2$ of n processes randomly start at time $19 \cdot xtime/80$ to $xtime/4$. In the simulation, the ending time $etime_i$ of each process p_i is obtained. The execution time ET_i of each process p_i is $etime_i - stime_i + 1$. The simulation ends at time $etime$ when every process terminates, $etime = max(etime_1, \ldots, etime_2)$. Eight process configurations $PF_{n1}, \ldots, PF_{n8}$ are randomly generated for each number n of processes.

There are variables pl_i, VC_i, $stime_i$, and $etime_i$ for each process p_i. The variable $stime_i$ and VC_i are randomly decided in each process configuration PF_{ng} as presented here. For each process configuration PF_{ng}, the simulation is done by the simulation algorithms shown in Algorithm 7. A variable CP_t stands for a set of active processes on a server s_t. Variables EE_t and AT_t denote the energy consumption [Wtu] and active time [tu] of each server s_t, respectively. A variable EE shows the total energy consumed by the servers $s_1, \ldots, s_4$. A variable n_t denotes number of active processes on a server s_t. ET_i denotes the execution time of each process p_i and ET indicates the total execution time of n processes. Initially, time $\tau = 0$, $ET_i = 0$ for each process p_i, and $EE_t = AT_t = 0$ for each server s_t. At each time τ, if a process p_i starts, i.e. $stime_i = \tau$, a server s_t and a virtual machine vm_h on the server s_t are selected in one of the algorithms, e.g. DM(*). Here, $CP_t = CP_t \cup \{p_i\}$. The variable EE_t is incremented by the power consumption $NE_t(n_t) - minE_t$ [W] for number n_t ($=|CP_t|$) of active processes on the server s_t at each time τ. The variable AT_t is incremented by one if $n_t > 0$. Then, if a process p_i terminates on a server s_t at time τ, $ET_i = \tau - stime_i + 1$. Time τ is incremented by one. These steps are iterated until every process terminates.

When the simulation ends, EE_t shows the total energy [Wtu] consumed by each server s_t and AT_t stands for the total active time [tu] of each server s_t. The total energy consumption TEE of the servers is $EE_1 + EE_2 + EE_3 + EE_4$. The variable TET indicates the total execution time of n processes, i.e. $ET_1 + \ldots + ET_n$. The average execution time AET of each process is TET/n.

5.2   Evaluation Results

For each number n of processes, eight process configurations $PF_{n1}, \ldots, PF_{n8}$ are randomly generated. For each process configuration PF_{ng}, the total energy consumption TEE and total active time TAT of the four servers and the total execution time of n processes are obtained in the simulation. Then, the average values of TEE, TAT, and TET are calculated for the eight process configurations $PF_{n1}, \ldots, PF_{n8}$.

Figure 4 shows the total energy consumption $TEE = EE_1 + \ldots + EE_4$ [Wtu] of the servers $s_1, \ldots, s_4$ for number n of processes. The total energy consumption TEE of the RD algorithm is almost the same as the RR algorithm. In the SM(1) and DM(1) algorithms, the servers consume more energy than the SGEA algorithm. In the SGEA algorithm, each process p_i is issued to a virtual machine on a server s_t where the expected energy consumption of not only the host server s_t but also the other servers is minimum. In addition, the virtual machine does not migrate. The total energy consumption TEE of the SGEA algorithm is smaller than the half of the total energy consumption TEE of the RR and RD algorithms. In the SM(*) and DM(*) algorithms, a group of multiple virtual machines migrate from a host server to a guest server. Here, the total energy consumption TEE of the servers more slowly increases than the other algorithms even if the number n of processes increases. The total energy consumption TEE of the DM(*) algorithm is smaller than the SM(*) algorithm and

---

Algorithm 7. Simulation Algorithm

Input : P = set of processes $p_1, \ldots, p_n$;
Output: TEE = total electric energy consumption;
1   TAT = total active time of server;
2   AET = average execution time of processes;
3 $EE = 0$; $ET = 0$;
4 **for** every process p_i, $state_i$ = Idle;
5 **for** every server s_t,
6      $EE_t = AT_t = 0$;
7      $CP_t = \phi$;
8 $\tau = 0$;
9 **while** *there is some active or idle process* **do**
10   **if** *there is a process p_i where $stime_i = \tau$* **then**
11   **select** vm_h on s_t in one of the algorithms like DM(*);
12          $state_i = Active$; $pl_i = VC_i$;
13          $CP_t = CP_t \cup \{p_i\}$;
14   **else**
15   **for** *each server s_t where $CP_t \neq \phi$* **do**
16          $n_t = |CP_t|$;
           /* number of active processes on s_t */
17          $EE_t = EE_t + NE_t(n_t) - minE_t$;
18          $AT_t = AT_t + 1$;
19          $cr = NSR_t(n_t) / n_t$; /* process computation rate   */
20   **for** *each active process p_i in CP_t* **do**
21              $pl_i = pl_i - cr$;
22   **if** $pl_i \leq 0$ **then**
23                  $state_i = Terminated$;
24                  $etime_i = \tau$;
25                  $ET_i = etime_i - stime_i + 1$;
26                  $CP_t = CP_t - \{p_i\}$;
27   **else**
          /* advance time τ */
28      $\tau = \tau + 1$;
29 $TEE = EE_1 + \ldots + EE_m$;
30 $TAT = AT_1 + \ldots + AT_m$;
31 $AET = ET_1 + \ldots + ET_n$;

---

is smallest in the algorithms. For example, the total energy consumption TEE of the DM(*) algorithm is about 50% of the RD and RR algorithms, 20% of the SM(1) algorithm, 15% of the DM(1) algorithm, and 5% of the SGEA algorithm for $n = 2,000$. The servers consume the smallest energy in the DM(*) algorithm than the other algorithms.

Figure 5 shows the total active time $TAT = AT_1 + \ldots + AT_4$ [tu] of the servers $s_1, \ldots, s_4$ for the number n of processes. The total active time TAT of the RR algorithm is same as the RD algorithm. The total active time TAT of the SGEA algorithm is shorter than the SM(1) and DM(1) algorithms but longer than the SM(*) and DM(*) algorithms. The total active time TAT of the DM(*) algorithm is about 45% of the RD and RR algorithms and about 5 to 10[%] shorter than the SM(*) and SGEA algorithms. This means, the servers are more lightly loaded in the dynamic group migration DM(*) algorithm than the other algorithms.

Figure 6 shows the average execution time AET [tu] of number n of processes. AET is $(ET_1 + \ldots + ET_n)/n = TET/n$. The average execution time AET of processes in the SM(1) and DM(1) algorithms is about 40% smaller than the RR and RD algorithms but is longer than the SGEA, SM(*), and DM(*) algorithms. The average execution time AET of processes in the DM(*) algorithm is the shortest in the algorithms. In the DM(*) algorithm, the average execution time AET of processes is about 5 to 10[%] shorter than the SGEA and SM(*) algorithms.

As shown in Figs. 4, 5 and 6, the total energy consumption TEE and total active time TAT of the servers and the average execution time AET of the processes can be more reduced in the DM(*) and SM(*) algorithms than the other algorithms. Especially, the TEE, TAT, and AET are the smallest in the DM(*) algorithm compared with the other algorithms. This means, the total energy TEE of the servers and the average execution time AET of the processes can be reduced by migrating a group of multiple virtual machines from a host server to a guest server.

Table 2. Parameters of servers.

Parameters	s_1	s_2	s_3	s_4
np_t	2	1	1	1
nc_t	8	8	6	4
nt_t	32	16	12	8
CRT_t [vs/tu]	1.0	1.0	0.5	0.7
$maxCR_t$ [vs/tu]	32	16	6	5.6
$minE_t$ [W]	126.1	126.1	87.2	41.3
$maxE_t$ [W]	301.3	207.3	136.2	89.6
bE_t [W]	30	30	16	15
cE_t [W]	5.6	5.6	3.6	4.7
tE_t [W]	0.8	0.8	0.9	1.1

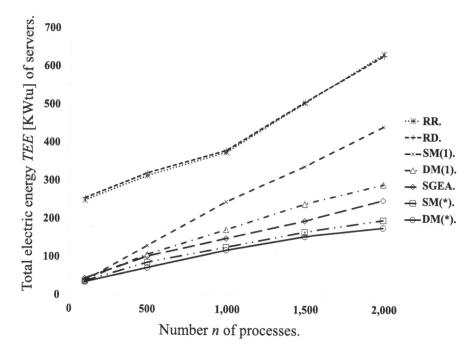

Fig. 4. Total electric energy consumption TEE ($m = 4$, $\sigma = 5$, $maxNVM_t = 10$).

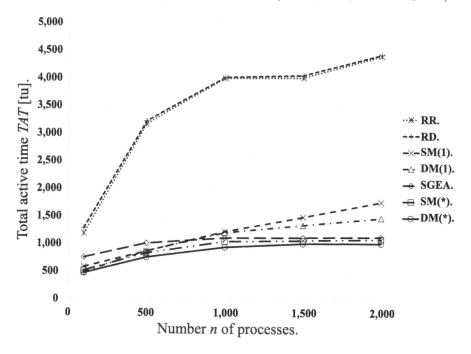

Fig. 5. Total active time TAT ($m = 4$, $\sigma = 5$, $maxNVM_t = 10$).

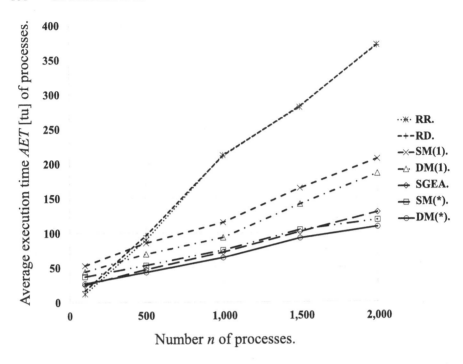

Fig. 6. Average execution time AET of processes ($m = 4$, $\sigma = 5$, $maxNVM_t = 10$).

6   Concluding Remarks

We have to reduce the total energy consumption of information systems to reduce carbon dioxide emission. Especially, clusters of servers are getting scalable like cloud computing systems and servers consume more energy than clients. Hence, it is critical to reduce the energy consumed by servers. In this paper, we discussed the virtual machine migration approach to reducing the electric energy to be consumed by servers to perform application processes. In this paper, we proposed the static migration SM(v) and dynamic migration DM(v) algorithms where a group of at most v virtual machines migrate from a host server to a guest server. In the DM(v) algorithm, virtual machines are dynamically resumed and suspended as the number of active processes increases and decreases, respectively. On the other hand, the number of virtual machines is invariant in a cluster in the SM(v) algorithm. In the evaluation, we showed the total energy consumption and total active time of servers and the average execution time of processes can be mostly reduced in the DM(*) algorithm compared with other algorithms. By migrating multiple virtual machines from a host server to a guest server and dynamically suspending and resuming virtual machines, the total energy consumed by all the servers and the average execution time of processes can be reduced compared with static migration and non-migration algorithms.

Acknowledgement. This work was supported by Japan Society for the Promotion of Science (JSPS) KAKENHI 15H0295 and Grant-in-Aid for JSPS Research Fellow grant 18J10022.

References

1. A virtualization infrastructure for the Linux kernel (kernel-based virtual machine). Kernel-Based Virtual Machine. https://en.wikipedia.org/wiki/
2. Duolikun, D., Enokido, T., Takizawa, M.: An energy-aware algorithm to migrate virtual machines in a server cluster. Int. J. Space Based Situated Comput. **7**(1), 32–42 (2017)
3. Duolikun, D., Nakamura, S., Enokido, T., Takizawa, M.: An energy-efficient dynamic live migration of multiple virtual machines. In: Barolli, L., Kryvinska, N., Enokido, T., Takizawa, M. (eds.) NBiS 2018. LNDECT, vol. 22, pp. 87–98. Springer, Cham (2019). https://doi.org/10.1007/978-3-319-98530-5_8
4. Duolikun, D., Nakamura, S., Watanabe, R., Enokido, T., Takizawa, M.: Energy-aware migration of virtual machines in a cluster. Advances on Broad-Band Wireless Computing, Communication and Applications. LNDECT, vol. 2, pp. 21–32. Springer, Cham (2017). https://doi.org/10.1007/978-3-319-49106-6_3
5. Duolikun, D., Watanabe, R., Enokido, T., Takizawa, M.: A model for migration of virtual machines to reduce electric energy consumption. In: Proceedings of the 19th International Conference on Network-Based Information Systems (NBiS 2016), pp. 50–57 (2016)
6. Duolikun, D., Watanabe, R., Enokido, T., Takizawa, M.: An eco algorithm for dynamic migration of virtual machines in a server cluster. In: Barolli, L., Enokido, T., Takizawa, M. (eds.) NBiS 2017. LNDECT, vol. 7, pp. 42–54. Springer, Cham (2018). https://doi.org/10.1007/978-3-319-65521-5_4
7. Duolikun, D., Watanabe, R., Enokido, T., Takizawa, M.: Energy-aware dynamic migration of virtual machines in a server cluster. In: Barolli, L., Xhafa, F., Conesa, J. (eds.) BWCCA 2017. LNDECT, vol. 12, pp. 161–172. Springer, Cham (2018). https://doi.org/10.1007/978-3-319-69811-3_14
8. Duolikun, D., Watanabe, R., Enokido, T., Takizawa, M.: An eco migration algorithm of virtual machines in a server cluster. In: Proceedings of IEEE the 32nd International Conference on Advanced Information Networking and Applications (AINA 2018), pp. 271–278 (2018)
9. Duolikun, D., Watanabe, R., Enokido, T., Takizawa, M.: Energy-efficient replication and migration of processes in a cluster. In: Proceedings of the 12th International Conference on Complex, Intelligent and Software Intensive Systems (CISIS 2018), pp. 118–125 (2018)
10. Elnozahy, E.N., Kistler, M., Rajamony, R.: Energy-efficient server clusters. Power Aware Comput. Syst. **2325**, 179–197 (2003)
11. Enokido, T., Aikebaier, A., Deen, M., Takizawa, M.: Power consumption-based server selection algorithms for communication-based systems. In: Proceedings of the 13th International Conference on Network-based Information Systems (NBiS 2010), pp. 201–208 (2010)
12. Enokido, T., Aikebaier, A., Takizawa, M.: A model for reducing power consumption in peer-to-peer systems. IEEE Syst. J. **4**(2), 221–229 (2010)
13. Enokido, T., Aikebaier, A., Takizawa, M.: Process allocation algorithms for saving power consumption in peer-to-peer systems. IEEE Trans. Ind. Electron. **58**(6), 2097–2105 (2011)

14. Enokido, T., Aikebaier, A., Takizawa, M.: An extended simple power consumption model for selecting a server to perform computation type processes in digital ecosystems. IEEE Trans. Ind. Inform. **10**(2), 1627–1636 (2014)
15. Kataoka, H., Nakamura, S., Duolikun, D., Enokido, T., Takizawa, M.: Multi-level power consumption model and energy-aware server selection algorithm. Int. J. Grid Util. Comput. **8**(3), 201–210 (2017)
16. Kataoka, H., Duolikun, D., Enokido, T., Takizawa, M.: Multi-level computation and power consumption models. In: Proceedings of the 18th International Conference on Network-Based Information Systems (NBiS 2015), pp. 40–47 (2015)
17. Kataoka, H., Duolikun, D., Enokido, T., Takizawa, M.: Energy-aware server selection algorithm in a scalable cluster. In: Proceedings of IEEE the 30th International Conference on Advanced Information Networking and Applications (AINA 2016), pp. 565–572 (2016)
18. Kataoka, H., Sawada, A., Duolikun, D., Enokido, T., Takizawa, M.: Simple energy-efficient server selection algorithm in a scalable cluster. Advances on Broad-Band Wireless Computing, Communication and Applications. LNDECT, vol. 2, pp. 573–584. Springer, Cham (2017). https://doi.org/10.1007/978-3-319-49106-6_56
19. Mittal, N., Garg, K., Ameria, A.: A paper on modified Round-Robin Algorithm. Int. J. Latest Technol. Eng. Manag. Appl. Sci. **5**(11), 93–98 (2015)
20. McEwen, A., Cassimally, H.: Designing the Internet of Things. Wiley, Chichester (2013)
21. Negus, C., Boronczyk, T.: CentOS Bible, 1st edn. Wiley, Indianapolis (2009)
22. Oma, R., Nakamura, S., Duolikun, D., Enokido, T., Takizawa, M.: An energy-efficient model for fog computing in the Internet of Things (IoT). Internet Things Eng. Cyber Phys. Hum. Syst. **1–2**, 14–26 (2018)
23. Rafaels, R.J.: Cloud Computing: From Beginning to End, Create Space Independent Publishing Platform (2015)
24. Watanabe, R., Duolikun, D., Enokido, T., Takizawa, M.: Energy-aware virtual machine migration models in a scalable cluster of servers. In: Proceedings of IEEE the 31st International Conference on Advanced Information Networking and Applications (AINA 2017), pp. 85–92 (2017)
25. Watanabe, R., Duolikun, D., Enokido, T., Takizawa, M.: A simply energy-efficient migration algorithm of processes with virtual machines in server clusters. Int. J. Wirel. Mob. Netw. Ubiquitous Comput. Dependable Appl. **8**(2), 1–18 (2017)

Unsupervised Deep Learning for Software Defined Networks Anomalies Detection

Ahmed Dawoud[(⊠)], Seyed Shahristani, and Chun Raun

School of Computing, Engineering, and Mathematics,
Western Sydney University, Sydney, Australia
a.dawoud@westernsydney.edu.au

Abstract. Software-Defined Networks (SDN) initiates a novel networking model. SDN introduces the separation of forwarding and control planes by proposing a new independent plane called network controller. The architecture enhances the network resilient, decompose management complexity, and support more straightforward network policies enforcement. However, the model suffers severe security threats. Specifically, a centralized network controller is a precious target for the attackers for two reasons. First, the controller is located at a central location between the application and data planes. Second, a controller is software which prone to vulnerabilities, e.g., buffer and stack overflow. Hence, providing security measures is a crucial procedure towards the fully unleash of the new model capabilities. Intrusion detection is one option to enhance networking security. Several approaches were proposed, for instance, signature-based, and anomaly detection. Anomaly detection is a broad approach deployed by various methods, e.g., machine learning. For many decades intrusion detection solution suffers performance and accuracy deficiencies. This paper revisits network anomalies detection as recent advances in machine learning particularly deep learning. The study proposes an intrusion detection framework based on unsupervised deep learning algorithms. The framework consists of an unsupervised deep learning phase followed by simple clustering algorithms, e.g. k-means. Our results showed accuracy over 99%, that is a significant improvement in detection accuracy.

Keywords: Software-Defined Networks · Deep learning · Anomalies detection · Autoencoders

1 Introduction

The conventional communication networking model consists of three planes. i.e., management, control, and forward planes. The management plane supports network monitoring and configuration. The control plane populates forwarding tables on the physical devices. Consequently, the forward plane switches packets to ingress and egress ports based on the forwarding tables. For decades, both the control and the forward planes are integrated into the same networking devices, for instance—switches or routers. The conventional model provided efficiency from a performance perspective. However, current networks became excessively complicated, and there is a necessity to adopt a more resilient architecture [1].

© Springer-Verlag GmbH Germany, part of Springer Nature 2019
N. T. Nguyen et al. (Eds.): TCCI XXXIII, LNCS 11610, pp. 167–178, 2019.
https://doi.org/10.1007/978-3-662-59540-4_9

Software-Defined Networks (SDN) networking model detaches control and forward planes [2]. The devices provide forwarding capabilities to switch the data flow, while the control plane is decoupled to introduce a new entity called the network controller. The forward plane located at the bottom of the stack includes hardware devices, e.g., switches, routers, and firewalls and intrusion detection systems (IDS). The devices do not possess the software intelligence needed to fill the forwarding tables. The network logic independently relocated to the controller layer.

The controller abstracts the devices and provides resources required to programme low-level forwarding devices. Controller aka Network Operating system (NOS) provides services like network state, and topology information. Additionally, the controller provides northbound, and southbound APIs. The northbound API to facilitate communication with the applications. Whereas, the southbound API to provide accessibility between the controller and forwarding devices. OpenFlow is a defacto SDN southbound protocol [3].

The application plane resides on the top of the SDN model stack. Network programmability is a fundamental privilege achieved by SDN model, where applications in the top plane can access the physical devices through the controller. Programmability facilitates and accelerates the innovation with an enormous number of network applications, e.g., monitoring, traffic engineering, security, and cloud applications. Centralisation is an essential feature of the SDN model. A controller is a central entity which provides a global view of the entire network; it eases the management and policies enforcement process.

Additionally, it decreases the faults in configuring and deploying the network policies. The centralisation enhances the network resilience and interoperability, for instance, multiple of devices from various industrials can be integrated and abstracted in one network. However, the controller introduces new security threats.

Network anomalies detection systems used several methods, for instance, statistical, and machine learning methods. Machine learning algorithms, e.g. supported Vector machines SVM, and Principal Components Analysis PCA (with various variations) has been used for attacks detections. However, the precision was not industrially applicable. Likewise, classical neural networks did not show exceptional precision results. However, recent advances in machine learning specifically, advancements in training deep neural networks, are promising. Anomalies detection is an area where machine learning widely contributed. However, few studies investigate the DL applicability for network anomalies detection.

Deep Learning (DL) is deep neural network architecture; the deepness term refers to multi hidden layers between the input and output layers. A deep network is a neural network with hidden layers between the input and output layers. Empirically more hidden layers mean more features to detect. Deep neural networks existed for a long time, however; it was not possible to train the network for three reasons, i.e., Vanishing Gradient Decent in the backpropagation algorithm, poor generalisation, and computation power.

This paper introduces a framework to enhance the security of SDN. The framework is anomalies detection based on machine learning. We use Autoencoders, at the first phase as the unsupervised algorithm, then we use the output as input for a simple clustering algorithm. Hence, the deploying Autoencoders as a pre-processing phase boosts the accuracy results.

The next section discusses the SDN model and related security threats. The third section investigates the deep learning and its current anomalies detection solution for network security. The fourth section represents our proposed framework. The fifth section is experimental for the framework implementation and results in analysis with confusion matrices.

2   SDN Security Threats

Security threats are critical challenges in conventional networking systems. The threats are intensifying in SDN networks. The model's many advantages are accompanied by additional threats that were not possible in the traditional networks. Kloti et al. have conducted a security analysis for the OF protocol [4]. The study has deduced that denials of services attacks have threatened the flow tables and the communication channels; as the attacker flood those components with OpenFlow rules and requests.

Additionally, tampering attacks have substantially targeted the flow tables on the devices by installing rules from untrusted sources. For The southbound OpenFlow protocol, the study exposed various attacks derived from the SDN standard protocol, for example, flow tables and on the devices control channels between the devices and controller affected by a denial of service attacks (DoS). Application privilege conflicts propagate to flow rules. The control channel between the controller and the switch is initiated as a TCP connection, with an option for encryption protocol Transport Layer Security (TLS) to secure the channel. Without an encryption method, the communication between the controller and the forwarding devices are exposed to a man in the middle attacks.

Kreutz et al. concluded seven threats vector for SDN [5]. Three threats are directly linked to the controller itself shown in Fig. 1 as follow,

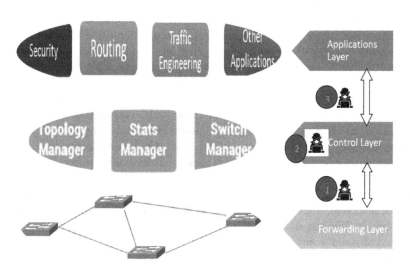

Fig. 1. SDN controller threats

1. Attacks on the communications between the controller and the data plane devices.
2. Attacks on the controller vulnerabilities
3. Attacks on the controller originated from untrusted applications

3 Anomalies Detection and Deep Learning

Intrusion Detection Systems are software or hardware systems dedicated to monitoring the traffic for security threats. Standard intrusion detection process includes three phases, collecting data from the network, analyzing, and then launch a proper response if a threat exposed. There are three approaches to analyze the collected traffic named signature-based, anomaly detection, and specification based. Firstly, signature-based, whereas a system has a database of predefined violations' signatures, and the system matches those signatures against the network activity signatures. Secondly, anomalies or outlier analysis, the system concerns about differentiate between the normal and abnormal patterns. For the system, normal activities are identified in a baseline profile, which the system develops in a learning phase. Thirdly the stateful protocol analysis, in this method a predefined pattern of protocols' behaviour is established, a comparison is made between network activities and the expected behaviour defined by protocols, and in the case of profile violation, an alert is raised. A combination of methods is used to maximize the IDS performance [6]. A significant weakness in the signature-based method is the inability to detect new attacks while anomaly detection has a higher false alarms rate. The majority of the commercial implementations use a hybrid approach [7].

Anomalies or outliers are unexpected patterns. In the context of networking, the intrusions or attacks are classified as unusual behaviour [8]. So at any point, the majority of the traffic is normal. Several approaches were adopted. e.g. statistical methods, machine learning, and biological models. The proposed framework adopts a machine learning approach.

Recently, deep learning has revived the neural networks. It has been successfully applied in various areas. e.g., objects and speech recognition [9]. The recent advances in DL started in 2006 by a pre-training step using restricted Boltzmann Machines (RBM) [10]. Later, various algorithms were proposed to solve the generalization problem these solutions include Rectifier Linear Units (ReLU) and dropouts. DL algorithms are classified into supervised and unsupervised. In supervised learning, the training dataset contains the input data and data labels. This approach is suitable for classification, and regression tasks. In the unsupervised, only an unlabeled dataset is available. Unsupervised applications include clustering, dimensionality reduction, and noise removal. For network anomalies detection we believe the unsupervised approach has the following advantages.

Unsupervised can detect the internal representation of the dataset; this conforms to the online detection. Theoretically unsupervised algorithms will discover the unprecedented threats. We can use the unsupervised method as a pertaining phase before supervised or Reinforcement Learning (RL).

Unsupervised DL algorithms include Autoencoder and Restricted Boltzmann Machines (RBM).

An autoencoder is a neural network that consists of two phases.

An encoder is a deterministic mapping function f_θ that transforms an input vector x into hidden representation y.

$\theta = \{\mathbf{W}, b\}$, where $\mathbf{W}$ is the weight matrix and, b is bias

$$f_\theta(x) \approx x'$$

A decoder reconstructs the hidden representation z (encoder's output) to x' via g_θ. Autoencoder measures the reconstruction error between x' (reconstructed) and the input x and to minimize this error (information loss) to make x' as close as possible to x.

$$J(W) = \sum ||x_n - x_n'|| \tag{1}$$

$J(W)$ is the cost function whose goal is to minimize the cost

Arg min $(J(W))_{\{w, w', b, b'\}}$

Where w and b are encoder weights and biases respectively, and w', b' are weights and biases for the decoder.

Various functions can be used as cost functions for example squared error. The cost function optimization, several options are available for instance stochastic gradient descent SGD and AdamOptimizer.

Fiore et al. used a semi-supervised deep learning tool for network anomalies detection [11]. Authors introduced a discriminative form of restricted Boltzmann machines. The results were not promising specifically when testing the DRBM in a new network. Several research papers focus on improving classical machine learning algorithms with deep learning. Salama et al. used a Deep Belief Network (DBN) as a dimensionality reduction tool for Support Vector Machines (SVM) classifier [12]. The authors claimed a hybrid approach achieve approximately 93% accuracy where the SVM and DBN scored 88% and 90% respectively. In another comparative study, authors compare three traditional algorithms, i.e., Bays networks, C4 and SVM against a hybrid SVM-RBM algorithm. The results showed the superiority of the hybrid method with several attack detection, e.g., DoS and user root attacks [13]. In a broader comparative study on anomalies detection, the authors presented a deep structured energy-based model; The study compares their algorithms in two different decisions boundaries against five severe anomalies detection algorithms including PCA and SVM. The authors go further step by applying their algorithm to various data types, i.e., static, sequential, and spatial datasets [14]. Among the static datasets, they choose the KDD99 network dataset. Their results showed comparable or better performance to methods like PCA and kernel PCA.

4   Detection Framework

The detection framework is positioned at a control plane. Figure 2 shows the architecture of the framework; where the IDS is a module of the controller plane. This architecture support centralisation and flexibility. The implementation of the system is beyond the scope of this paper, as the primary goal is to investigate the accuracy of the algorithm.

We used Tensorflow (TF) as a deep learning development library. Tensorflow is matrices flow in a graph model. TF graph consists of nodes and edges; nodes represent mathematical operations, edges represent multi-dimensional data arrays (tensors).

KDD99 is the most used dataset in machine learning and intrusion detection. The dataset represents real network traffic collected data. The dataset includes 4898431 traffic records for the training, 311029 records for testing. The dataset contains four types of attacks,

Figure 3 depicts the workflow of the simulation. The first stage of the experiments is to build the AE network. The AE consists of two passes, the encoder, and the decoder. Both the encoder and decoder consist of multiple layers. The dataset is loaded into Tensorflow tensor dimension (Training samples, 41), where 41 is some features in a single data samples (input). The weight and biases implemented as tensors for the encoder and decoder. The dimension of weighs and biases depends on the number of neurons (units in the hidden layer). For instance, if we decode the input into five units, this means we will have (41, 5) tensor where 41 input units (features of one network traffic record), and same dimensions will be used in the decoder.

The next step is to train the network; in the forward pass, we use the logits as an activation function. Then we apply the activation function to reconstruct the record from the decoded units, weights, and biases for the output. The next step is to compare the original data against the reconstructed output.

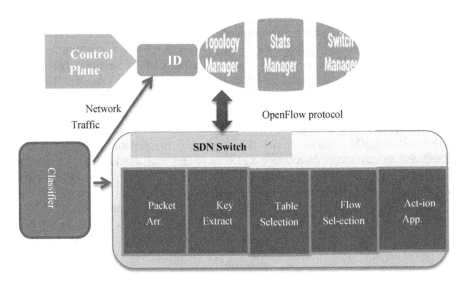

Fig. 2. Proposed location of the detection system in SDN model.

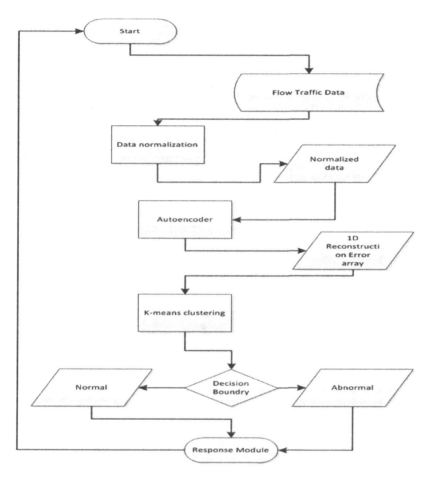

Fig. 3. Framework flow diagram

A cost function is used to compute the data loss, for instance, the squared error function. The third step is to minimise the cost (in our case data loss). Several optimisation algorithms are used to minimise the loss or reconstruction rate. For example, we used Adam optimiser. Once the network settles after various sweeps of data chunks (batches), the second phase testing is on the network with the testing sample and try to reconstruct the data.

For the anomalies detection, the data loss between the input and the reconstructed record is computed. Figure 4 depicts the reconstruction error for each test sample. RE of similar samples are close; the AE successes in finding a pattern in the data. Defining a threshold is not practically applicable, instead of clustering REs into a set of clusters. In the training phase, the network supposed to train on normal traffic, if an input did not belong to one of the previous clusters, it will be classified as an anomaly.

The performance of the algorithm varies depending on various criteria.

- Type of the data, whether the input is binary or decimal.
- Activation function, for example, sigmoid works better with binaries while Relu is good for decimals.
- The cost function, for instance, squared error, and cross entropy
- Optimizer, Gradient Descent, Adam optimize, SGD (figure below shows cost optimization using two different optimizers). The autoencoder aims to minimize the reconstruction error over multiple sweeps of the input data. The y-axis represents the data loss calculated by the cost function (squared error), while the x-axis represents the data sweeps. The graph shows the loss is decreased till it reaches the minima.

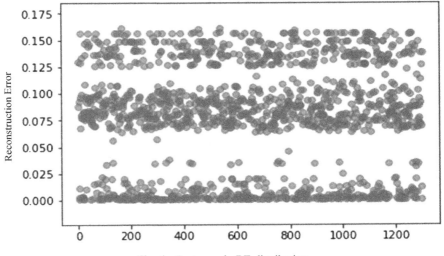

Fig. 4. Test sample RE distribution

Figure 5 shows the framework had deduced the cluster. It is noticeable we have separated clusters for RE ranges. Table 2 shows the framework prediction. As some testing samples increase the accuracy declines; the main reason for this is the number of training samples. If the framework sees more training sample the accuracy expected to increase.

For testing, the samples contain normal and abnormal traffic. The output was clustered; in perfect results, those clusters only include normal or abnormal data. For example, Table 1 shows the predicted clusters for 1300 samples.

Table 2 summaries statistics for the experiments. The first table represents the results for AE conjunction with K-means and shift means algorithms. The accuracy represents how often the framework is correct. The highest accuracy in the table achieved by AE and k-means and the samples number was at the lowest. A remarkable note here, the accuracy declines as the number of samples increases. The F1 score

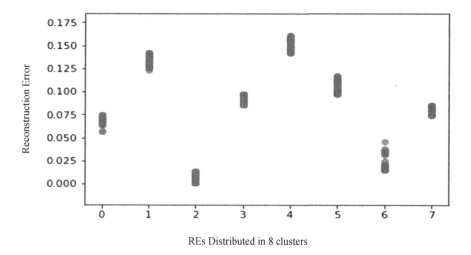

REs Distributed in 8 clusters

Fig. 5. RE distribution in clusters

Table 1. 800 input in 8 clusters, each cluster contains normal or abnormal with the possibility of false positive and false negative

Cluster 1	Normal	139	Abnormal	3
Cluster 2	Normal	4	Abnormal	183
Cluster 3	Normal	0	Abnormal	302
Cluster 4	Normal	172	Abnormal	0
Cluster 5	Normal	0	Abnormal	150
Cluster 6	Normal	100	Abnormal	2
Cluster 7	Normal	0	Abnormal	61
Cluster 8	Normal	184	Abnormal	0

Table 2. Statistical metrics for various testing iterations

	AE 1300 KM	AE MS 1300	AE KM 800	AE MS 800	AE KM 400	AE MS 400
Sensitivity	0.9917	0.9932	0.9974	0.9974	1	1
Specificity	0.9943	0.9789	1	0.9952	1	0.9808
Precision	0.9933	0.975	1	0.9947	1	0.9796
Negative predictive value	0.9929	0.9943	0.9976	0.9976	1	1
False positive rate	0.0057	0.0211	0	0.0048	0	0.0192
False discovery rate	0.0067	0.025	0	0.0053	0	0.0204
False negative rate	0.0083	0.0068	0.0026	0.0026	0	0
Accuracy	0.9931	0.9854	0.9988	0.9963	1	0.99
F1 score	0.9925	0.984	0.9987	0.996	1	0.9897

Table 3. Confusion matrix components

		Predicted	
		Normal	Abnormal
Actual	Normal	True positive TP	False negative FN
	Abnormal	False positive FP	True negative TN

considers the precision (true positive results/total true positive by the framework) and recall (no of true positive results in the total sample). AE achieved F1 and accuracy higher than 98.5%

To summarise the performance of a framework, the confusion matrix consists of columns and rows that list the number of testing samples as either predicted or actual ratios. Table 3 is a general description of the confusion matrix, where we have two classes normal and abnormal.

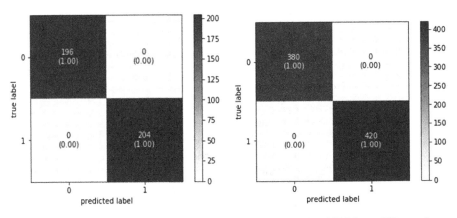

Fig. 6. AE and K-Means 400 samples   **Fig. 7.** AE and K-Means 800 samples

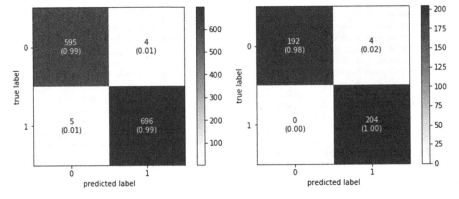

Fig. 8. AE and K Means 1300 samples   **Fig. 9.** AE and shift means 400 samples

To validate the results the second phase was done in two different clustering algorithms K-means and shift means. The confusion matrices for both with different samples sizes are listed below (Figs. 6, 7, 8, 9, 10 and 11).

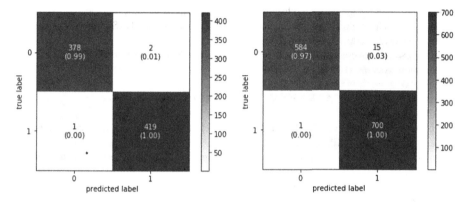

Fig. 10. AE and shift means 800 samples   **Fig. 11.** AE and shift means 1300 samples

5 Conclusion

Deep learning algorithms achieved a breakthrough in neural networks. With a strong record of successful applications, deep learning is a promising approach for network anomalies detection. The paper showed the potential of unsupervised deep learning to enhance the security of SDN.

Network anomalies detection is an area where DL can improve the detection precision. In this paper, we proposed a semi-supervised DL based detection framework for discovering the network abnormalities. The framework employs the unsupervised deeply learning Autoencoder algorithm at the first phase, and a simpler algorithm, K-means or means-shift, during the second phase.

Autoencoders calculate a reconstruction error for network traffic records. Then a K-means or shift means cluster REs. Our approach showed robust prediction with reasonable training data. AE with K-means scored the best accuracy and precision over 99%.

References

1. Kreutz, D., Ramos, F.M.V., Esteves Verissimo, P., Esteve Rothenberg, C., Azodolmolky, S., Uhlig, S.: Software-defined networking: a comprehensive survey. Proc. IEEE **103**(1), 14–76 (2015)
2. Open Networking Foundation (ONF): (2015). https://www.opennetworking.org/
3. McKeown, N., et al.: OpenFlow: enabling innovation in campus networks. SIGCOMM Comput. Commun. Rev. **38**(2), 69–74 (2008)

4. Klöti, R., Kotronis, V., Smith, P.: OpenFlow: a security analysis. In: 2013 21st IEEE International Conference on Network Protocols (ICNP), Goettingen, pp. 1–6 (2013)

5. Kreutz, D., Ramos, F.M., Verissimo, P.: Towards secure and dependable software-defined networks. In: Proceedings of 2nd ACM SIGCOMM Workshop Hot Topics Software Defined Network, pp. 55–60 (2013)

6. Ghorbani, A.A., Lu, W., Tavallaee, M.: Network Intrusion Detection and Prevention Concepts and Techniques. Advances in Information Security, vol. 47. Springer, US (2010). https://doi.org/10.1007/978-0-387-88771-5

7. Mudzingwa, D., Agrawal, R.: A study of methodologies used in intrusion detection and prevention systems (IDPS). In: 2012 Proceedings of IEEE Southeastcon, pp. 1–6, 15–18 March 2012

8. Chandola, V., Banerjee, A., Kumar, V.: Anomaly detection for discrete sequences: a survey. IEEE Trans. Knowl. Data Eng. **24**(5), 823–839 (2012)

9. Krizhevsky, A., Sutskever, I., Hinton, G.: ImageNet classification with deep convolutional neural networks. In: NIPS (2012)

10. Hinton, G.E., Osindero, S., Teh, Y.: A fast learning algorithm for deep belief nets. Neural Comput. **18**, 1527–1554 (2006)

11. Fiore, U., Palmieri, F., Castiglione, A., De Santis, A.: Network anomaly detection with the restricted Boltzmann machine. Neurocomputing **122**, 13–23 (2013)

12. Salama, M.A., Eid, H.F., Ramadan, R.A., Darwish, A., Hassanien, A.E.: Hybrid intelligent intrusion detection scheme. In: Gaspar-Cunha, A., Takahashi, R., Schaefer, G., Costa, L. (eds.) Soft Computing in Industrial Applications, pp. 293–303. Springer, Heidelberg (2011). https://doi.org/10.1007/978-3-642-20505-7_2

13. Dong, B., Wang, X.: Comparison deep learning method to traditional methods using for network intrusion detection. In: 2016 8th IEEE International Conference on Communication Software and Networks (ICCSN), Beijing, pp. 581–585 (2016)

14. Zhai, S., Cheng, Y., Lu, W., Zhang, Z.: Deep structured energy based models for anomaly detection. In: Balcan, M.F., Weinberger, K.Q. (eds.) Proceedings of the 33rd International Conference on International Conference on Machine Learning - Volume 48 (ICML 2016), vol. 48, pp. 1100–1109. JMLR.org (2016)

15. Tavallaee, M., Bagheri, E., Lu, W., Ghorbani, A.: A detailed analysis of the KDD CUP 99 data set. In: 2009 IEEE Symposium on Computational Intelligence for Security and Defense Applications, CISDA 2009, pp. 1–6 (2009). https://doi.org/10.1109/CISDA.2009.5356528

Author Index

Printed in the United States
By Bookmasters